SHAKESPEARE, FROM STAGE TO SCREEN

How is a Shakespeare play transformed when it is directed for the screen? Sarah Hatchuel uses literary criticism, narratology, performance history, psychoanalysis and semiotics to analyse how the plays are fundamentally altered in their screen versions. She identifies distinct strategies chosen by film directors to appropriate the plays. Instead of providing just play-by-play or film-by-film analyses, the book addresses the main issues of theatre/film aesthetics, making such theories and concepts accessible before applying them to practical cases. Her book also offers guidelines for the study of sequences in Shakespeare adaptations and includes examples from all the major films from the 1899 *King John*, through the adaptations by Olivier, Welles and Branagh, to Taymor's 2000 *Titus* and beyond. This book is aimed at scholars, teachers and students of Shakespeare and film studies, providing a clear and logical apparatus with which to examine Shakespeare screen adaptations.

Sarah Hatchuel is Lecturer in English at the University of Paris I Panthéon–Sorbonne and Teaching Assistant in Film Studies at the University of Paris VII. She is the author of *A Companion to the Shakespearean Films of Kenneth Branagh* (2000) and has published several articles on the aesthetics of Shakespeare on screen.

SHAKESPEARE, FROM STAGE TO SCREEN

SARAH HATCHUEL

CAMBRIDGE
UNIVERSITY PRESS

PUBLISHED BY THE PRESS SYNDICATE OF THE UNIVERSITY OF CAMBRIDGE
The Pitt Building, Trumpington Street, Cambridge, United Kingdom

CAMBRIDGE UNIVERSITY PRESS
The Edinburgh Building, Cambridge, CB2 2RU, UK
40 West 20th Street, New York, NY 10011–4211, USA
477 Williamstown Road, Port Melbourne, VIC 3207, Australia
Ruiz de Alarcón 13, 28014 Madrid, Spain
Dock House, The Waterfront, Cape Town 8001, South Africa

http://www.cambridge.org

First published 2004

Printed in the United Kingdom at the University Press, Cambridge

Typeface Adobe Garamond 11/12.5 pt.   *System* LATEX 2$_\varepsilon$ [TB]

A catalogue record for this book is available from the British Library

Library of Congress Cataloguing in Publication data
Hatchuel, Sarah.
Shakespeare: from Stage to Screen / Sarah Hatchuel.
p.   cm.
Includes bibliographical references (p. 177) and index.
ISBN 0 521 83624 7
1. Shakespeare, William, 1564–1616 – Film and video adaptations.   2. English drama – Film and
video adaptations.   3. Film adaptations.   I. Title: Shakespeare, from Stage to Screen.   II. Title.
PR3093.H37   2004
822.3'3 – dc22   2004040791

ISBN 0 521 83624 7 hardback

In memory of Bijou

Contents

Acknowledgments

I am greatly indebted to Dr Kevin De Ornellas for reading carefully and critically every draft of this work and for making useful suggestions at every stage of my writing. I wish to express my deepest gratitude to Professor Pierre Iselin, who supervised my doctorate at the University of Paris IV Sorbonne, who trusted me when I came to English studies after five years of management and economics and who welcomed me to his seminars on Elizabethan theatre. To him I owe my research philosophy. I am extremely grateful to Dr Nathalie Vienne-Guerrin, University of Rouen, with whom I have started co-organizing a series of conferences on 'Shakespeare in performance/on screen' in Rouen. Her support and friendship have been very precious to me. I am grateful to Professor Elisabeth Angel-Perez, Professor Francis Bordat, Professor Russell Jackson and Professor Michèle Willems who were external advisers at my Ph.D. viva and whose invaluable advice I used to adapt my thesis into the present book. I owe many thanks to Mark Thornton Burnett, Professor at Queen's University of Belfast and Director of the Kenneth Branagh Archive, for making constructive remarks on my book proposal and encouraging the project. I owe a great debt of gratitude to Sarah Stanton and the two anonymous readers for Cambridge University Press without whom publishing this book would not have been possible. I wish to thank Jude Tessel for being such a prompt and efficient proof-reader at the first stage of my writing, and Margaret Berrill for her diligent and astute copy-editing.

Not least, I offer my heartfelt thanks to all the people who bring happiness to my life: Kevin De Ornellas, Annie Ganansia-Ganem, Andrée Ganansia, Fernand Ganem, Isabelle Gonzalez, Nicolas Louvet, Natacha Moenne-Loccoz, Nathalie Vienne-Guerrin and Caroline Wilmot.

I am grateful to Kenneth Branagh who gave me permission to include extracts from his publications. Quotes from his *Much Ado About Nothing by William Shakespeare: Introduction and Notes on the Making of the Film* (1993) and *Hamlet: Screenplay, Introduction and Film Diary* (1996), published by Chatto & Windus, are also reprinted by permission of The Random House Group Ltd. Extracts from Leon Garfield's Shakespeare Stories (London: Victor Gollanz, 1985) are reprinted by permission of Penguin Books Ltd. I am very grateful to Professor Lisa Hopkins, editor of *Early Modern Literary Studies*, for permission to draw on my article 'Leading the Gaze: From Showing to Telling in Kenneth Branagh's *Henry V* and Hamlet', *EMLS* 6.1 (May 2000) <http://www.shu.ac.uk/emls/06-1/06-1toc.htm>. Quotations from William Shakespeare's plays are from *The Riverside Shakespeare*, Second Edition, ed. G. Blakemore Evans, J. J. M. Tobin. Boston, MA: Houghton Mifflin Company, 1997.

CHAPTER I

Shakespeare, from stage to screen: a historical and aesthetic approach

THE HISTORY OF SHAKESPEARE PRODUCTIONS

In order to understand the aesthetic stakes of screen adaptation, this book first examines the theatrical presentation of Shakespeare's plays from the Renaissance to the present. Over the centuries, theatre progressively introduced elements and techniques that foreshadowed (or were appropriated by) cinematic devices. Pictorial elements established a separation between the actors and the audience, and used focusing processes that had certain similarities to film narrative techniques. Several stages, both historical and in terms of aesthetics, took place in the transition between the plays performed on the Elizabethan stage and their screen adaptations. The Restoration marked the beginning of this slow transition by introducing the first pictorial elements into Shakespeare's plays. Then, the eighteenth-century stage not only introduced the aesthetic of spectacle and 'tableau', but also established a physical separation between actors and spectators. Finally, performances in the nineteenth century put extreme realism on the stage and developed the processes of focus and fast changes between different concomitant plots.

It is important to define what we mean by 'realism' before moving any further. In literature, theatre and cinema, two meanings of realism co-exist. One concerns the content of the work, i.e. the subject matter. In this case, the realist play, film or text aims at reconstructing a certain social background by emphasizing its everyday aspects and banishing any idealist fairy-tale extravaganza. The other meaning deals with a representational form that seeks to give a convincing impression of reality, creating the effect of being 'just like life', whether the subject matter is quotidian or exotic in time and/or place.[1] Throughout this book, the term will be used in this second meaning.

---

[1] See Pam Morris, *Realism* (London: Routledge, 2003), pp. 1–6, and Paul Cobley, 'Realist Representation', in *Narrative* (London: Routledge, 2001), pp. 88–116.

According to Nicholas Vardac, author of the seminal 1949 work *Stage to Screen*, the development of cinema was encouraged by the desire to go even further into realistic, credible presentation.[2] For Vardac, the stage aesthetic inaugurated at the Restoration, then asserted by Garrick and Irving, would have anticipated cinema techniques. According to Ben Brewster and Lea Jacobs, authors of the 1997 book, *Theatre to Cinema*, the processes used by cinema would not have been anticipated. The new medium would have simply borrowed certain techniques which were popular in the theatre at the moment of its emergence. In their 1996 book *Shakespeare: An Illustrated Stage History*, Jonathan Bate and Russell Jackson support this theory when they acknowledge the theatrical legacy of cinema: 'The appeal of spectacle combined with and legitimised by historical information and edifying morality was inherited by the early cinema especially in such "epic" films as D. W. Griffith's *Intolerance* (1915).'[3] In any case, the two arguments concur in bringing to the fore the intimate relationship between the cinema and the nineteenth-century stage. Cinema gradually took over from the spectacular theatre productions of the time. At first, cinema lacked the technology to compete with the elaborate special effects of extremely realistic theatre productions, but at the time of World War I it certainly started to compete strongly with theatres as it acquired the same potential for visual illusion. In the following history of Shakespeare production, the major aesthetic changes that followed one another and extended into screen adaptations will be pointed out.

The Shakespeare stage, or the absence of realistic illusion

At the start of *Henry V*, the Chorus calls upon the 'imaginary forces' (Prologue 18) of the audience to go beyond the limitations of the stage and to create the battlefield in their mind's eye. Shakespeare's plays were, indeed, written for a very particular mode of presentation, far from film realism. At the end of the sixteenth century and the start of the seventeenth, Elizabethan popular plays were performed on an open-air stage, during the day, in a circular or polygonal construction in which the spectators stood in the stalls or sat in the galleries. All parts were played exclusively by male actors who occupied a bare stage where space and time were

---

[2] See Nicholas Vardac, *Stage to Screen* (Cambridge, MA: Harvard University Press, 1949), p. xx: 'The necessity for greater pictorial realism in the arts of theatre appears as the logical impetus to the invention of cinema.'

[3] See Jonathan Bate and Russell Jackson, eds., *Shakespeare: An Illustrated Stage History* (Oxford University Press, 1996), p. 118.

suggested verbally. This absence of a realistic frame avoided the need to change sets between scenes. Acting was, therefore, continuous, and the scenes of Elizabethan plays followed one after the other with fluid rapidity. Visual aids to imagination were minimal and inherent in the architecture of public theatres: a roof painted above the stage represented the sky and the divine; a trapdoor under the floor evoked hell. The presentation of the plays showed a constant distancing between the sign and its meaning, as well as an absence of illusionist intention. Music sometimes accompanied stage action to create a particular atmosphere. Music was used when heavy props were carried on stage, covering the noise of machinery and adding a spectacular flourish to the sudden apparitions.[4] However, musicians and singers always remained visible to the spectators, thus impeding any establishment of illusion.[5] Shakespeare plays included singing interludes which were always made visible and noticeable. The aim of these interludes was less to create emotion in the audience than to reveal the supposed feelings of the character(s) on stage after listening to the music or the song.

In his 1992 book, *The Shakespeare Stage*, Andrew Gurr advances, as the only concessions to realism, sponges filled with vinegar and hidden under the armpit to simulate wounds, the use of water and smoke, and the sound and visual imitation of thunderstorms.[6] Some props, such as pretences of trees or rocks, could also be brought on stage,[7] but their dramatic functioning was more a matter of metonymy than realistic imitation. According to Gurr, the large majority of Elizabethan plays were performed on a stage that was entirely bare, a challenge that called for the playwright's maximum linguistical skills.[8]

However, parallel to the public theatres, private indoor venues – such as the Blackfriars – opened for a more affluent audience. The performances were candle-lit, and used illusionist processes inspired by the masques of the time with elaborate sets and machinery. This aesthetic trend continued after the Restoration.

The Elizabethan public theatre, with its thrust stage, established a privileged relationship with the audience on three sides nearly encircling the action. Most spectators saw the play being performed in a metatheatrical set composed of other spectators. By its mode of presentation, Elizabethan

---

[4] See Cécile De Banke, *Shakespeare Stage Production Then and Now* (London: Hutchinson, 1954), pp. 79–80.
[5] See J. L. Styan, *The English Stage: A History of Drama and Performance* (Cambridge University Press, 1996), p. 99.
[6] See Andrew Gurr, *The Shakespeare Stage* (Cambridge University Press, 2nd edn 1992), pp. 182–6.
[7] *Ibid.*, pp. 191–2. [8] *Ibid.*, p. 191.

theatre emphasized the breaking of illusion and the notion of shared ritual. The spectators attended both the play and the stage activity surrounding and creating the play. The boundary was blurred between art and life, between the actor and the spectator: both were united in the same communion of entertainment and imagination. The stage of the Elizabethan public theatres was characterized by its absence of separation between the space where the play was performed and the space occupied by the public. As opposed to the architecture of the Italian proscenium theatres, it did not feature any framing or encasing. The thrust stage put the actors in intimate contact with the audience. The difficulty of creating realistic illusion resided in the very proximity of the participants. According to Gurr, 'The players . . . lacked the facilities for presenting the pictorial aspects of illusion because they were appearing in three dimensions, not the two that the proscenium-arch picture-frame establishes.'[9] The physical reality of performance was, in fact, much too patent to create the illusion of simulated reality.

Elizabethan drama, therefore, played with the spectators and their permanent awareness of theatrical illusion. *Mises-en-abyme* (i.e. embedded structures) – which could take the form of masques or plays within plays – added a second level of dramatic action, while a Chorus, a Prologue or an Epilogue could directly call out the spectators and alienate them from the action. The actors' soliloquies and asides were conventions that established intimacy with the public while signalling the devices of theatre. The spectators intervened regularly during the performance, participating in the action with their own reactions.[10] Fiction was thus designated as such. The deceit and trickery that are part of acting were pointed out by the *mise-en-scène* itself.

A comparison between cinema and the Elizabethan stage reveals minor common points and major differences. In the cinema, as in the Renaissance theatre, scenes move on with great rapidity and fluidity. A film, like a theatre production in Shakespeare's time, can go quickly from a battle scene to a discussion behind closed doors inside a palace. Yet, cinema differs from Elizabethan public theatres in the absence of physical interaction between the actors and the audience, and in the high level of realism it can reach. Moreover, while the architecture of Elizabethan theatres allowed the spectators to see the action from different angles, cinema offers a single

---

[9] *Ibid.*, p. 180.
[10] *Ibid.*, p. 226: 'Hisses or "mewes", as well as applause, were given freely, and not only at the end of the play.'

frontal viewpoint, and, through editing and camera moves, mandates how the action will be seen.[11]

The Restoration stage, or the generalization of the decorated set

In 1660, with the Restoration, English theatres reopened. They had been closed – at least officially – since 1642, following an edict adopted by the parliamentary opposition to the king. With Charles II back on the throne after his exile in France, the aesthetics of theatre and opera, very popular in continental Europe, started to spread into England. Charles II allowed women to go on the stage: female characters in Shakespeare plays were, from now on, played by actresses. Shakespeare's texts were revised and rewritten by William D'Avenant, an actor–manager who adapted them to the taste of a restricted audience, essentially composed of aristocrats. The theatres were private, indoor and lit by candles. The stage curtain, which was not present during Shakespeare's time, was introduced, but it was not used to create illusion. It was raised at the beginning of the performance and dropped only at the end of the show: the audience could still see the changing of sets between scenes.

The Restoration stage was still largely based on an intimate relationship between actors and spectators. It did not aim to reach a realistic representation of the action. Metatheatrical effects were still as numerous as they were before. Theatres had a very small capacity and the front stage still thrust out into the auditorium, as in the Elizabethan time. Each spectator was still very close to the actors, and attended a play performed among other spectators. However, the stage began to undergo some important transformations. The surface area of the apron (or thrust stage) was reduced in favour of the back stage, though the dimness of the light did not yet allow the actors to linger in a space that was too far away from the spectators.[12] The lighting was still limited to candelabra hanging from the ceiling and probably some front-stage footlights. But it already allowed for effects of chiaroscuro that delighted an audience fond of novelty. The reduction of the thrust stage was coupled with the introduction of music and pictures. Although the set elements were not physically present, they were painted on shutters at the back of the stage. These shutters were changed regularly

[11] See Michael W. Shurgot, *Stages of Play: Shakespeare's Theatrical Energies in Elizabethan Performance* (London: Associated University Presses, 1998), p. 17: 'The multiplicity of visual perspectives in an Elizabethan public theatre intensified the role of each spectator as an autonomous "maker of meaning".'

[12] See Hazelton Spencer, *Shakespeare Improved* (New York: Frederick Ungar, 1963), pp. 51–5.

during the course of the play. This evolution was a step towards the Italian stage, also known as the proscenium stage, a direct legacy of the opera, in which the actor–singers had to face the conductor to follow the beat. The development of stage machinery and the frequent accompaniment of the acting with music, songs and dances also contributed to importing the aesthetic of opera into Shakespeare production.[13] In William D'Avenant's production of *Macbeth*, the three witches sang, danced and soared in the air thanks to a system of ropes and trapezes.[14] Some particularly melancholic soliloquies and dialogues could be accompanied by instrumental music to make emotions more intense.[15] However, this was still a long way from the time when music came from an unseen pit. The musicians who accompanied the action with their instruments stood in an upper gallery that the spectators could see. Musical moments were admittedly more frequent, but they remained in view.

The Restoration stage was the result of several influences, both English and continental. It was inspired by court masques, Elizabethan private theatres, French theatrical practices and Italian opera. It was still based on a very strong relationship with the audience, and did not work in the mode of realism. Yet, by introducing the first decorated elements, the Restoration stage was at the root of a trend that would continue during the centuries to come. The stage, which was above all a place of verbal enunciation, became a space where set design and music gained in importance after the Restoration.

The eighteenth-century stage, or the separation between actors and spectators

The eighteenth-century stage set a tradition that already foreshadowed filmic illusion. At the start of the eighteenth century, the system of painted shutters was developed. The shutters slid along rails to facilitate placement during the performance, and were positioned on the stage at various distances to create *trompe-l'œil* effects.[16] Painted landscapes or interiors seemed to get smaller according to the natural laws of perspective, and merged into a distant point on the horizon. The presentation of plays, therefore, began to strive to transcend the physical limits imposed by the stage, creating imaginary spaces.

---

[13] See Bate and Jackson, *Shakespeare*, p. 46.   [14] See Hazelton Spencer, *Shakespeare Improved*, p. 93.
[15] Curtis A. Price, *Music in the Restoration Theatre* (Anne Arbor, MI: UMI Research Press 1979), p. 7.
[16] See Styan, *English Stage*, p. 274.

As theatre-going started to become more popular, actor–managers sought to save space in order to increase the theatre capacity to accommodate increasing numbers of spectators. New seats took the place of a part of the front stage, the surface area of which was again decreased.[17] The actors then began to move away from the audience and insert themselves into more and more realistic scenery. This trend intensified in the middle of the century when actor–manager David Garrick wished to establish a complete separation between the actors and the audience. In 1748, he tried to prevent the spectators from sitting on the stage. This habit disturbed the actors in their movements, as they had to apologize each time that they bumped into a spectator. Theatrical illusion was thus compromised for a few seconds several times during a performance. However, the audience, tied to the tradition, resisted Garrick's innovating calls, which remained unheeded for fourteen years. They were finally successful in 1762 when Garrick increased the size of his theatre, the Drury Lane. The spectators, satisfied by the comfort offered by the new auditorium, finally accepted that they would no longer sit on the stage.[18] So, from 1762 onwards, dramatic action took place without any physical interaction with the public. For the first time, a virtual fourth wall was created between the stage and the auditorium. Audience passivity began to be encouraged. The actors played as if protected in a world of their own. They progressively left the front stage to merge into more and more elaborate tableaux.[19] This movement was then intensified due to the progress in lighting. In 1765, Garrick brought back a new technique from Europe. The candles were made more luminous by tying small tin reflectors on them that could be pointed onto different parts of the theatre. This process facilitated not only the lighting of action at the back of the stage but also variations in luminous intensity in order to suggest different times of day.[20] By focusing the audience's attention on a particular action, it anticipated the function of modern spotlights.[21]

In the eighteenth century, the curtain was used to hide the machinery and to prepare special effects without the audience noticing anything. It

[17] *Ibid.*, p. 277, and Richard W. Bevis, *English Drama: Restoration and Eighteenth Century 1660–1789* (London and New York: Longman, 1988), p. 195.

[18] See Cecil Price, *Theatre in the Age of Garrick* (Oxford: Basil Blackwell, 1973), p. 95.

[19] See Iain Mackintosh, *Architecture, Actor and Audience* (London and New York: Routledge, 1993), p. 36.

[20] See Bevis, *English Drama*, p. 196, and Cecil Price, *Theatre in the Age of Garrick*, p. 81.

[21] See Russell Jackson, 'Shakespeare on the Stage from 1660 to 1900', in *The Cambridge Companion to Shakespeare Studies*, ed. Stanley Wells (Cambridge University Press, 1986), p. 195.

emphasized the impressions of surprise and realism, and worked in the mode of waiting and expectation. At the time, the curtain became the material sign of the separation between stage and auditorium, stimulating curiosity and the desire for disclosure.[22] When it is raised, it unveils a picture that lends itself well to realism. Painted scenery was naturally inserted in a rectangular stage, and revealed through successive disclosures. In the eighteenth century, the aesthetic of the tableau was clearly formed in relation to a pictorial vision of the theatrical stage. Garrick's avowed objective was to reach the highest level of emotion and realism. To achieve it, he exploited all the possibilities of stage machinery. He introduced visual and sound devices that made special effects more and more convincing. Paradoxically, it was through devices ever more ingenious and artificial that the theatre attempted to imitate life in the most believable way, by inserting the characters in scenery as real as the actors. With a window-pane at the back of the stage, Garrick even found a way of showing real passers-by walking in the street alongside the Drury Lane Theatre.[23] In his production of *King Lear*, the storm scene was interspersed with thunder and bright flashes of lightning, and took place in a tormented landscape painted on shutters. Theatre sets were conceived as gigantic painted frescos. The use of lighting simulated the faint light of the moon, the brightness of the sun and even volcanic eruptions. Between fairy magic and near naturalism, Garrick set a tradition that portended the theatrical evolution of the nineteenth century and the processes of film illusion. Garrick's merging of naturalism and magic is somehow predictive of modern cinema, in which special effects are usually not produced for their own sakes, but to make situations even more plausible and natural. This was not the case during the early days of cinema, as the newly created medium took two different directions: everyday naturalism and magical illusion. The naturalistic trend was introduced by the Lumière Brothers – originally photographers – who attempted to reproduce as faithfully as possible daily events such as a train arriving at a station or workers leaving a factory. The magical tendency appeared with Georges Méliès – a former magician – whose films focused on ostensible special effects, such as the famous shot of the rocket landing on an anthropomorphic moon. Special effects would progressively become less obvious and stylized, and would be designed to give a heightened impression of reality, thus eventually making the two aesthetic trends much harder to differentiate.

---

[22] See Patrice Pavis, 'Rideau', *Dictionnaire du théâtre* (Paris: Editions Sociales, 1980), p. 338.
[23] See Cecil Price, *Theatre in the Age of Garrick*, p. 83.

The nineteenth-century stage, or the era of romantic realism

The nineteenth-century stage adapted itself to a more and more popular audience. Performances aimed at reaching the most credible realism through more and more spectacular means. At the start of the century, Charles Kemble's Shakespeare productions resorted to impressive human as well as material means. The character of Coriolanus in the eponymous play was thus surrounded by a crowd of one hundred and fifty extras. If Shakespeare used verbal rhetoric to create the impression of a throng around Coriolanus, this new theatre aesthetic used above all a visual and literal rhetoric.[24]

Between 1830 and the end of the nineteenth century, actor–managers reigned over the theatre. They cut and rewrote Shakespeare's texts in order to favour spectacle even more. Actor–managers considered Shakespeare plays as stories to be illustrated. The spectators felt the need for some visual help; so much so that they expected to see faithful reconstructions of history.[25] In the programme of the production of *Henry V* directed by William Macready in 1839, it was written: 'The narrative and descriptive poetry spoken by the Chorus is accompanied with Pictorial Illustrations from the pencil of Mr Stanfield.'[26] Macready also used a new illusionist process called the 'Diorama' to illustrate Henry's journey to France.[27] The 'Diorama' was a set fixed to a moving wall in the background, which unwound vertically or horizontally according to the actors' movements, giving the feeling that the characters were walking or running.[28] This mechanism foreshadowed the cinematic device of the lateral tracking shot in which the camera follows the displacing action. This move from verbal poetry to literal illustration was clearly seen in actor–manager Charles Kean's spectacular, realistic, historical productions.[29] Kean strongly believed in the educational virtues of his productions. To guarantee the accuracy of his reconstructions, he handed out to the spectators leaflets that summed up his historical research.

[24] See Bate and Jackson, *Shakespeare*, p. 99.
[25] See Alicia Finkel, *Romantic Stages: Set and Costume Designs in Victorian England* (Jefferson and London: MacFarland, 1996), p. 33.
[26] Quoted by Finkel, *Romantic Stages*, p. 10.
[27] See George Rowell, *The Victorian Theatre 1792–1914* (Cambridge University Press, 1978), p. 16.
[28] See Michael R. Booth, *Theatre in the Victorian Age* (Cambridge University Press, 1991), p. 81: 'The panorama unrolled as a single or double canvas from one side of the stage and was rolled up on the other; it was popular for depicting a journey or a change of natural setting, in Shakespeare as well as pantomime.'
[29] See Richard Schoch, *Shakespeare's Victorian Stage: Performing History in the Theatre of Charles Kean* (Cambridge University Press, 1998), p. 53.

In the history of English theatre 1880 was an important date as it marked the complete disappearance of the apron, whose surface had been gradually reduced since the Restoration. The Haymarket Theatre in London was the first venue in which the actors played on a stage totally encased and protected from the spectators. Producer Squire Bancroft surrounded the stage with a golden frame, making it resemble a huge animated picture.[30]

Productions included extensive instrumental music to intensify emotion during the dialogues. Yet, in contrast to the Restoration and eighteenth-century stages, the musicians could no longer be seen by the audience. The pit music they produced did not belong to the world of the play. By convention, the characters were not supposed to hear it. This addition of music, which foreshadowed extradiegetic music in cinema, was a sign of the increasing taste for melodrama, a popular theatrical genre at the time, which used atmospheric music in relation to the action and the characters' feelings to facilitate the creation of emotion.[31] Actor–managers, in order to please a larger audience, offered a romantic treatment of Shakespeare's plays.

Romanticism, a term first used in literature, has extended to all artistic forms. It was originally an artistic movement that can be dated more or less accurately depending on the country where it took place, but the notion also covers a general aesthetic tendency in literature and arts that has survived well beyond the time of the movement itself. Romantic works generally put the stress on the individual, a melancholic feeling of loneliness, and personal emotions. They are based on a desire to escape in time and in space, reflecting a longing for the infinite and inserting human beings in wild landscapes. Frenzied grandiloquence and intense events are combined with a sinking into the mind.[32] Romantic works thus usually associate opposite genres, often uniting epic with intimacy, tragedy with comedy. The romantic movement, which historically wishes to free itself from conventions, does not accept the hierarchy of genres nor the classical rule of the three unities. In the nineteenth century, Shakespeare's plays, with their combination of tragedy and farce, were therefore considered as romantic dramas, and performed as such. Actor–manager Henry Irving used Shakespeare texts to produce extremely romantic *mises-en-scène* with

---

[30] See Richard Southern, 'The Picture-Frame Proscenium of 1880', *Theatre Notebook* 5.3 (1951), 60.

[31] See Finkel, *Romantic Stages*, p. 4.

[32] See Anne Souriau, 'Romantique/Romantisme', in *Vocabulaire d'esthétique*, ed. Etienne Souriau (Paris: Presses Universitaires de France, 1990), pp. 1248–51. See also the definition of 'romanticism' in *The Bedford Glossary of Critical and Literary Terms*, ed. Ross Murfin and Supryia M. Ray (Boston, MA: Bedford Books, 1997), pp. 350–3.

very realistic devices. Performances climaxed in stunning visual interpolations and featured sets in three dimensions with real trees, real animals and even water in the form of small lakes or falling rain. The Sadler's Wells Theatre was famous for its water tanks that allowed phenomena of rain or storm, shipwrecks, fountains and waterfalls to be simulated on stage.[33] With Irving, the spectators were encouraged to watch Shakespeare's plays as if they were real, moving pictures. The actors did not play in front of mere painted shutters, but became part of magnificent compositions by famous painters of the time, such as Lawrence Alma-Tadema, Ford Madox Brown or Edward Burne-Jones. The sceneries and stage effects became more and more important, almost as essential as the actors themselves. This transformation of the stage into an immense animated picture was a major artistic phenomenon of the nineteenth century.

The profusion of realistic elements came with elaborate lighting effects. Gaslight (in 1817), then electric limelight (from 1885 onwards) were not extraneous to this new mastery of light. It allowed the actors to be seen perfectly even at the back of the stage, and focused the spectators' concentration in a way unmatched until then. While the auditorium remained in the dark, the stage could go from the brightest light to the most frightening gloom. This variation in light allowed not only the creation of a particular atmosphere for each scene, but also an increase in the rhythm of the play. Turning the light down to near darkness amounted to lowering the curtain, thus making fast changes of sets possible without the audience witnessing the manipulation. In Henry Irving's productions, a mysterious castle could suddenly be replaced by a beautiful garden or a spooky crypt. The rapidity with which a tableau was replaced by another – thanks to rail systems and hydraulic mechanisms – soon became a feature of the nineteenth-century stage as essential as visual and sound realism. This effect, called 'wand change', gave the impression of miraculous and immediate apparitions.[34] The lighting variations made the alternation of different narrative lines possible, creating a 'cross-cutting' effect indicative of film cutting and editing. Irving's 1882 production of *Romeo and Juliet* used these new techniques, which had certain similarities to various cinematic processes: the 'tableaux' foreshadowed the freeze frame and slow motion of cinema, while changes of scenery were executed very quickly, giving a feeling of cinematic *découpage* through fading out (the stage darkened completely before the new scenery appeared), fading in (first in the dark, the scenery appeared progressively) and even cross-dissolving (one set disappeared slowly while

[33] See Styan, *English Stage*, pp. 307–8. [34] See Vardac, *Stage to Screen*, p. 17.

a new one appeared behind or in front of it). These dissolves were achieved
with transparent fabric, painted on each side. When the lighting angle
began to change, it let a different painting appear.[35] At the very end of
the nineteenth century, the theatre found a way to intensify the focus on
a character or a particular action at a given time due to a new device. In
1892, American Steele MacKaye invented the 'proscenium-adjuster' which
opened and closed the proscenium stage at a stroke. It anticipated the different shot scales in the cinema, becoming the forerunner of medium and
close shots.[36] Just before the emergence of the cinematograph, Shakespeare's
plays were performed in a theatrical context that favoured fiction and liter-
alness over meta-drama and imagination. The theatre actors were included
in a world almost as real as themselves, while the spectators were invited
to contemplate this world from a voyeuristic position, without any direct
participation. Shakespeare's plays were, therefore, presented without their
original interaction with the public. The fourth wall had become completely watertight between the reality of the auditorium and the idealism of
the stage. There was no way to progress towards greater illusionist realism
without going into another mode of presentation, into another medium.
Appearing at the end of the nineteenth century, cinema seemed to have
superseded the realistic trend of nineteenth-century theatre productions,
fulfilling the need of the public for naturalism.

From the talking stage to the silent screen

Herbert Beerbohm Tree, an actor–manager who fervently defended the
spectacular aesthetic of realism for staging Shakespeare's plays, was the first
to carry out the transition to cinema. In 1899, William Kennedy-Laurie
Dickson, an Edison protégé, shot scenes from Tree's production of *King
John* for advertising purposes. This first silent transfer of Shakespeare scenes
to the screen inaugurated the movement from a verbal to a visual point of
view. The aim of the new medium was not to communicate Shakespeare's
language but to tell the stories of the plays by including scenes either non-
existent or only described in the original plays. Two forms of Shakespeare
adaptations could then be rapidly distinguished: films that favoured the
means of theatre and concentrated on the actors, the sets and the *mise-
en-scène*; and those that used the camera with the intention of cinematic
creation.

---

[35] See Booth, *Theatre in the Victorian Age*, p. 81.   [36] See Vardac, *Stage to Screen*, p. 143.

At the beginning, cinema was used to record stage productions. The first kind of adaptations, therefore, worked in the mode of filmed theatre. The camera remained fixed, and the shooting was frontal. Everything was done to reproduce the theatrical experience and to immortalize the acting of great players. In 1900, the performance of Sarah Bernhardt as Hamlet was thus recorded by Maurice Clément. Generally, these films, which did not free themselves from a theatre *mise-en-scène*, conveyed the implicit idea that the stage performance was already a complete work in itself, and that their only function was to 'photograph it' in order to preserve it. As opposed to filmed theatre, cinematic art implies three different kinds of movements: the displacement of the characters – the only move that can also be found on stage – the movements of the camera, and the succession of shots within the film. The point is no longer the representation of reality alone, but the *way* of representing this reality. What is at stake is the creation of a particular vision of the world, the insertion of action into a certain strategy of perception. In 1908 and 1909, the screen adaptations of *The Tempest* (directed by Percy Stow) and *A Midsummer Night's Dream* (directed by J. Stuart Blackton and Charles Kent) displayed some elaborate editing, fading and superimpositions. Fades notably created realistic or magical effects during the shipwreck, Ariel and Puck's tricks and Bottom's asinine transmogrification.[37] In 1917, an Italian adaptation of *Hamlet* directed by Eleuterio Rodolfi lingered in close-ups over the characters' faces. It also experimented with the technique of superimposition to give flesh to Yorick's skull for a few seconds, a device that would be found again in Kenneth Branagh's 1996 *Hamlet*.

The twentieth-century stage: minimalism and neo-realism

Until the beginning of World War I, the theatre tried to compete with the cinema in terms of realism. Herbert Beerbohm Tree continued to mount Shakespeare's plays in a spectacular way until 1910. His productions featured an impressive series of tableaux of accurate historical reconstructions, insisting on the pathos of the plots and based on the glorification of a single character that he generally played himself.[38]

Yet, after the war, actor–managers like Irving or Tree were abandoned by their investors who did not believe in the productions' profitability any

---

[37] These films can be seen on *Silent Shakespeare*, a VHS released by the British Film Institute in 1999.
[38] See Finkel, *Romantic Stages*, p. 99, pp. 102–6.

longer. Theatre directors then progressively neglected romantic spectacle and realistic reconstructions, and turned to symbolism and abstract minimalism. As photography freed painting from the constraints of representational art, cinema seems to have obliged theatre to work again on symbols and on the verbal. The development of cinema relieved theatre from attempting to reach perfect realism. Stage productions, therefore, replaced imitation and reconstruction with interpretation and minimalism. At the turn of the century, William Poel suggested that Shakespeare's plays were written to be played as they were in the Elizabethan period.[39] He then strove to produce the plays using the original texts and removing every realistic element from the set. In 1901, Poel played *Henry V* with Elizabethan costumes on a bare stage, with curtains and a small gallery as the only elements of the set. The way of performing Shakespeare's plays returned to its original aesthetic simplicity. In the twenties, director Tyrone Guthrie reacted against the illusion of the proscenium stage and the voyeuristic phenomena it induced.[40] He rediscovered not only the aesthetic simplicity but also the structure of the Elizabethan stage by staging the shows on a bare and thrust stage.[41] According to J. L. Styan, stage history in England has accomplished a circular journey since the Renaissance: 'In one important sense, the radical English stage we see at the end of the twentieth century is returning to the simplicity it knew in its beginning.'[42] Freed from realistic responsibilities by the cinema, stage productions again put the stress on the metatheatrical nature of the plays.

However, if this return to a less spectacular and photographic presentation characterizes the theatre in the twentieth century, several stage productions, much less radical, are still attracted to naturalism. In his 1993 book, *Looking at Shakespeare: A Visual History of Twentieth-Century Performance*, Dennis Kennedy accounts for a return to pictorial realism (which he calls 'neo-pictorialism') from 1975, when the *mises-en-scène* again favoured a frontal point of view, chiaroscuro lighting and realistic sound effects.[43] While the first film productions imported techniques from the stage, theatre productions are now sometimes influenced by realistic cinema.

[39] See Robert Speaight's book, *William Poel and the Elizabethan Revival* (London: William Heinemann, 1954).
[40] See Styan, *English Stage*, p. 361.
[41] See Tyrone Guthrie, *A Life in the Theatre* (London: Readers Union, 1961), pp. 179–80.
[42] Styan, *English Stage*, p. 414.
[43] See Dennis Kennedy, *Looking at Shakespeare: A Visual History of Twentieth-Century Performance* (Cambridge University Press, 1993), pp. 288–302.

SHAKESPEARE AND THE TALKING MOVIES

If the silent era produced many screen adaptations of Shakespeare plays in the United States as well as in Europe, the birth of the talking picture led to a noticeable decrease in the number of adaptations. Paradoxically, while this technique gave directors the possibility of doing justice to plays based on the verbal, the interest in Shakespeare's texts started to decline. There are three reasons for this phenomenon. The first one is purely financial: the sound technique was expensive and necessitated longer shooting time. As a consequence, the general number of film productions dropped. The second is linked to the history of cinema. When it emerged, this new medium sought legitimacy and respectability.[44] For directors and producers, filming theatre performances or adapting plays represented ways of winning acclaim. The more cinema proved that it constituted a credible art form in itself, capable of producing works specially conceived for it, the less appeared the need to film or adapt theatre plays. The third reason lies in the Shakespeare text itself. With the talkies, the question was raised whether the Elizabethan language was suitable to the medium of cinema. Wouldn't the idiosyncratic, old-world nature of Shakespeare dialogues prevent cinema from reaching its aim of verisimilitude? The wish to adapt the plays for the screen seems to have been inhibited by the fear of some unfortunate interaction between the words of Shakespeare and the film medium.

What is a 'Shakespeare film'?

Writing a concise history of Shakespeare adaptations from the beginning of talking cinema to our days requires, first of all, a definition of 'Shakespeare screen adaptations'. It is relatively easy to define what a screen adaptation is. It has been shot on film and has been shown in a cinema on a big screen. Moreover, it takes advantage of the possibilities offered by editing and camera effects to present a personal and highly subjective vision of the play. However, defining the notion of a 'Shakespeare film' is much more difficult. What does this expression mean exactly? Is it a film inspired by the story of a Shakespeare play? Is it a film that uses Shakespeare's text? Is it a film that features some scenes from one of the plays? Or is it a film which talks about a play? Roger Manvell in his 1979 book, *Theater*

---

[44] See Robert Hamilton Ball, *Shakespeare on Silent Film* (London: George Allen and Unwin, 1968), pp. 39–40.

and Film, proposes a system of six stages of adaptation, depending on their distance from stage productions.[45] Jack Jorgens in his 1977 book, *Shakespeare on Film*, offers his own taxonomy by distinguishing between a theatrical mode, a realistic mode and a filmic mode.[46] In the theatrical mode, the dramatic text is emphasized, as in a plain record of a theatre performance. In the realistic mode, the stress is put on spectacle, landscapes and settings, very much as in Franco Zeffirelli's adaptations. Finally, the filmic mode can be found in visually expressive films with extensive imagery and cinematic (almost poetic) skills, such as the Kozintsev or Welles appropriations. Parallel to this first classification, Jorgens has conceived three other categories: presentation (in which the director tries to convey the original play with as little alteration as possible), interpretation (in which the director shapes the play according to a specific view) and adaptation (in which the original play becomes only a source material for a new, but related, work of art). However, the drawback, according to Kenneth S. Rothwell, is that these categories 'sometimes overlap and cross one another'.[47] In fact, every Shakespeare film can be considered as an adaptation as it moves away from the original play in one way or another. Essentially, there are four main types of adaptation, though their boundaries will often overlap. In the corpus of Shakespeare adaptations on screen, it is possible to identify:

(1) Adaptations that use the original English text but transform it more or less extensively through cutting, changing the order of scenes, importing cues from another play, etc. Films by Laurence Olivier (*Henry V, Hamlet, Richard III*), Orson Welles (*Macbeth, Othello, Chimes At Midnight*) and Kenneth Branagh (*Henry V, Much Ado about Nothing, Hamlet, Love's Labour's Lost*) belong, for example, to this category.

(2) Free adaptations that use a translation of the text. This is the case of *Hamlet* (1964) and *King Lear* (1970), both directed by Grigori Kozintsev, whose dialogues were translated into Russian by Boris Pasternak. Akira Kurosawa's films, *Throne of Blood* (1957) and *Ran* (1985), adapted respectively from *Macbeth* and *King Lear*, stand at the extreme limit of this category, as the dialogues and some situations are quite distant from the original text.

---

[45] Roger Manvell, *Theater and Film: A Comparative Study of the Two Forms of Dramatic Art, and the Problems of Adaptation of Stage Plays into Films* (Cranbury: Associated University Presses, 1979), pp. 36–7.

[46] Jack Jorgens, *Shakespeare on Film* (Bloomington: Indiana University Press, 1977), pp. 7–16.

[47] Kenneth S. Rothwell, *A History of Shakespeare on Screen* (Cambridge University Press, 1999), p. 218.

(3) Films whose frameworks are inspired by plots of Shakespeare plays. Shakespeare's text is either completely absent or only present in a few scenes. Two major films retain excerpts from the plays by which they were inspired. John Madden's *Shakespeare In Love* (1998) is essentially inspired by *Romeo and Juliet* and *Twelfth Night*, from which numerous extracts are drawn to tell an imaginary love story between Shakespeare and a young aristocrat. In the same way, Tom Stoppard's *Rosencrantz and Guildenstern Are Dead* (1990) tells the story of *Hamlet* seen from the viewpoint of the Prince's two friends by retaining only some scenes of the play. Other films are based on Shakespeare plots but totally suppress the original text. The musical, *West Side Story*, directed in 1961 by Robert Wise and Jerome Robbins, follows the plot of *Romeo and Juliet* to tell the tragic love story of an American and a young Puerto Rican, but no Shakespeare text is spoken. Another example is Fred McLeod Wilcox's *Forbidden Planet* (1956), a science-fiction film whose story very much resembles that of *The Tempest* but which does not use a single word from the text. Some men in a spaceship land on an unknown planet and discover a genius inventor there. He lives in complete autarchy with his daughter and a robot that evokes Ariel's servitude, but without the same burning desire to escape.

(4) Films in which the characters play Shakespeare roles, direct or teach a Shakespeare play. In these cases, extracts from Shakespeare's texts appear in some scenes, but the story of the film does not follow the plot of a play. In 1995, Branagh directed *In The Bleak Midwinter*, in which amateur actors mount a production of *Hamlet* in a disused church. The film offers numerous excerpts from the play during the rehearsals and the performance. Yet, the general framework does not correspond to that of *Hamlet*, but to that of the actors fighting against their own emotional, financial and psychological problems. In Penny Marshall's *Renaissance Man* (1994), an instructor played by Danny DeVito teaches *Hamlet* to a group of uneducated American soldiers. Again, several extracts of the play are heard during the lessons but the film's general storyline is very different from that of the Danish prince. It is also possible to cite John McTieman's *Last Action Hero* (1993) in which Arnold Schwarzenegger delivers the 'To be, or not to be' soliloquy; Peter Weir's *Dead Poets Society* in which high school pupils play in *A Midsummer Night's Dream*; or even Alan Parker's *Fame* (1980), where the auditions that the students must go through before their admission to the School of Dramatic Arts abound in extracts from *Romeo and Juliet*.

But one should not imagine that these borrowings from Shakespeare represent a recent phenomenon. Original screenplays have been calling on Shakespeare extracts for a long time. The most famous examples date, in fact, from the forties and fifties. In 1942, the spy comedy, *To Be or No To Be*, directed by Ernest Lubitsch, opens on a performance of *Hamlet*. Each night, an actor playing the part of the wavering prince has the surprise of seeing one of the spectators get up and go when he starts delivering the 'To be, or not to be' monologue. The soliloquy stands, in fact, as a signal for the actor's wife (cast as Ophelia) to inform an amorous and flattering admirer that she is free to receive him in her dressing room. This film situation obviously overlooks the Shakespeare play, as Ophelia is supposed to appear on stage immediately after the end of the famous soliloquy. If the original succession of scenes on stage was followed, the actress would not have much time to dally with her admirer.[48] This comic borrowing from Shakespeare can also be found in George Sidney's *Kiss Me Kate* (1953). Two actors, married in real life, whose tempestuous relationship very much resembles that of Kate and Petruchio, play in a musical inspired by *The Taming of the Shrew*.

According to the definition one decides to use, the expression 'Shakespeare film' can therefore cover adaptations that more or less respect the plot and the original text; films that respect the plot but use a translated, adapted text; films whose framework is inspired by the plot of a play but which may not retain one single word of the text; and films that use Shakespeare extracts but whose framework does not follow the plot of any play. In his 1998 book, *Unspeakable ShakeXXXspeares*, Richard Burt compiles and analyses hundreds of borrowings from Shakespeare that can be found in Hollywood films, TV series (for example *Star Trek*) and even in exploitative, pornographic movies. For this historical and aesthetic study, only Shakespeare films from the first and second categories will be retained, i.e. adaptations which are based entirely on Shakespeare plays, using both plots and texts. Films that make very limited references to plots and texts will not be examined here. However, every taxonomy has its limits. It is always difficult to distinguish between limited or 'complete' borrowing, especially since the majority of adaptations based entirely on plays use, in fact, only half of the original text. But it seems more relevant to restrict the study to the adaptations which have as many common points as possible

---

[48] See Robert F. Willson, 'Lubitsch's *To Be or Not To Be* or Shakespeare Mangled', *Shakespeare on Film Newsletter* 1.1 (December 1976), pp. 2–3; p. 6.

with the original plays. It is, then, easier to analyse how those plays are modified when they go through the film directors' prisms, and to identify which methods are chosen to put the images and Shakespeare's text in context.

Film directors have, generally, used two strategies to associate the visual with the verbal in a Shakespeare adaptation: literal illustration and/or metaphorical association. Literal illustration consists of showing pictorially what is expressed textually. Images can either replace the words (the transposition is complete between oral and visual) or work in association with them (images come to reinforce or contradict the spoken words). In the case of metaphorical associations, the succession of images carries visual analogies, giving birth to a meaning which transcends literal significance. These analogies can be engendered by images that break narrative continuity or by pictorial effects achieved through lighting, camera moves, dissolves or editing. Several forms of metaphors can be identified: those that can be noticed through repetition, insistence (for example, with close-ups, sequence shots or unusual angles) or amplification (with visual distortions such as enlarging effects).[49] In Shakespeare films, the specificity of metaphorical associations resides in the absence of simultaneity between the visual and the verbal: visual metaphors do not occur at the same time as the words which have inspired their creation. The connections have to be established by the spectators themselves. The audience can see an image and remember the dialogues to which it is linked, or see an image and wait for the spoken words that will come and justify its appearance.

As the following concise history of Shakespeare adaptations will argue, these two strategies of associating the visual and the verbal are at the core of some essential differences between film directors and their works.

The thirties: irreverence and extravaganza

The earliest feature-length talking Shakespeare film is an adaptation of *The Taming of the Shrew*, filmed in 1929, with Mary Pickford and Douglas Fairbanks in the respective roles of Katharina and Petruchio. Its faithfulness to Shakespeare's text is quite relative. The film is indeed famous for the addition of cues written by Sam Taylor or borrowed from Garrick's adaptation in the eighteenth century, *Catherine and Petruchio*. The producers considered that these were more natural, more credible and, therefore,

---

[49] See Francis Vanoye and Anne Goliot-Lété, *Précis d'analyse filmique* (Paris: Nathan, 1992).

more adapted to the medium of cinema. In 1935, Max Reinhardt and William Dieterle directed a version of *A Midsummer Night's Dream*. The film appropriates *A Midsummer Night's Dream* (*Incidental Music*) by Felix Mendelssohn as a soundtrack; magical elements of the Shakespeare comedy are retained and even enhanced. The scenes taking place in the forest contrast with the town scenes through diaphanous, dream-like visual effects. Transparent fairies dance on clouds, and Puck can take every shape, from a dog to a boar, or to a little flame moving as fast as lightning.

A year later, George Cukor adapted *Romeo and Juliet* with Leslie Howard and Norma Shearer in the title roles. The use of close-ups isolates the lovers from the other characters, and the alternation of shots showing their two faces produces a loving complicity of the gazes. The dialogue in which Friar John tells Friar Lawrence that he could not warn Romeo (v.ii) is replaced by literal illustrations. An interpolation shows how Friar John visited the house of a plague victim and had to remain locked up to avoid spreading the epidemic. This realism finds its counterpoint at the start of the film, which anticipates the opening of Laurence Olivier's *Henry V* a few years later. The camera flies above a painted village, getting closer and closer to attend a reading in some kind of theatre. The film is thus openly presented as a piece of fiction.

Laurence Olivier and Joseph Mankiewicz: between theatre and cinema

Olivier's *Henry V*, released in 1944, was the first Shakespeare film to be shot in colour. The film includes both interpolations with theatre sets and evidently realistic sequences such as the battle of Agincourt, a moment very reminiscent of a Hollywood western. Olivier also adapted *Hamlet* in 1948 and *Richard III* in 1955, two films which again combine theatrical *mise-en-scène* (with continuous shots and artificial sets), and film direction (with camera movements and changes of focal distance). Joseph Mankiewicz also alternates between these two modes in his 1953 *Julius Caesar*, with Marlon Brando as Marcus Antonius. The medium of cinema allows the impressive crowd sequences to be realized, importing the familiar aesthetic of the Hollywood epic. But some dialogue scenes are closer to a stage approach. The camera moves less and the number of different shots is reduced. Yet, if Olivier starts with a theatrical *mise-en-scène* and tries to make it sometimes cinematic, Mankiewicz attempts, on the contrary, to bridle his filmic style for fear of betraying the spirit of the play. Francis Bordat has cogently noticed that: 'Olivier seems to fear that there is not enough cinema in his theatre, while Mankiewicz is afraid that there is not enough theatre in his cinema.'[50]

Orson Welles: textual reconstruction and visual metaphors

Orson Welles opts for a resolutely cinematic style in his three Shakespeare adaptations, *Macbeth* (1946), *Othello* (1952), and *Chimes At Midnight* (1965), which is inspired by the two parts of *Henry IV*, *Henry V* and *The Merry Wives of Windsor*. Welles cuts the text, transforms verse into prose, changes the order of scenes, rarefies soliloquies and slices up some cues to allocate them among several characters. Welles constructs new texts and adapts them to a very personal filmic style, marked by fast editing, chiaroscuro effects, oblique shots, extreme high and low angle shots and a great depth of field – meaning that a large zone is in focus. Welles's strategy of adaptation is based above all on metaphorical associations, creating connections between textual and visual elements separated in time. In *Othello*, for example, the metaphors of the net and the trap run through the whole film. Shadow and light effects project square patterns onto Othello's face, which is also seen under some lattice-work when he speaks to Iago. Desdemona is often shown through the netting of her wrought iron window. When Iago chases Roderigo in the Turkish baths, he keeps jabbing his sword through the lattice-work that allows water to drain away, and finally wounds Roderigo mortally. The spectator is invited to make the connection with Iago's objective, already announced in the film. The character has revealed his plan to use Desdemona to catch all his enemies: 'And out of her own goodness make the net / that shall enmesh them all' (ii.iii.361–2). The visual metaphor is even more obvious at the start of the film which shows the end of the story. The film opens on the funeral procession which accompanies Othello and Desdemona to their grave. Iago is suspended in a cage dangerously swinging in front of the castle walls. Caught in his own trap, Iago is filmed through the bars of this torture cage. The film thus operates a back-and-forth move between visual metaphors that take place before the text to which they are linked, and metaphors that take place after. Welles's strategy is, therefore, not merely illustrative. It manages to associate words with images within the film, but dissociates them through time.

---

[50] Francis Bordat, 'Table ronde sur "Shakespeare et le cinéma"', in *Shakespeare et le cinéma, Actes du Congrès 1998 de la Société Française Shakespeare*, ed. Patricia Dorval and Jean-Marie Maguin (Paris: ENS, 1998), p. 197.

From the fifties onwards, adaptations of Shakespeare become more and more diversified. Some directors favour sets, historical reconstruction and literal illustration; others transpose the plays to unusual times and spaces, while preferring metaphorical associations; some others, finally, adopt an *avant-garde* vision and stop insisting on the plot's logic.

Franco Zeffirelli: realistic frames and literal illustrations

Franco Zeffirelli, who started his career as a stage designer, attaches particular importance to the environment in which the action takes place, and to the creation of a naturalistic universe. *The Taming of the Shrew* (1966) with Elizabeth Taylor and Richard Burton in the title roles works mainly on realism. The original metatheatrical induction scene with Christopher Sly is suppressed. Only references to it are included during the film, but they are integrated in the story itself. When Lucentio and servant Tranio arrive in Padua for the first time, they walk under a cage on which there is a sign reading 'Drunkard' and that houses an intoxicated lout reminiscent of Sly. Burton's rough, crude and inebriated portrayal of Petruchio is also very reminiscent of Sly's drunkenness. The film lingers on the hectic, social and commercial activity that reigns in the town of Padua. The camera often stops on the extras, creating several small plots within the main story. Zeffirelli creates two labyrinths, one outside (in the Padua alley-ways) and the other inside (in Kate's house). Set design becomes as important as the story protagonists, providing a series of physical obstacles to seduction when Petruchio chases his 'prey'. Images supplant text due to literal interpolations. Long speeches relating facts are often transformed into purely visual moments, as when Kate is married to Petruchio or when she falls into the mud while travelling to her husband's home.

In *Romeo and Juliet* (1968), the director carries on with this construction of a realistic world and reconstructs the town of Verona during the Renaissance. In 1990, he locates *Hamlet* in the twelfth century, following the Saxo Grammaticus legend of Prince Amleth, one of the play's sources. Elsinore is a real medieval castle (in fact situated not in Denmark but in Northern Scotland) whose ramparts and interiors recall the claustrophobic atmosphere in Olivier's *Hamlet*. Literal illustrations come to replace whole pieces of the text. For example, Ophelia's speech to Polonius relating Hamlet's visit to her chamber is suppressed in its entirety, and replaced by its signified, i.e. the scene of the visit itself. In his three adaptations, Zeffirelli thus favours literal illustration with text deletion. Peter Hall, Tony

Richardson, Peter Brook, Roman Polanski and Grigori Kozintsev all make more original choices, both in terms of design and visual strategy.

Towards avant-garde *Shakespeare films*

At the end of the sixties, Peter Hall and Tony Richardson endeavoured to move away from fairy-tale-like or realistic designs. In his 1969 *A Midsummer Night's Dream*, Hall removes all magical effects and enchanting landscapes. Inspired by a theatre production that he directed for the Royal Shakespeare Company, he creates the world of a forest full of mud in which the characters get stuck. Richardson also took his cue from his own stage production (at the Round House Theatre in London) when he adapted *Hamlet* for the screen in 1969. The main originality of this adaptation resides in the choice of staying in the Round House Theatre to shoot the film. No effort is made to create a realistic architecture. The camera focuses not on the environment, but on the characters' faces, scrutinizing their emotions and reactions. The actor becomes the very centre of the film.

This search for a more austere design can also be found in Brook and Polanski's works which situate their respective adaptations in a remote period, right after prehistory. Brook's *King Lear* (1971) shows a king eminently pathetic and overwhelmed. Visual metaphors run all through the film. Blurred images and dissolves to black, either progressive or sudden, reflect Lear's lack of discernment and Gloucester's enucleation at the same time. In his 1971 *Macbeth*, Polanski conceives a cruel and pagan world, between the Neolithic and the Middle Ages, in which earth, water, fire and stone dominate. These elements are also the base for Grigori Kozintsev's adaptations, *Hamlet* (1964) and *King Lear* (1970). Natural elements become the source of metaphors, and film techniques are used to serve an ideological fight for the freedom of expression. In Kozintsev's *Hamlet*, immediately adjacent to a rough sea and isolated in the landscape, Elsinore becomes a prison of stone where corruption and spying rule. The film starts with a long interpolation of Hamlet riding home after the death of his father. Like so many other adaptations, it focuses on the theme of imprisonment with the metaphor of the drawbridge recalling a giant jaw swallowing Hamlet. In *King Lear*, the eponymous character is also isolated. With very frequent long shots, Kozintsev insists on the king's vulnerability by losing the frail figure in landscapes again dominated by stormy elements.

With director Akira Kurosawa, Shakespeare's text is rewritten and adapted to the context of medieval Japan. *Throne of Blood* (1957) retains only the mere plot of *Macbeth* to construct an eerie universe where the characters get lost in misty labyrinths. In 1985, *Ran*, inspired by *King Lear*, is as free an adaptation. The king's daughters are replaced by sons, and interpolations show samurai warriors fighting violently in the middle of infinite plains or fires. Again, the characters have difficulty in finding their way in landscapes deprived of any clear markers.

In 1979, not only do the characters have difficulty in finding their bearings, but so do the spectators. Derek Jarman's *The Tempest* is an *avant-garde* adaptation which attempts to redefine what cinema is. The plot is made opaque, images from documentaries are mixed with those of the fiction, and Prospero's island becomes a series of dark rooms in a large residence. The spectator loses all sense of direction, and watches the transformation of each room into a pictorial, well-organized and almost motionless composition. The magic of cinema is replaced by the elaboration of visual tableaux in front of the camera.[51]

In the seventies and eighties, Shakespeare screen adaptations are thus rare and relatively far from the original texts. Placed in Russian and Japanese contexts, or presented as *avant-garde* experiments, the films undergo heavy rewriting and transposition. More traditional adaptations are then realized for another medium, that of television, for which the BBC produced the whole Shakespeare canon.

Kenneth Branagh: the return of realism

At the end of the eighties, director Kenneth Branagh worked against the tide of the *avant-garde* trend of Shakespeare films. He directed *Henry V* (1989), *Much Ado About Nothing* (1993), *Hamlet* (1996) and *Love's Labour's Lost* (2000) with an admitted goal: that of presenting Shakespeare's works in a most accessible and popular way. Branagh, à la Garrick or Irving, wishes to present Shakespeare's texts in a way that can please a large audience, and adopts the familiar style of Hollywood realism. By introducing numerous realistic interpolations, he situates each film in a particular film genre. *Henry V* becomes a war film whose spectacle is hardly questioned by the Chorus's interventions. *Much Ado About Nothing* is filmed in Tuscany like a light comedy, full of sun and ebullience. *Hamlet* turns into an epic thriller. Finally, *Love's Labour's Lost* explores the genre of the musical. Moreover, Branagh takes advantage of the techniques offered by the cinema: his

---

[51] See the article by Russell Jackson, 'Shakespeare's Comedies on Film', in *Shakespeare and the Moving Image*, ed. Anthony Davies and Stanley Wells (Cambridge University Press, 1994), pp. 107–9.

adaptations always display important aesthetic work with camera moves, editing, dissolves and slow-motion.

This fascination with energetic movement denies any fixedness. Nevertheless, if Branagh's films avoid static 'staginess', they present 'theatrical' effects in the sense of a large, operatic amplification of the form.[52] Examples are numerous – the extremely long travelling shot during the *Non Nobis* song at the end of *Henry V*, the 'Overture' in slow-motion at the start of *Much Ado About Nothing*, or the sequence which ends the first part of *Hamlet* with the backward movement of the camera and the distorted sound perspective – Hamlet's voice is rising while his body is disappearing in the distance. In all cases, the effect is huge, relying on its impulse and momentum, on its strength and evidence. In his films, Branagh often combines the visual strategies of literal illustration and metaphorical association. As opposed to directors like Zeffirelli, Branagh introduces literal illustrations without necessarily suppressing the original text. Image and text are thus superimposed, raising questions of redundancy. Illustrations, which are generally very explicit, are considered as aids to facilitate the understanding of the story and language. They never contradict what is said, but rather come to confirm it. For example, in his 1996 *Hamlet*, Branagh illustrates the guard Barnardo's words, 'When yond same star that's westward from the pole' (1.i.36), with a shot of the sky, and those of Horatio, 'But look, the morn . . . / Walks o'er the dew' (1.i.166–67), with a shot of the rising sun. At first, these illustrations can be considered superfluous and redundant. They seem naively and pointlessly to reduplicate what is already signified by the text. These images, however, do not work like mere illustrations of the word 'sky'. They can play an important part in the global vision that is offered by the film. They contribute to importing some elements that go beyond simple denotation. In fact, they carry a series of connotations – that is, a set of emotional values linked to the perception of the sky at this exact point in the movie. For a moment, the film frees itself from the interior space of Elsinore to show the horizon and the stars. The actions of men are thus presented under a cosmic sign. They are situated in the infinite of the universe, underlining their vanity. The celestial images in *Hamlet* appear as a means to make the film 'breathe', to carry the story, as well as the spectator's gaze, towards some limitless exterior. In a 1998 interview, Branagh said that he borrowed this technique from David Lean, who directed such epic

---

[52] See Pierre Berthomieu and Sarah Hatchuel's article, '"I Could a Tale Unfold", I Could a Tale Enlighten: Kenneth Branagh ou l'art de la clarté', in *Shakespeare et le cinéma, Actes du Congrès 1998 de la Société Française Shakespeare*, ed. Patricia Dorval and Jean-Marie Maguin (Paris: ENS, 1998), pp. 131–40.

movies as *The Bridge on the River Kwai* (1957), *Lawrence of Arabia* (1962) and *Doctor Zhivago* (1965):

It is obvious that I've been influenced by Lean. His epic movies are built around six or seven long shots of immense landscapes, but also on close-ups. In fact, we can convince the audience that they are watching a film much bigger than it really is. You have to choose the right moment to show the grandiose shot.[53]

Therefore, the celestial shots, which at first can seem trivial, serve to introduce epic effects into the film. Literal illustration can thus help to root the film in a specific, cinematic genre, to link it to well-known films which already ring in the public's collective imagination. In *Hamlet*, metaphorical associations also come to forge connections between the verbal and the visual. They work on the themes of the mirror and the prison, based on Hamlet's famous cues: 'for any thing so o'erdone is from the purpose of playing, whose end, both at the first and now, was and is, to hold as 'twere the mirror up to nature' (III.ii.19–22) and 'Denmark's a prison' (II.ii.243). The symbol of the mirror is an intriguing metaphor in a play where the characters are mirror images of one another, and are, in a metatheatrical way, confronted by their own doubles played on stage in the play within the play. In Branagh's vision, Elsinore becomes a world of two-way mirrors, reflecting the paranoia of an opulent and narcissistic realm. Two-way mirrors are, by nature, double. On the one hand, they reflect the image that one expects to see; on the other hand, no one can see through the mysteries that they retain behind them.

Visual associations also exploit the theme of the prison. Throughout the film, Branagh includes shots of characters filmed behind bars, prisoners of the closed world of Elsinore. Hamlet is filmed through the palace gates when the Ghost appears before him; Claudius is seen through the lattice-work of the confessional after confessing his crime; Ophelia is filmed screaming behind Elsinore's portal when her father's corpse is carried out of the palace. Even Elsinore's palace is often tightly framed through and located behind its own gates: the trope of prison conquers the entire dramatic and filmic space.

Branagh therefore combines two approaches. One aims at giving the film an appearance of historical reality so that the characters' actions seem to step out of a document from the period. The other uses expressive and metaphorical means to accentuate this reality. Lighting, framing, editing and music add a specific connotation that goes beyond the simple showing

---

[53] Quoted in French by Pierre Berthomieu, in *Kenneth Branagh: traînes de feu, rosées de sang* (Paris: Editions Jean-Michel Place, 1998), p. 196. My translation.

of characters and objects. Branagh appropriates Shakespeare plays into a universe which is both firmly rooted in reality and highly stylized.

Branagh's approach has undoubtedly influenced the wave of Shakespeare films in the nineties. Most of these new adaptations present readings of the plays according to two major principles. The first principle is to film Shakespeare in an accessible way by finding a relationship of immediate support for the story and characters in order to clear away the effect of strangeness produced by Shakespeare's language. The second principle is to shoot the plays like cinema films, expressing with cinematic means a vision not yet explored. Like Branagh's, the films directed by Oliver Parker, Trevor Nunn, Richard Loncraine, Baz Luhrmann and Michael Hoffman follow those two principles. However, other directors such as Peter Greenaway or Christine Edzard differentiate themselves from this tendency by proposing adaptations very far from classical realistic narrative.

The nineties: between avant-garde *and realistic cinema*

Many directors followed Branagh on the path to realism in the course of the last decade. In *Othello* (1995), Oliver Parker proposes a naturalistic representation of Venice and Cyprus. He adopts a literal style which slips towards voyeurism when the hero's epileptic trance gives rise to a fantasy interpolation. Explicit images show Desdemona and Cassio making love, thus raising the problem of knowing if what is shown on screen has really taken place or not. In 1996, Trevor Nunn also included several interpolations in his *Twelfth Night*. The most notable one is the opening sequence of the shipwreck in which the twins get separated. Nunn, famous stage director and ex-artistic director of the Royal Shakespeare Company, has not hesitated to explore the possibilities of film naturalism.

In the same year as Nunn's *Twelfth Night*, Richard Loncraine's *Richard III* was released on the big screen. It also opens with a major interpolation. The bunker in which King Henry VI and his son have taken refuge is stormed by Richard and his tanks. The characters move about in an imaginary world, but one which evokes the rise of fascism in the thirties in a very realistic way. Battersea Power Station, an iconic, mammoth edifice in London (which was built in the 1930s, but is now abandoned), is transformed into a Hitlerian palace and ends up as the scene of an apocalyptic fight in which Richard falls into hell, swallowed by the flames of an explosion. Throughout the film, Loncraine introduces visual metaphors essentially based on the insults uttered by Queen Margaret. Her part being entirely suppressed, visual metaphors are somehow there to compensate for her absence. If Margaret does not appear physically in the film, her presence is felt through the showing of the bestial metaphors that she normally uses in her speeches. In the original play, Margaret calls Richard a pig when she talks to him: 'Thou elvish-mark'd, abortive, rooting hog!' (I.iii.227). Then she speaks of him as a spider when addressing herself to Queen Elizabeth: 'Why strew'st thou sugar on that bottled spider / Whose deadly web ensnareth thee about?' (II.iii.241–2). These images are materialized several times in the course of the film. When he presents himself as devoted to Richard's cause, James Tyrrell gives food to a real pig; Richard is then seen with the horrible head of a boar in another collaborator's nightmare; when Lady Anne is shown dead in her bed with her eyes wide open, a spider crawls on her face, as a symbol of Richard's victory over her. To insist on the eponymous character's double and serio-comical nature, Loncraine skilfully exploits the possibilities offered by editing. The first soliloquy, 'Now is the winter of our discontent', is presented in two parts. In the first part, Richard begins his speech while he is not alone but in an extremely public place – the royal court. The first verses are delivered as Machiavellian compliments. In the second part of the sequence, Richard starts to express his true frustration. The monologue ends in the most private space – the toilets. The brutal cut and the extreme contrast between the two places display not only a comical aspect but also emphasize the character's hypocrisy and two-facedness.

The year 1996 was a prolific one for Shakespeare films since Baz Luhrmann's *William Shakespeare's Romeo + Juliet* was also released, above all intended for a teenage American audience. Action is transposed to an American beach town in our time or in a near future, where urban violence reigns. The style of musical clips can be found in the saturation of colours, the brutality of editing and the violence of zooming. Realism comes with extremely apparent cinematic effects as well as explicit references to other films. The beginning of the film is marked by the use of a relatively rare technique in modern films, that of the wipe, in which an image comes to push and replace the previous one by making it slide horizontally. The first confrontation between the Montagues and Capulets is highly reminiscent of films directed by Sergio Leone or John Woo. Musical accompaniment (guitar and disturbing whistling) reminds the audience of Ennio Morricone's scores; the close-up in slow-motion of Tybalt's boot crushing a still smoking match clearly evokes the characters of Clint Eastwood and Charles Bronson in Leone westerns. When the fight starts, rapid cutting, slow-motions, quick-motions and shots showing the characters leaping and using several weapons at the same time strongly recall the film aesthetic used by Woo, with spectacular, daring and stylized fights.

In 1999, Michael Hoffman retreated to a more traditional style with *A Midsummer Night's Dream*. This version is very reminiscent of Branagh's *Much Ado About Nothing*, with its landscapes (both films were shot in Tuscany), lightness of tone and the construction of a past, imaginary period.

Parallel to this wave of Shakespeare films following the Hollywood canons, directors including Christine Edzard, Peter Greenaway and Adrian Noble continued the *avant-garde* and experimental tendency of the seventies and eighties. In 1991, Greenaway directed *Prospero's Books*, an eminently metafilmic adaptation of *The Tempest* in which the density of visual signs becomes more essential than the story of the film. Prospero – played by John Gielgud – inherits all the cues, and rules over a world full of references to the Italian Renaissance. Strangely enough, the film also includes numerous literal illustrations of the text and situations. The audience is shown Prospero and Miranda's happy past, Sycorax's delivery of Caliban, and even Alonso's thoughts when he imagines Ferdinand's drowning. If Greenaway plays on pictorial abundance, Edzard opts for minimalism. Her adaptation of *As You Like It*, in 1992, locates the play in an urban environment at the end of the twentieth century. The deficiency of greenery from the visual world of the film serves to give notice to the un-natural, environmentally depleted space of contemporary inner cities. In the audience's mind's eye, the forest is maybe all the more visible because of its absence.

Naturalism is also disturbed in the version of *A Midsummer Night's Dream* directed by Adrian Noble in 1996. Noble largely followed a theatre production that he had mounted for the Royal Shakespeare Company in 1994. The film juxtaposes theatrical concepts and cinematic techniques. The whole story is, in fact, the dream of a little boy. He looks at every scene as an astonished spectator, and sometimes intervenes in the characters' environment by making the moon turn, or pulling the curtains to reveal the amateur performance of 'Pyramus and Thisbe'. The little boy thus becomes a second director, pulling the strings of his own dream-like creation.

Half-way between the Hollywood tendency and the *avant-garde* trend, stands Al Pacino's *Looking For Richard* (1996). It both attempts to make Shakespeare more popular through a pedagogical approach, and offers a resolutely unusual adaptation. The film is at the same time a fiction which uses every cinematic technique to tell Richard's fate; a testimony to the place of Shakespeare in our society, and a documentary on the very shooting of the fiction.

The turn of the millennium: high technology and the blending of times

During 2000, Michael Almereyda's *Hamlet* and Julie Taymor's *Titus* were released, both displaying a highly personal vision of the plays through the extensive use of metaphorical associations. At the start of Almereyda's *Hamlet* (starring Ethan Hawke as the Danish prince, and transposed to our time in New York), the chairman of multimedia company Denmark Corporation has just died and his young brother announces his takeover of the firm and his marriage with Gertrude at a press conference. In this modern, high-technological context, the film is mainly based on the themes of espionage and the spreading of false information. In Shakespeare's play, misinformation is troped in the recurrent image of the ear. The symbolic ear of the Danish people has been intoxicated by Claudius's lie. The Ghost first mentions this figurative poisoning before even referring to the literal poisoning that he was victim of:

> 'Tis given out that, sleeping in my orchard,
> A serpent stung me, so the whole ear of Denmark
> Is by a forged process of my death
> Rankly abus'd.   (I.v.35–8)

> Upon my secure hour thy uncle stole,
> With juice of cursed hebona in a vial,
> And in the porches of my ears did pour
> The leprous distillment.   (I.v.61–4)

The country's intoxicated ear becomes a literal motif with the poisoning of the king, then becomes a trope again, since Hamlet's ear is symbolically poisoned by his father's secret.[54]

In Almereyda's film, not only the ears but also the eyes are poisoned via modern high technologies: Claudius's first speech is delivered in front of journalists and cameras during a press conference; surveillance cameras watch every move of the characters inside Elsinore Hotel; and Ophelia is forced by Polonius to wear hidden microphones when she brings back the love letters to Hamlet. These devices are updated equivalents of Branagh's

---

[54] See Pierre Iselin's article, '*Hamlet* and the Rhetoric of Secrecy', in *Hamlet*, ed. Pierre Iselin (Paris: Didier Eruditions – CNED, 1997), p. 144.

two-way mirrors that allow characters to see and hear without being noticed. Mediated spying is thus at the core of Almereyda's production. Communication itself becomes mediated through technological tools: Hamlet advises Ophelia to go to a nunnery by leaving messages on her answering machine; the closet scene ends up on the phone while Hamlet is already trying to hide Polonius's body; and the character of Osric is replaced by a fax machine announcing the forthcoming duel. Another strong metaphorical association in the film makes the audience share Hamlet's feeling of imprisonment through the low-angle, oblique shots of New York skyscrapers oppressively surrounding the character.

In Taymor's *Titus*, styles of architecture are extremely varied as they are part of the film's strategy of blending times from ancient Rome to the present. Modern buildings co-exist alongside coliseums. The wild, decadent feeling of the thirties and the fascist style of the forties are merged with Roman design. Different worlds collide in the eclectic means of transport – tanks, chariots, horses, motorcycles. The robes of Roman senators are combined with modern-day suits, and the weapons are both technologically advanced and old-looking. Several scenes are constructed around this contrast between old and new: Vegas-like lighting can thus illuminate archaic ruins. In this production, the scenery is very often a metaphor for the characters' state of mind. When Titus pleads for the life of his two sons, he is physically presented at the crossing of ancient Roman roads, reflecting a psychological turning point. Similarly, a swamp of mud and burnt logs stand as a metaphor for the brutalizing of the ravaged Lavinia.

But all through the film, metaphors are essentially based on the themes of bodily dislocation and bestiality. The numerous human sacrifices and amputations in the play give rise, in Taymor's production, to a series of stunning images of body parts. Sculptures of hands and feet can be spotted among various ruins. Arms, legs and torsos swirl in a nightmarish fire that regularly appears between the characters of Tamora and Titus to reflect their hate and desire for revenge. Animal imagery is used to mirror the textual metaphors that are already present in the text to describe the characters. Taking her cue on Titus's belief that 'Rome is but a wilderness of tigers' (iii.i.54) and Lucius's assertion that Aaron is a 'ravenous tiger' (v.iii.5), Taymor often fills the frame with wild animals hunting or being hunted. The rape of Lavinia is notably evoked in a stylized flashback in which two tigers pounce on a deer. Lavinia is already troped as this helpless animal in the *double-entendre* words of her father: 'It was my dear' (iii.i.91).

This brief history of Shakespeare on screen has shown that the aesthetic strategies employed in adapting the plays can differ greatly from one another. Nevertheless, whether the films work on literal illustrations or metaphors, they generally concur in their use of interpolation, focus and editing to construct a world of fiction whose illusion is rarely disclosed. In the following chapters, the consequences of cinema aesthetics on Shakespeare's plays are examined. In chapter 2, interpolation, focus and editing raise questions of narrative and narration. Chapter 3 examines how most film directors elaborate, from Shakespeare plays, classical fictions in which semiotic elements are combined to create a realistic, melodramatic world. Chapter 4 considers the ways film directors have tried to find screen equivalents to Shakespeare's metatheatrical devices in order to defamiliarize the spectators with the plays and encourage them to reach an alienated state of critical distance. Chapter 5 analyses the construction of screenplays written for several adaptations of *Hamlet*. It looks at how the dramatic text of the original play becomes coated with a subtext that appropriates quasi-novelistic aspects, alternating between dialogues, narrator interventions and focused narrative. The purpose is to bring to light different ways of 'telling' and then to determine their ideological consequences. Finally, chapter 6 offers five detailed aesthetic comparisons between key scenes from different adaptations of the same play. It aims at identifying distinct aesthetic strategies chosen by film directors to appropriate the same scene, suggesting some guidelines for the study of sequences in Shakespeare adaptations.

CHAPTER 2

From theatre showing to cinema telling

This chapter appropriates theories of literary and film narratology as well as the concepts of film semiotics to analyse how Shakespeare plays are transformed when they are adapted to the screen. Adapting Shakespeare plays on screen always involves a shift from one enunciative system to another. Given its verbal nature, theatre is generally considered to be more able to 'tell', whereas cinema is usually thought to be more able to 'show' through the semiotic diversity of images and sounds that it can convey. Nevertheless, film studies have reached the conclusion that cinema merges the acts of showing and telling, and introduces the figure of an exterior narrator.[1]

Several directors of Shakespeare adaptations have positioned themselves in a narrative trend that guides the audience's concentration. Baz Luhrmann, director of *William Shakespeare's Romeo + Juliet*, is convinced that 'Everything is about telling the story.'[2] For Julie Taymor, who directed *Titus*, the point of film-making is 'not just the story but how you tell the story'.[3] In an interview in *American Theatre*, Ian McKellen explains what experience director Richard Loncraine brought to the project of adapting *Richard III* for the screen:

I'm not an expert practitioner. Fortunately, director Richard Loncraine is. He made 400 fabulous commercials for a start. I'm a huge fan of commercials. Telling a story very quickly, grabbing the audience's attention, that's all part of movie making – it's all part of how to do Shakespeare.[4]

---

[1] See André Gaudreault, *Du littéraire au filmique: système du récit* (Paris: Méridiens Klincksieck, 1988); André Gaudreault and François Jost, *Cinéma et récit II* (Paris: Nathan, 1990); François Jost, *L'œil-caméra. Entre film et roman* (Presses Universitaires de Lyon, 1987); Francis Vanoye, *Cinéma et récit I: récit écrit, récit filmique* (Paris: Nathan, 1989).

[2] Interviewed by Paul Adamek on 3 November 1996. <http://www.omnileonardo.com/bazinterview96. html> Accessed 1 June 2003.

[3] Interviewed by Joel Snyder. <http://arts.endow.gov/explore/Taymor/Taymor.html> Accessed 29 May 2003.

[4] Norman Allen, 'McKellen on Richard III', *American Theatre* (April 1996), 34.

For Branagh as well, cinema, like theatre, must be used above all for narrative purposes. In a 1993 interview, he said:

When you work in the theatre, you must have a very clear obligation *to tell a story* because you can't tell the audience 'I want you to look there'. In movies, you can cut from that, to that, to that and you can't look anywhere else. Whereas in the theatre, you have the whole space. You have to be very *aware* of *how to tell a story*.[5]

Branagh clearly reveals the influence of cinema aesthetics on the theatre. It seems that, for him, theatre must attempt to achieve cinema's abilities. But, at the same time, Branagh establishes a significant difference between stage and screen: telling a story on screen would be much easier. Roman Polanski shares this opinion when he states in a 1998 interview:

The stage just doesn't allow you to tell your story in the way you would necessarily want to tell it, whereas the film allows you to tell it in any way. If there is some kind of retrospective narration, for example, you can use a flashback, which you cannot on the stage.[6]

Film editing is considered to be a very useful device for constructing a story. *Montage* and camerawork turn a show into a narrative in which space is fragmented through time. After examining the concepts of telling and showing, this chapter explores how film directors have used cinematic narrative techniques to modify the nature of Shakespeare's plays.

THE CONCEPTS OF SHOWING AND TELLING

The notion of showing and telling are rather delicate and fluctuating. The first definitions were advanced by Plato and Aristotle. In Book III of *The Republic*, Plato relates a discussion between Socrates and Adeimantus concerning the different styles of telling. Narration (*diegesis*) is defined as what is expressed by storytellers and poets, who tell stories aloud to their audience:

– And a narrative it remains both in the speeches which the poet recites from time to time and in the intermediate passages?
– Quite true. (Book III, 393b)[7]

[5] In an interview given on Canal + in *Le journal du cinéma* on the French release of *Peter's Friends* in January 1993. Personal video archive. My italics.
[6] Interviewed by Gary Crowdus in 'Shakespeare in the Cinema: a Film Directors' Symposium, with Peter Brook, Sir Peter Hall, Richard Loncraine, Baz Luhrmann, Oliver Parker, Roman Polanski and Franco Zeffirelli', *Cineaste* 24.1 (1998), 49.
[7] Plato, 'The Republic III', in *The Portable Plato*, ed. Scott Buchanan, trans. Benjamin Jowett (Harmondsworth: Penguin Books, 1976), p. 376.

Two modes of telling would, therefore, exist. When the poet delivers speeches belonging to some characters, 'this assimilation of himself to another, either by the use of voice or gesture, is the imitation of the person whose character he assumes' (393c). Telling is thus achieved through imitation, a mode of enunciation which finds its most extreme example in the theatre, either in tragedy or comedy. In contradistinction to this, when the poet recites the text between the speeches, he speaks with his own voice, without pretending. He achieves simple telling. In Plato's *The Republic*, narration can happen when a single storyteller speaks in his own name (simple *diegesis*), or when he imitates characters (mimetic *diegesis* or *mimesis*). Imitation (*mimesis*) is thus considered a branch of narration (*diegesis*).

Aristotle, in *Poetics*, adopts a very different approach. For him, the poet would always imitate:

[I]t is possible to represent the same objects in the same medium but in different modes. Thus they may be imitated either in narration (whether the narrator speaks at times in an assumed role, which is Homer's way, or always in his own person without change) or in a mode in which all the characters are presented as functioning and in action.[8]

Aristotle does not distinguish between two modes of narration, but between two modes of imitation. The poet can imitate either by telling (whether he impersonates other characters or remains himself) or by simulating the actions of characters. *Mimesis* includes every kind of performance, whether the poet remains a strict narrator or plays parts. As opposed to what can be read in Plato's *The Republic*, *diegesis* is considered a branch of *mimesis*. Theatre does not have a narrative status any longer. It would only fall within the province of imitation.

Current notions of telling and showing use Plato's categories of simple *diegesis* and mimetic *diegesis*, adapting them to new artistic forms such as novels or films. In order to take into account the evolution of concepts and to avoid any confusion of vocabulary, the terminology established by Gérard Genette in his 1980 book, *Narrative Discourse*, will be adopted. Genette proposes to designate by *story* the narrated events (or narrative content), by *narrative* the account that organizes the events in a particular order and filters them through some specific perspective, and by *narration* the very act of telling and producing the story.[9]

---

[8] Aristotle, *Poetics*, 1448a, trans. James Hutton (Toronto: W. W. Norton, 1982), pp. 46–7.
[9] See Gérard Genette, *Narrative Discourse: An Essay in Method*, trans. Jane E. Lewin (Ithaca, NY: Cornell University Press, 1980).

Film theorists often use the term *diegesis* instead of story to designate the narrative content of a movie. This term, far away from its ancient definition, can be applied to classical, narrative cinema. In this cinematic mode, the story frees itself from filmic enunciation so well, that it seems to become autonomous and to take the shape of a real world. Diegesis refers to a story as a pseudo-world, as an imaginary universe in which elements go together to form some globality.[10] Diegesis eventually swallows the story, inserting it into a universe that simultaneously embraces the succession of events, the geographical, social and historical frame and the general atmosphere in which the action unfolds.

The notion of 'narration' applies to the discourse which tells a story – that is a mode of enunciation which calls for a speaker and a listener.[11] Narration is necessarily the product of an enunciative, telling authority which can sometimes reveal the artificial nature of filmic illusion. According to Robert Scholes and Robert Kellogg, in their 1966 book, *The Nature of Narrative*, 'narrative art requires a story and a story-teller'.[12] They oppose that situation to drama which is 'a story without a story-teller'.[13] Telling implies the existence of a discursive authority which delivers the story in a given time. Narrative art, then, involves two temporal dimensions: it inscribes the time of the tale into the time of narration itself.[14] For example, a story that takes place over twenty years can be narrated in a film that lasts two hours. There cannot be any narrative without a succession of words or images arranged through time. The following study reveals this double temporality and this discursive authority in Shakespeare screen adaptations. It argues that the cinematic techniques used by film-makers introduce some narrative elements into Shakespeare's plays, transforming their purely mimetic aspects.

EDITING AND NARRATION

Identifying a double temporality comes down to finding in what phase of its making a film can play with time. A movie is usually made in three stages. The first stage can be compared to theatrical direction and organizes what takes place in front of the camera (acting, *mise-en-scène*, setting). The

---

[10] See Jacques Aumont, Alain Bergala, Michel Marie and Marc Vernet, *Esthétique du film* (Paris: Nathan, 1999), p. 81.
[11] See Patrice Pavis, 'Narration', *Dictionnaire du théâtre* (Paris: Editions Sociales, 1980), p. 260.
[12] See Robert Kellogg and Robert Scholes, *The Nature of Narrative* (New York and Oxford: Oxford University Press, 1966), p. 240.
[13] *Ibid.*, p. 4.   [14] See Genette, *Narrative Discourse*, p. 35.

second stage concerns the actual camerawork during the shooting – it is a framing process. Then, during the third stage, the filmed images are linked together – an assembling and editing process. According to some film scholars, the second framing stage would still belong to showing, as it does not have any temporal freedom: the time of the story would always be the same as the time of narrative.[15] In this formulation, only the third editing stage is the source of narration in the movies. Cinema would, in fact, weaken the mere iconic aspects of images through the act of assembling them. This idea has some historical grounds. As Harry Geduld writes in his 1975 book, *The Birth of the Talkies*, 'The silent film was not silent. Before 1928 movies were customarily accompanied by one or more of the following: sound effects, music played by live performers; live singers, speakers, or actors; and phonograph recordings.'[16] It seems that a kind of 'movie lecturer' would at times provide narration in the form of elementary exposition, while actors behind the screen would give performances.[17] Noel Burch, in his 1981 article 'How We Got Into Pictures', attests the importance of the lecturer who explained and commented on the action.[18] While Burch suggests that the narrating lecturer would have disappeared around 1912–14, Norman King believes that 'he continued in existence for rather longer, at least in rural areas'.[19] It would seem that the extended exploitation of editing techniques added a visual narration which became integrated into the image track, while suppressing the need for the oral narration of the lecturer.[20] In fact, a film owes to editing to be something other than a mere reproduction of some pre-existing show. Editing bodies forth a discursive, organizing authority, necessarily subsequent and exterior to the filmed event. It introduces the figure of a 'virtual narrator' who leads the spectators by the hand and orchestrates the focus of their gaze. As opposed to theatre where, most of the time, the spectators must organize their own vision of things and events, this cinematic narrator leads the gaze.[21] By focusing in turn on particular objects, particular characters or particular actions, it can shape space at will,

---

[15] See, for example, André Gaudreault, *Du littéraire au filmique: système du récit* (Paris: Méridiens Klincksieck, 1988), p. 126.

[16] Harry Geduld, *The Birth of the Talkies: From Edison to Jolson* (Indiana University Press, 1975), p. 30.

[17] *Ibid.*, pp. 41–2.

[18] See Noel Burch, 'How We Got into Pictures: Notes Accompanying Correction Please', *Afterimage* 8–9 (1981), 24–38.

[19] Norman King, 'The Sound of Silents', in *Silent Film*, ed. Richard Abel (London: The Athlone Press, 1996), pp. 31–2.

[20] See Paul Cobley, *Narrative* (London: Routledge, 2001), pp. 155–8.

[21] It is to be noted, nevertheless, that modern theatre frequently uses spotlights to guide and concentrate the spectators' attention, introducing a certain kind of focus within the stage organization.

create different levels of realities, and reorganize the succession of events in time.

The editing techniques used by film directors and their consequences on Shakespeare's plays will be examined from four angles: editing as a producer of meaning; editing as an ordering process of the story and the narrative; editing as a producer of different narrative rhythms; and, finally, editing as a process facilitating alternate points of view and, therefore, managing the quantity of information given by narrative about the story.

Editing as a producer of meaning

Editing produces meaning, whether it expresses an idea or an emotion by the shock of two images put together, or acts subtly to generate diegesis. Juxtaposition of images gives birth to a denoted meaning (the story in itself) and a connoted meaning (effects of comparison, parallelism or causality between the shots) at the same time. This semantic function of editing was notably examined by theorist Béla Balazs and film director Sergei Eisenstein. In his 1929 book, *Theory of the Film*, Balazs explains how images are contextualized through editing, and are thus inscribed in a series of associations that grant them their meaning.[22] Balazs even thinks that two images chosen at random, and then juxtaposed, will be linked inevitably in the spectators' mind by an induced stream of meaning. The spectators would inevitably weave a coherent thread between two succeeding images. Through editing, a shot would therefore become necessarily the sequel of the previous shot.

According to Eisenstein, bringing two shots together is always more meaningful than two shots seen separately.[23] Editing becomes, for the director, a tool which helps give a certain vision of reality and manipulates spectators. Eisenstein considers each juxtaposition of images to be a stimulus provoking a precise reaction in the audience. He thus attempts to use editing as a producer of ideas and emotions by increasing the number of analogies and metaphors. In his film *Battleship Potemkin* (1926), Eisenstein inserts, for example, shots of sculpted lions – the first one is asleep, the second is standing, the third is showing its teeth – to generate the idea of popular rebellion. By controlling the psychological effect produced by his films, Eisenstein wishes to win the audience's fidelity to the cause he supports. The capacities of editing are exploited for ideological purposes.

---

[22] See Béla Balazs, *Theory of the Film*, trans. Edith Bone (New York: Dover Publications, 1970), p. 119.
[23] See J. Dudley Andrew, *The Major Film Theories: An Introduction* (Oxford University Press, 1976), p. 52.

Such expressive, metaphorical editing is used extensively by Orson Welles in his three Shakespeare adaptations. In *Chimes at Midnight*, the battle of Shrewsbury is filmed with extremely rapid cuts that reflect the soldiers' blows and frenzy. Instead of showing literal violence, Welles uses editing to create a striking impression of war. In *Othello*, when Iago is asked to give the 'ocular proof' of his accusation, the increase in tension comes with an acceleration in editing. Othello's fury finds an equivalent in the raging sea down at the bottom of a sheer cliff. Editing establishes an obvious metaphorical connection between Othello's agitation and the high, virulent waves. Later in the film, fast cutting turns the Turkish baths into a maze. The series of shots fragments space, emphasizing the vulnerability of Roderigo's body in a location where any sort of marker is lost. After the murder, Welles cuts to images of water running in great quantities. Editing replaces blood by a powerful metaphor directly linked to the place of the murder. During the final fight in *Macbeth*, a close-up on the terrified face of Macbeth, expectant of Macduff's stroke, is instantly followed by a shot of Macbeth's statue being decapitated with a sword. The actual killing is not shown. The physical decapitation is only implied, and combined immediately with Macbeth's symbolic fall from power.

In his *Hamlet*, Branagh also uses this kind of expressive editing based on analogy. While the Danish prince decides to mount a play to prove Claudius guilty, he moves closer to a small model theatre. As he promises himself to catch the conscience of Claudius, Hamlet releases a trapdoor on the tiny stage, making the model king disappear. The following shot reveals the real Claudius opening a door. This immediate juxtaposition associates Claudius with a puppet that Hamlet wishes to dispatch to the world of the dead. The image of crossing – by going through a (trap) door – is also kept, thus preserving the progression of the film.

The editing of Richard Loncraine's *Richard III* works not only on visual but also on sound analogies to add pace to the film. An example is a series of shots when Earl Rivers – Queen Elizabeth's brother – is assassinated. Just as a knife is thrust through the bed into his chest during sexual intercourse, Rivers's mad screaming is followed by a shot of a whistling train passing through the countryside and bringing the Prince of Wales to town. Editing dissolves the two sounds – the screaming and the whistle – into one. The sudden cutting renders the unexpected murder even more shocking while inserting it into Richard's long-term strategy: Rivers's death is only a step to power, preceding the elimination of the princes. The image of the whistling train is then followed by a shot of the Duke of York innocently playing with a model train, close to his mother Queen Elizabeth; two messengers quickly come to announce Rivers's death. This time, editing is based less on sound than pictorial analogy. The visual transition from one train to another helps the story to progress without interruption. In the course of a few, rapid shots, the film moves from the murder of Rivers to its announcement to his sister, while presenting the two princes as Richard's future targets, unaware of the looming danger.

The visual chain thus acquires an internal logic, with consecutions, causal links and thematic reminders which establish a strong parallel with a written chain. Film theorist Christian Metz believes that the invisible narrator of a film is 'very similar to a novelist, exterior to the facts that are told; the invisible film narrator unwinds the image track before the very eyes of the spectators in the same way as the novelistic narrative lines up sentences which go directly from the author to the reader'.[24] As a consequence, while it would be easy to think that cinema has certain similarities to theatre since actions are mimed and presented by actors, it appears that cinema is somehow closer to the novel by the very unwinding of its images. The semantic function of images generates effects of punctuation or demarcation, of linearity or alternation. The alternating technique of cross-cutting (also called parallel editing) allows the audience to simultaneously follow two narrative lines that occur in different places, thus revealing the narration to be omniscient through omnipresence, since, in David Bordwell's words, 'the narration knows that something important is happening in another line of action'.[25] In Branagh's *Hamlet*, the speech in which the eponymous hero apologizes to Laertes before the final duel is punctuated with synchronic inserts where Fortinbras's army invades the Palace of Elsinore. The film's end thus presents an interpolation with a centrifugal development of the original play. It links a private duel inside to a national war outside.

At the end of his *Romeo + Juliet*, Baz Luhrmann chooses to have Juliet wake up before Romeo dies. He uses cross-cutting to separate two narrative lines unfolding in the same place at the same time. While Romeo believes his love to be dead, close-ups on Juliet's fingers moving slightly and on her opening eyes come to inform the audience that she is conscious again. These close-ups on Juliet's moving fingers recall the classic film trope of the awakening monster as in James Whales's *Frankenstein* (1931). Shots alternatively focus on despairing Romeo who is looking elsewhere, and on Juliet who smiles at the sight of her new-found lover. When Juliet finally

[24] Christian Metz, *Essais sur la signification au cinéma*, vol. 2 (Paris: Klincksieck, 1981), p. 54. My translation from French.
[25] David Bordwell, Janet Staiger and Kristin Thompson, *The Classical Hollywood Cinema* (London: Routledge, 1985), p. 48.

touches Romeo, he has just been swallowing the poisonous drink. Editing here generates dramatic irony, emphasizing the tragic bad timing as Romeo fails to notice what is happening. Cross-cutting makes the audience almost believe that an alternate, happy ending might be possible, that the two narrative lines could ultimately meet while both lovers are still alive.

Directors also resort to alternated editing without necessarily adding narrative lines that are absent from the original play. In Trevor Nunn's *Twelfth Night*, Act II, scene iii, in which Andrew, Feste, Maria and Toby are up at night singing and drinking, is cut several times with shots of Act II, scene iv, in which Orsino gives Viola/Cesario his opinions and advice on love. Instead of presenting the two long scenes in succession, Nunn prefers to create a fast cinematic rhythm, cutting from one place to the other. The alternation emphasizes the contrast between the two situations: one is noisy, but informal; the other is more intimate, but composed and rigid. Branagh also uses editing to reorder the chronology that is offered by the text. In his 1996 *Hamlet*, Act III, scene ii presents the play-within-the-play, and ends with Hamlet's soliloquy "'Tis now the very witching time of night' (III.ii.388) in which he plans to visit his mother to be 'cruel' to her, but not 'unnatural' (III.ii.395). In Act III, scene iii, Claudius is enraged after the performance of 'The Mousetrap'. He speaks to Rosencrantz and Guildenstern about the strategy that he will choose to deal with Hamlet's apparent lunacy. He then finds himself alone to confess his sins. In the film, Branagh disrupts the chronology of events. He drops Hamlet's soliloquy at the end of scene ii, and moves immediately to the beginning of scene iii. After filming Claudius walking towards the chapel to confess, the camera returns to Hamlet while he promises to spare his mother. The film then goes back to Claudius to hear his confession. In a 1997 article, 'Kenneth Branagh's Film of *Hamlet*: the Textual Choices', Russell Jackson considers that this choice of editing generates extra time. It suggests, indeed, that Claudius has already spent a certain amount of time in deep thought before starting to pray aloud.[26] Editing, here, dilates the time of the diegesis. Branagh offers a new arrangement of space and time by reordering the unfolding of the play in the course of cinematic narrative.

Flashbacks: editing as an ordering process

Directors can also dilate time by inserting flashbacks. This insertion has an influence on the organization of narrative and on the succession of

---

[26] See Russell Jackson, 'Kenneth Branagh's Film of Hamlet: the Textual Choices', *Shakespeare Bulletin* 15.2 (Spring 1997), 38.

events within diegesis. Flashbacks, indeed, create images whose place in the chronology of the story is located before their appearance in the narrative. With flashbacks, editing allows directors to explore the past. In this respect, cinema strongly differs from theatre, a medium which is linked to the inexorable succession of time and hardly allows a turning back of the clock. Even if some theatrical productions, inspired by recent screen adaptations, begin to import past scenes in their directing choices, they nevertheless uphold the integrity of the plot's forward progression. For example, Jean-Louis Benoit's 1999 production of *Henry V* inserted scenes from the *Henry IV* plays to remind the audience of the king's debauched past, but those scenes were not 'real' flashbacks as they were confined to the very start of the play, thus protecting the linear nature of the action. Unlike the theatre, the cinema easily works as a visual, time-exploring machine by reordering events within the chronology of the story.

Directors often use this possibility to illustrate moments when characters relate past events. In Parker's *Othello*, when the Moor explains to the Duke and senators how he won Desdemona's heart, a scene from the past shows Othello and Desdemona meeting, talking and finally kissing. These interpolated images help to present the Moor as a trustworthy character whose allegations can be visually confirmed. Flashbacks also serve to insert nostalgic reminders, as in Luhrmann's 1996 *Romeo + Juliet*. When the two lovers are reunited in death, past images document the happy time that they had together, from their first encounter on each side of the fish tank, to their kiss under water. With this journey into the past, Luhrmann constructs the idea of an eternal love, continuing even beyond death. In Branagh's *Henry V*, flashbacks recall the king's careless days, helping to elaborate the character of Falstaff and his former friendship with Henry. In his *Hamlet*, the love story with Ophelia is developed through several flashbacks which punctuate the movie with the mode of the straight cut. But when Hamlet holds Yorick's skull and starts to remember the past, the flashback is introduced with a dissolve to evoke the effort of memory. Yorick's skull regains the living flesh of the Jester – memorially embodied through the comedian, Ken Dodd: we shift to another time dimension for a few seconds, while the object itself – the skull – remains the same. In Branagh's as well as in Olivier's version of *Hamlet*, the Ghost's tale of the murder is illustrated by an interpolated flashback. In Olivier's adaptation, the images are presented as Hamlet's own mental representation of the spectre's words: a close-up shows Hamlet closing his eyes, and a transition subtly leads to the flashback. In Olivier's film, the Ghost's story is thus entirely mediated through Hamlet's thoughts. The murder is offered to the eyes rather than to the ears, satisfying the audience's scopic urge through the character's imagination. Branagh also inserts a flashback but its origin is made less explicit and obvious than in Olivier's version. As it follows a shot of the Ghost and not of Hamlet, it is legitimate to wonder what the nature of this flashback is. As Bernice W. Kliman writes: 'as Branagh presents the flashcuts, the possibility of omniscience is always present: what we see is what happened rather than what happened filtered through the Ghost's perception'.[27] Nevertheless, if one takes into account the fact that Branagh's film-making generally works within classical filmic narration, the flashcuts should be analysed in the light of David Bordwell's views on flashbacks in his 1985 book *Classical Hollywood Cinema*:

> Classical narration admits itself to be spatially omnipresent, but it claims no comparable fluency in time. The narration will not move on its own into the past or the future. Once the action starts and marks a definite present, movements into the past are motivated through characters' memory [. . .] The narration simply presents what the character is recalling.[28]

Bordwell's definition would seem to rule out the possibility of omniscience. The flashbacks would not provide information on what really took place. But the uncertainty still remains as far as whose memory is concerned. Are the flashcuts mere illustrations which only commit the author of the tale – the Ghost? Or are they created by the imagination of him that listens – Hamlet? Only this ambiguity of the source allows the doubts regarding Claudius's actual guilt to be preserved: despite the showing of the murder, it is not certain that this act truly happened.[29]

The opposites of flashbacks, i.e. flashforwards, are quite rare in movies in general, and in Shakespeare adaptations in particular. The process of memory and recalling is, indeed, more natural and common than the process of premonition and anticipation. However, director Baz Luhrmann uses one flashforward in his version of *Romeo + Juliet*. As Friar Lawrence rehearses to Juliet his idea for saving her and Romeo, he is filmed in front of the very events he imagines. Behind him, the audience indeed sees a sleeping Juliet, Paris discovering her dead in bed, a burial ceremony, a letter being written to Romeo, a Juliet who wakes up and a smiling Romeo. Showing these images at this point of the story allows Luhrmann to cut the scene

---

[27] Bernice W. Kliman, 'The Unkindest Cuts: Flashcut Excess in Kenneth Branagh's Hamlet', in *Talking Shakespeare*, ed. Deborah Cartmell and Michael Scott (Houndmills: Palgrave, 2001), p. 157.

[28] Bordwell *et al.*, *Classical Hollywood Cinema*, p. 30.

[29] For a discussion on the ambiguity of interpolations in Branagh's *Hamlet*, see David Kennedy Sauer's article, 'Suiting the Word to the Action: Kenneth Branagh's Interpolations in *Hamlet*', *Shakespeare Yearbook* (1997), 325–48.

in which the Capulets lament over Juliet's body, in order to accelerate the events at the end of the film. The flashforward also presents some images that will be seen later, such as Juliet opening her eyes, thus highlighting interesting discrepancies between what Friar Lawrence plans and what the real outcome will be.

Narrative rhythms

If film editing allows diegetic chronology to be mastered, it can also play with the double temporality of narrative, with the discrepancy between story-order and narrative-order. Through ellipsis, slow motion and flash-back, it can compress, dilate or visit the time of diegesis in a way unmatched in the theatre. According to Gérard Genette in *Narrative Discourse*, there are four main narrative rhythms. Each one establishes a particular relation between the time of narration and the time of the story (equivalent to diegetic time in film studies). In the *pause*, the storyteller contemplates one event extensively: the time of narration is 'infinitely' longer than diegetic time. In the *scene*, both times are equal, displaying isochronic action. In the *summary*, the action speeds up and is often presented in a series of episodes which are distant in time: the time of narration is shorter than diegetic time. Finally, in the *ellipsis*, a period of time is entirely suppressed between two different actions: the time of narration is 'infinitely' shorter than diegetic time. Shakespearean dramatic material is obviously composed largely of isochronic scenes. Nevertheless, the plays are far removed from the classical pattern: they rarely present a unity of action, time and place. They may feature more or less significant ellipses between two scenes. In *Hamlet*, the audience does not know exactly how much time has passed between the moment when Hamlet is sent into exile in iv.iv and the moment of his return in v.i. Depending on interpretations, this ellipsis can suppress a diegetic interval of several days to several years. Moreover, Shakespeare introduces prominent narrative effects to accelerate or to simply stop the course of time. In *Henry V*, the metadramatic character of the Chorus sums up whole pieces of history, hastens action or offers commentaries between two scenes, thus giving rise to narrative pauses. Shakespeare's plays also display returns to the past (retrospection or *analepsis*) and forward moves into the future (anticipation or *prolepsis*).[30] At the start of *Henry V*, clerical figures recall at length the dissolute past of their monarch, which was presented on stage in the two parts of *Henry IV*; and when *Henry V* ends, the

---

[30] See Genette, *Narrative Discourse*, p. 40.

Chorus evokes the future loss of the realm of France, presented on stage in the three parts of *Henry VI*. Like cinema, Shakespeare makes time flexible, dilating or compressing it at will, returning to the past or visiting the future. Yet he achieves these effects in an exclusively verbal mode. The metaphorical and poetical use of language creates no exterior visions on stage but interior visions in the minds of the spectators. Quite distinctly from theatre, cinema works on time visually and literally, again with the help of editing. Elliptical cuts can simulate the passing of time. The audience is then left to imagine the suppressed action.

Screen adaptations sometimes reflect ellipses which are already more or less present in the Shakespeare text – or invent some from scratch. An example of the former case can be found in Branagh's *Henry V*, when the king ends his prayer to the God of Battles. A fade-out evokes the passing of time between the nocturnal soliloquy and the beginning of the battle on the following morning. Such an effect is very similar to the end of a chapter in a novel: it signals that one part of the film is over and suggests a transition. The presence of such a fade-out at this moment in the film reveals a deep break within diegesis, as well as within the experience of the English king. As Henry doesn't know what the battle has in store for his army, the image dissolves to black, reinforcing loneliness and doubt. The following sequence starts abruptly: the light of day contrasts with the night of the previous scene. The battle of Agincourt is soon to begin, and the French are stationed on top of a hill to observe the ground. The black screen is thus immediately followed by another shot, this time without any progressive fade-in. This produces an effect of forward movement similar to that of musical 'attack'.[31] If Branagh here mirrors the Shakespeare text by evoking the passing of time between the end of the prayer and the beginning of the battle, some of his other adaptations present elliptical effects in a scene meant to remain isochronic in Shakespeare's original play. Branagh's cinematic style, based on uninterrupted movement and energy, lends itself well to ellipses which suppress all minor actions from a film. In *Hamlet*, Barnardo, Horatio and Marcellus come to warn the prince of the apparition. The discussion begins in the palace hall, but ends up in Hamlet's private room, as if a couple of minutes had passed by. This elliptical effect occurs when Hamlet encourages his companions to further deliver a discreet, detailed report of the event. At that point, Branagh modifies both the time of the story and the time of narration. He first creates the impression of

[31] This idea of the musical 'attack' after a fade to black is developed in Robert Edmonds's book, *The Sights and Sounds of Cinema and Television: How the Aesthetic Experience Influences Our Feeling* (New York, London: Teachers College Press, 1992), p. 60.

time passing by, a time which does not exist in Shakespeare's play, thus introducing an effect of diegetic dilation. The rhythm of narrative then displays a temporal reduction: the action that happened during that virtual time is not revealed to the audience.

In Kozintsev's *Hamlet*, the passing of time is expressed through the regular filming of a chiming clock with traditional figures of the Dance of Death. The King, the Queen, the Courtier and the Peasant pass in front of the audience's eyes, until the hooded figure of Death appears with its scythe. The repeated showing of the Dance of Death in the film implies an endless repetition: there is no beginning, there is no end; there is just an eternal renewal of the same cycle. For Kozintsev, ellipsis and the passing of time serve to remind the spectators that death is the ultimate fate of all human beings. As Hamlet puts it, 'your fat king and your lean beggar is but variable service, two dishes, but to one table' (IV.iii.23–4). Kozintsev's emphasis on the chiming clock reflects the text in which the great ones (Alexander, Caesar) as well as the most simple ones (Yorick the jester) are subject to the levelling power of Death.

On film, treating a sequence episodically is another way to compress the time of narration. This kind of sequence, composed of a chronological series of brief isolated scenes, stands for Genette's 'summary', in which the amount of narration is less than that of the story. The episodic sequence appears as a chronological film segment composed of several shots that are obviously temporally connected.[32] A sequence constructed by differing episodes is generally used to present a short cut of slow, predestined evolutions. It may be defined as 'frequentative' if it aims at suggesting the repetition and/or monotony of one action. In that case, the shots are often linked by dissolves to simulate the passing of time. In his *Hamlet*, Michael Almereyda adds an interpolated scene in which the prince is writing his poem, 'Doubt thou the stars are fire' (II.ii.116), to the 'celestial' Ophelia. The sequence is made episodic through discontinuous cuts. An image shows Hamlet writing while the words of the poem can be heard in voice-over. The following images still show Hamlet writing or pausing for inspiration, but in different positions, without any continuity of movement between the shots. This lack of aesthetic fluidity generates an impression of time passing between each image, while reflecting the difficulty of writing experienced by an amateur, clumsy poet. Another example of episodic sequence can be found in Peter Brook's *King Lear*. In the original play, Kent, who has been banished, returns to serve Lear in disguise, introducing himself in these terms:

[32] See Metz, *Essais sur la signification au cinéma*, vol. 1 (Paris: Klincksieck, 1978), p. 132.

I do profess to be no less than I seem, to serve him truly that will put me in trust,
to love him that is honest, to converse with him that is wise and says little, to fear
judgment, to fight when I cannot choose, and to eat no fish. (1.iv.13–17)

In Brook's film, this passage ceases to be part of a dialogue with Lear.
It becomes a monologue which Kent utters during an episodic sequence.
This scene shows the several phases of his physical transformation after
being banished. To each sentence of the short monologue corresponds a
shot separated from the other through time. To move from one shot to
the other, Brook moves the camera closer to Kent's face, fades to black and
then fades in again. The audience sees Kent cutting his hair with a knife,
burning a wooden stick, ruffling his hair, putting soot on his face, smoking
a pipe, putting on gloves and warming himself up near the fire at night.
During each shot, Kent speaks as if the thought has just occurred to him
through the very gestures he is accomplishing. Such an episodic sequence
suggests that this monologue took quite a long time to be delivered in its
entirety. Brook thus creates a phase of initiation. Banished and isolated in
the wilderness, Kent changes his former self into another. Turning his reply
to Lear into a time-fragmented monologue constructs some profession of
faith, emphasizing the character's determination and transformation. The
same kind of episodic sequence appears at the beginning of Trevor Nunn's
Twelfth Night. Nunn films Viola's transformation into a boy in different
shots separated through time: the beautiful long hair being cut, the corset
being removed and the breasts being painfully pressed flat under the clothes.
Through this chronological series of shots, Nunn stresses Viola's heart-
breaking decision to change physically. Deciding to appear as a boy is not
a mere game, but a resolution which has drastic, tormenting consequences
on her body. In *Henry V*, Branagh constructs an episodic sequence to evoke
an epic length. The march to Calais becomes an interpolated sequence in
which the soldiers' superhuman efforts are implied through a succession of
dissolved shots: exhausted men cross rivers under the rain and collapse in
the mud while regular inserts of a French map detail the army's advance.
Therefore, the passing of time is also evoked by a progression through
space.

Focusing and points of view: editing and identification

Editing influences the chronology of diegesis and the rhythm of narrative. Nevertheless, its functions go beyond the organization of diegetic
events within narration. By giving the director the possibility of alternating points of view during the unfolding of events, editing manages the

quantity of information given by narrative about the story. Directors can concentrate the attention of spectators in turn on the various characters, on their perceptions and reactions. In his 1992 book *The Sights and Sounds of Cinema*, Robert Edmonds identifies an essential difference between theatre and cinema: 'in the theatre . . . we are interested in *what* is happening on the stage . . . In film what we are interested in is the performers' reactions to what is happening in the drama.'[33] Therefore, contrary to dramaturgy which is based on action, cinema seems to be built more upon a succession of reactions. By alternating shots of action and shots of reaction, and by making the spectators' object of focus vary, it induces the mechanisms of identification which are generally so difficult to create in the theatre. But what does 'identification' in the cinema mean exactly? In order to avoid any terminological confusion, it is first necessary to establish a distinction between identification as a psychoanalytic concept and identification as a cinematic concept.

According to Freud, there are two kinds of identification: primary and secondary. Freud sets down primary identification as the very basis of the imaginary constitution of the I.[34] During the first years of the subject's life, this identification is the first form of affective link with the mother. At this oral stage, the child still makes no delineation between self and other. The differentiation between the subject and the object takes place during the 'mirror stage', a theory elaborated by Jacques Lacan. In his 1949 essay, 'The Mirror Stage as Formative of the Function of the I as Revealed in Psychoanalytic Experience', Lacan argues that the human being comes into the world without an ego – without an identity, without a sense of self separate from an other (its mother). After experiencing a fragmented reality through underdeveloped senses and motor skills, the infant discovers in the mirror his own image as well as the image of the (m)other who carries him or stands close to him.[35] The mirror stage ends the fantasy of the disjointed body since the child is faced with an image of itself as a totalized whole. Ego is born as the infant identifies with the image. However, because this image of a unified body does not yet correspond with the underdeveloped infant's physical weakness, it is seen as an Ideal I towards which the subject will always strive throughout his or her existence.

---

[33] Edmonds, *Sights and Sounds of Cinema*, p. 13.

[34] See Sigmund Freud, *The Essentials of Psychoanalysis*, ed. Anna Freud, trans. James Strachey (Harmondsworth: Penguin Books, 1986), pp. 452–61.

[35] See Jacques Lacan, *Ecrits: A Selection*, trans. Alan Sheridan (London: Tavistock Publications, 1977), pp. 1–7.

If the mirror stage ends the phase of primary identification, the Oedipus complex – when the child is between three and five years old – leads the way to the phenomenon of secondary identification. In *Five Lectures on Psycho-Analysis*, Freud explains how the child first models itself upon the parent of the same sex, whose place near the parent of the opposite sex it would like to take. The little boy admires his father but at the same time would like to supplant him. The relationship of identification, therefore, frequently assumes an aspect of hostility or, at least, ambivalence.[36] After the Oedipal phase, other forms of identification replace the relationships with the mother and the father. The subject abandons emotional investment in the parents and replaces it with a series of secondary identifications with admired characters, either in real life or in the course of cultural experiences. In secondary identification, we assimilate something from the other without realizing it; we are continually and unconsciously invaded by the personalities of others. This leads progressively to the internalization of a model which constitutes the 'Ideal I'. This process happens extensively during childhood but continues all through life. Secondary identifications thus allow one individual to play the parts of many people at the same time. Because of their Oedipal origins, these identifications always remain extremely ambivalent, prone to expressions of tenderness or desires of violence. In the end, the subject's personality is created through the diversity of its models, through the successes or failures of secondary identifications.

Film theorists such as Christian Metz and Jean-Louis Baudry have emphasized several analogies between the subject of psychoanalysis and the spectator in the cinema. Cinematic experience may be likened to the mirror stage in which the infant learns to recognize its own image. The framed and limited surface of the screen is similar to a mirror in which the spectators, fascinated by the reflection, experience the wholeness of the body, even though the bodies seen on the mirror-screen are not their own.[37] Metz also identifies a double identification in the cinema, primary cinematic identification and secondary cinematic identification. The adjective 'cinematic' is used to make the distinction between these concepts and those of Freudian psychoanalysis. Primary and secondary cinematic identifications are always part of Freud's secondary identification since they can only be experienced by a subject who went beyond the stage of differentiation between self and other, thus reaching the symbolic stage.

---

[36] See Sigmund Freud, *Five Lectures on Psycho-Analysis*, trans. James Strachey (Harmondsworth: Penguin Books, 1995), pp. 74–8.

[37] See Christian Metz, 'The Imaginary Signifier', in *Film and Theory: An Anthology*, ed. Robert Stam and Toby Miller (Oxford: Blackwell, 2000), p. 411.

In primary cinematic identification, the spectators identify with the sub-ject of their vision, with their own gaze. In other words, we experience ourselves as the privileged subject of the show.[38] In secondary cinematic identification, the spectators identify with the characters as figures of the self within the fiction, and as the focuses of emotional investment. As opposed to preconceived ideas, the spectators will not identify with a char-acter because it has a 'nice' personality, but because it is inserted in a certain situation or narrative structure which calls for identification. Identifica-tion is, in fact, less a psychological consequence than a structural one. According to the authors of *Esthétique du film*, 'each *situation* that springs up in the course of the film redistributes the places, proposes a new net-work, a new positioning of the *intersubjective relations* within the fiction'.[39] Consequently, secondary cinematic identification, just like psychoanalyti-cal secondary identification, is not a stable phenomenon: its focus changes several times during the film – whenever a new situation arises. Since identification precedes empathy and not the other way round, the specta-tors can find themselves frequently identifying with 'bad' characters. We can imagine ourselves in turn in the role of the victim experiencing fear and of the assailant experiencing sadism, in the place of the person who asks (expressing desire and lack) and of the person who receives the plea (experiencing narcissism), in the part of the one who knows (representing the parents) and of the one who learns (symbolizing the child).[40]

The mechanisms which regulate identification in the cinema lead back to film editing, since it offers the spectators a multiplicity of points of view in the course of one scene. It shapes space by alternating shots of action and reaction, notably with the technique of shots/counter-shots which consists of showing first a given field, then a spatially opposed field. For example, two characters face to face will be filmed by framing each face in turn. This process seems to be at the very root of secondary identification in the cinema, as it constantly shifts the focus of emotional investment. In 1946, the director Robert Montgomery attempted the experiment of filming only a private detective's point of view in subjective camera. He believed that the spectators would identify even more with the character. The film, *Lady in the Lake*, is, however, famous for its failure at the box-office. The lack of objective shots of the actor and the absence of shots/counter-shots would suppress, on the contrary, any possibility of identifying. Identification with a character seems to require a back-and-forth move between a shot and a

[38] *Ibid.*, p. 413.
[39] Aumont *et al.*, *Esthétique du film*, p. 192. My translation from French. Italics by the authors.
[40] *Ibid.*, p. 193.

counter-shot, between the focus on a character and the focus through the eyes of a character.[41] The spectators must know the character before they can interiorize the character's own gaze. They should be able to identify with themselves 'as pure act of perception' (primary cinematic identification) and should therefore see the characters, before being able to identify with them (secondary cinematic identification).

In their screen adaptations, directors often take advantage of the shot/counter-shot to develop a complex economy of the gaze. In Joseph Mankiewicz's *Julius Caesar*, reaction can even precede action. A shot of a woman screaming in the crowd is seen before the image of Mark Antony carrying Caesar's corpse out of the Capitol. Antony's entrance is thus announced by a violent response, and made more spectacular when it is finally revealed. During his speech, Antony is scrutinized by a throng that he must tame. Numerous reaction shots of the whole crowd or of individuals come to punctuate his words. Responses progressively move from threat and animosity to approval and support. When Antony pauses for a short while, he turns his back on the crowd. The camera shows the citizens still watching Antony who pretends not to comprehend the passions that he just aroused. Editing thus alternates shots of a crowd watching a single man, and shots of a man who discreetly spies on those he shrewdly manipulates. When Antony unveils Caesar's wounded body, a long tracking shot lingers in close-up on the citizens' gaze. The focus of emotional investment is subtly blurred between a powerful, threatening but genuine and compassionate crowd, and a lonely, passionate but secretive and machiavellian orator. In Branagh's *Hamlet*, the 'Mousetrap' scene presents reaction shots and even some reaction shots to the reactions, as some characters watch some other characters react. The characters keep spying on one another during the performance of the Players. For example, Horatio observes Claudius carefully through binoculars. In a 1996 interview for BBC Education, Branagh commented on this constant return of glances: 'It felt like a very strong scene to treat cinematically and we went in determined to cover it with endless numbers of angles. In editing, we could construct it and we've spent probably more time on that scene than any other in the picture.'[42]

This construction of drama through reaction is also the basis of the conclusion of Taymor's *Titus*. Taymor suddenly transfers the final slaughter over the banquet table from Titus's house to the dark Coliseum seen at the beginning of the film. Five reaction shots show groups of spectators on

---

[41] See Francis Vanoye, *Cinéma et récit 1: récit écrit, récit filmique* (Paris: Nathan, 1989), p. 146.
[42] See Branagh's interview on the *BBC Education* website: <www.bbc.co.uk/education/archive/hamlet/vision.htm>.

the steps of the monument watching the horrible, violent scene unfolding before their eyes. The audience in the Coliseum, as that in the cinema, silently witness the result of the cycle of hatred. Unlike Mankiewicz or Branagh, who use reaction shots to show the characters' changing emotions, Taymor works here with the shot/counter-shot pattern in a non-diegetic way, metacinematically reflecting the audience's gaze on the film.

In his 1991 book, *Still in Movement*, Lorne Buchman persuasively considers that this action/reaction structure which is so specific to film creates a space that is unknown in the theatre: the spectator has the opportunity not only to look through the eyes of the characters, but also to 'travel the intimate space between those eyes'.[43] In adaptations of *Henry V*, the warlike speeches have been treated differently as far as this travel of 'intimate space' is concerned. In 1944, Laurence Olivier retains theatricality by filming Henry's harangues in one take, with the camera moving back progressively. For Olivier, the camera had to be pulled back to provide 'space' for the vocal climax.[44] In contrast, Branagh's exhortations present the various reactions of the soldiers listening to their king in close-ups. Bernice W. Kliman has noticed this particular phenomenon in this *Henry V*: 'this film is less about action than about responding to action'.[45] The Harfleur speech includes six reaction shots, then a succession of shots showing galvanized soldiers. As far as the Saint Crispin speech is concerned, it includes three reaction shots followed by a series of shots revealing the enthusiasm of the soldiers, ready to rush to the battlefield. This alternation conditions identification both with the king and his subjects. The focus of emotional investment goes from the exhorting man to those who listen, from the one who orders to those who obey.

The same contrast between the display of all the characters in one shot and the alternation of shots/counter-shots can be found in the different versions of the wooing scene in *Richard III*. In Laurence Olivier's 1955 film, Richard and Anne share the camera field. There is no particular focus on one character or the other. Quite differently, Loncraine's 1995 production presents alternated focuses. The shots keep alternating between Anne and Richard, sharing each character's viewpoint. We shift from Olivier's theatrical perspective in which the spectators can choose their own focus, to more

[43] Lorne Buchman, *Still in Movement: Shakespeare on Screen* (Oxford University Press, 1991), p. 25.
[44] See Roger Manvell, *Theater and Film: A Comparative Study of the Two Forms of Dramatic Art, and the Problems of Adaptation of Stage Plays into Films* (Cranbury: Associated University Presses, 1979), p. 34.
[45] Bernice W. Kliman, 'Branagh's Henry: Allusion and Illusion', *Shakespeare on Film Newsletter* 14.1 (December 1989), 9.

emotionally involving (and manipulative?) phenomena of identification, which make the audience alternatively share Anne's dilemma and enjoy Richard's cunning plan.

When the camera shows a character and then this character's point of view, the spectators identify with their own gaze while identifying the subjective vision as that of the character momentarily absent from the screen. The image is thus made subjective by the very context of the film, through editing. In Welles's *Macbeth*, the alternation between shots of Macbeth and shots of the dagger that he sees before him turns an objective image into a subjective one. The shot of the dagger keeps getting out of and into focus, sharing Macbeth's viewpoint and paralleling his uncertainty about the object's actual presence. In his *Othello*, Welles notably uses subjective camera during the Moor's epileptic collapse after Iago's revelations. After filming a distressed Othello running on the battlements, Welles cuts to a low-angle shot that subjectively shows the character's perspective when he falls down onto the ground. Sometimes, the subjective shot is made less obvious. At the end of the film, Othello delivers his last speech directly to the camera. The monologue could be considered as addressed to the spectators only, until the next shot reveals Iago looking down. Othello is actually talking to him, and the shot is a subjective one. For a short while, the audience has completely shared Iago's viewpoint. The spectators are also acknowledged in Branagh's *Hamlet*, when Yorick's skull is shown facing the camera. The skull seems to reflect our own image, reminding us of the inevitable death of every being. But the previous shot of Hamlet's face informed us that the image of the skull is not objective: the skull is being looked at by the prince. The shot, transformed into a *memento mori* for the audience, is also made subjective by a contextualization that becomes feasible due to the availability of the resource of editing.

The changes in point of view often come along with variations in the scale of shots, which also participate in generating phenomena of identification. In the theatre, some processes such as the 'proscenium-adjuster' made possible a certain concentration upon one part of space, one object or one character, by reducing the audience's field of vision. The cinema, with the help of editing, can go further. In the course of one scene, it can modify the relation between the height of the frame and that of the character. The alternation of closeness and distance allows the character to be inserted within the narrative structure each time in a different way. It can be a figure among others in the frame, or become the central focus of identification by being isolated with a close-up. The establishing shot enables the geographic location where the action unfolds to be situated clearly; the long shot puts the emphasis on the set, and starts to make the action stand out; the medium long shot frames characters from head to toe; the medium close shot cuts the characters below the knees, stressing their gestures; and the close shot cuts the actors at the waist, emphasizing their expressions. Finally, the close-up frames the face, and the extreme close-up focuses on one particular part of the visage. The close-up not only helps to provide a closer view of reality, but also to reproduce the mental act of focusing. It would be tempting to study its effects on the audience with regard to proxemics, the science of face-to-face interactions elaborated by Edward T. Hall in his 1959 book, *The Silent Language*. Hall identifies four types of distances between the speaker and the listener, each generating a particular relation: *intimate* distance (within 1.5 feet) reserved for telling secrets, comforting others and love-making, *personal* distance (from 1.5 to 4 feet) used when talking to friends, *social* distance (from 4 to 12 feet) generally used for social gatherings, and *public* distance (beyond 12 feet) reserved for formal speeches, lectures and business meetings.[46] Hall's followers, such as Stuart Albert, have noticed that speakers have a stronger power of conviction when they get closer to their listener until they reach personal distance. But if they get too close, this power decreases.[47] It is, however, difficult to study the consequences of the scale of shots in the cinema by applying these theories. As opposed to the theatre, the spectators and actors in the cinema occupy distinct spaces that are separated by a radically watertight screen. While establishing shots are similar to the stage perspective, close-ups lead the audience to a space unknown in the theatre. This great proximity of the camera is quite essential to set the level of attention that a spectator grants to one character.[48] The close-up underlines the expressions, emphasizing the role of faces within diegesis. It intensifies the mechanisms of identification by creating an emotional face-to-face with the actor. As a shot associated with confidence and secrecy, it creates an intimate relationship with the characters.

In Peter Brook's *King Lear*, the characters are repeatedly filmed in extreme close-ups, as opposed to Grigori Kozintsev's version in which the protagonists are very often alienated from the audience in long shots. Brook particularly fixates upon the eyes of Gloucester and Lear, echoing the themes of literal and figurative blindness. Zeffirelli, in his adaptation of *The Taming of the Shrew*, also lingers in extreme close-ups on the eyes of Katharina spying

---

[46] See Edward T. Hall, *The Silent Language* (New York: Doubleday, 1959), pp. 204–9.
[47] See Stuart Albert, 'Physical Distance and Persuasion', *Journal of Personality and Social Psychology* 15.3 (1970), 265–70.
[48] See Aumont *et al.*, *Esthétique du film*, p. 197.

on her sister and on Petruchio at the beginning of the film. Through these shots, the film emphasizes Katharina's desire to control every situation, to master even action that takes place behind her back.

The alternation of close-ups and long shots can be extremely meaningful as well. For example, in Loncraine's *Richard III*, the wooing scene is composed of a series of close-ups of Richard and Lady Anne, but ends with a long shot of Anne alone in the mortuary. This abrupt change of scale stresses the character's confusion and loneliness. As the long shot suddenly reveals the corpse of Anne's father-in-law close to her, the sequence emphasizes Anne's difficulty in forgetting Richard's murders. This is far from Olivier's version in which the dead body is absent from the screen during the whole wooing scene. Anne is thus much more inclined to forget and become romantically involved with the murderer.

Branagh proposes particular interpretations of the plays of *Henry V* and *Hamlet* by playing on the scale of shots. *Henry V* favours close-ups and medium shots. Even when the film presents exterior scenes, the camera remains fixed mostly on the characters. The close-ups allow for a focus on King Henry, concentrating on his doubting, interior world. On the other hand, the film of *Hamlet* plays on contrasts. It alternates establishing shots revealing the frame of action and developing a centrifugal universe, and extreme close-ups exploring the tiny details of faces and insisting on flesh and death. Consequently, a representation of a mouth can stretch to the size of the whole screen: it is as if intimacy itself becomes epic. With a particular use of the scale of shots, Branagh therefore transforms the history play of *Henry V* into a tragedy of doubt, while the tragedy of *Hamlet* is turned into a military epic.

The alternation of subjective perceptions

Cinema's ability to make the scale of shots vary and to alternate points of view allows space but also the different perceptions of that space to be shaped. Whereas theatre can only present a single level of perceptible reality, movie editing can offer different visions of one event through the eyes of various characters. This aesthetic potential has some interesting consequences for the closet scene in *Hamlet*. In Shakespeare's play, the Ghost is supposed to be perceived by Hamlet only, and not by his mother, who remains bewildered by the words that her son addresses to an inaudible and invisible being. When this moment is performed in the theatre, the director must make a decision: either the Ghost is physically present on stage, or it is not. Yet, in the cinema, the Ghost can be both present *and* absent. Cinematic editing brings an essential element to that scene: it can change viewpoints and turn objectivity into subjectivity. Branagh's camera in 1996 – like Olivier's in 1948 and Zeffirelli's in 1990 – first shares Hamlet's point of view and shows the Ghost, then shares Gertrude's point of view and does not show it. The combination of these two experiences through editing makes two realities co-exist within the same space. According to Lorne Buchman, the alternation of subjective visions can reflect the Ghost's ambiguous state, an entity both present and absent, creating a dynamic tension between identification and alienation.[49] The spectators share the point of view of one character (Hamlet seeing and hearing the Ghost) and are brought to identify with him, only to turn to another point of view (Gertrude not perceiving the Ghost) which alienates them from the former.

But if editing makes this alternation of participation and distance possible, it also provides the chance to enter a character's interior dimension by showing both how he perceives space (through subjective camera shots) and what the very visions of his mind are. Unlike a theatre director, who can generally suggest mental images only through text, lighting effects, sound of voice and meaningful moves by the actors, the film director can literally penetrate the character's interior world. In *Looking For Richard*, Pacino makes the audience experience Richard's dream on the eve of the battle of Bosworth. The nightmare is visually composed of two different kind of images – those that were seen previously in the film and those that will be shown again later during the battle. Flashbacks of the murders Richard ordered and flashforwards of his own imminent death coalesce in a quasi-subliminal way to produce confusion, remorse and premonition all at the same time. In his *Hamlet*, Branagh reveals Ophelia's most secret thoughts. When the girl swears to her father that she will not see Hamlet any more, Branagh inserts some shots showing the loving relationship already consummated. Whether the images are memories or mere fantasies, they purport to display a real sinking into Ophelia's intimate space. They even suggest some grounds for her future descent into madness, since her father is to be murdered by the man with whom she has experienced her first love affair. In Baz Luhrmann's 1996 *Romeo + Juliet*, Romeo only begins to wake up from his wedding night when his mind recalls his killing of Tybalt the night before. Luhrmann cuts to brief images of the murder, emphasizing trauma and death over the new relationship of love. The director of the 1995 *Othello*, Oliver Parker, also explores the intimate thoughts of the

---

Moor during his epileptic crisis. As opposed to Welles, who films the scene in subjective camera from Othello's viewpoint, Parker presents the very visions of the disturbed mind. The audience doesn't witness what Othello sees any more, but what he imagines. The spectators are transported into a voyeuristic fantasy in which Desdemona sleeps with Cassio. The shots, revealing parts of the two bodies, entwined, are edited faster and faster, giving rise to a kind of delirious, orgasmic trance.

Through editing and superimposition, directors can also transform the thought of one character into a thought shared by several. In Branagh's *Henry V*, during the final scene in which the English and French monarchs are negotiating the peace, one shot of the English king is followed by a series of shots in flashback showing the characters who have died in the course of the film. Then, instead of coming back to the English king, Branagh cuts to the French king. This structure, which inserts nostalgic and mortuary reminders between shots of the two monarchs, turns the flashback into one single, common memory. In *Titus*, Taymor creates surreal, nightmarish images of fire and body parts, which are repeatedly superimposed between Tamora and Titus. These sequences delve into the landscapes of the characters' minds, while creating shared memories of violence and murder. Here, two illusions of interior realities are jumbled together.

The Shakespeare text and the limits of editing

In spite of the possibilities offered by editing for shaping space and time, some directors of Shakespeare films see *montage* as a hindrance to the dramatist's verbal flow. In his 1992 essay, 'Shakespeare on Film and Television', Robert Hapgood quotes Michael Birkett, the producer of Peter Hall's *A Midsummer's Night's Dream*, on the consequences of editing:

Peter Hall and I found in *A Midsummer Night's Dream* that there were several passages where, looking at the picture on a movieola,[50] without any sound, the cutting pattern seemed to be perfect. Hearing the sound track on its own, the rhythms of the speech also seemed to be fine. When the two were run together, however, the result seemed unsatisfactory.[51]

For Birkett, the edited succession of images breaks the harmony and rhythm of Shakespeare dialogues and monologues. Such belief in the wrongs of editing can be related to André Bazin's theories, which are

---

[50] Individual watching-and-listening appliance for editing film.
[51] Robert Hapgood, 'Shakespeare on Film and Television' in *The Cambridge Companion to Shakespeare Studies*, ed. Stanley Wells (Cambridge University Press, 1986), p. 277.

expounded in his book, *What is Cinema?* According to Bazin, cinema should reproduce reality, and respect its ambiguity as much as possible. In a normative discourse about what cinema should be, Bazin forbids editing 'When the essence of a scene demands the simultaneous presence of two or more factors in the action', that is when the event is highly ambiguous and unpredictable.[52] To illustrate his theory, Bazin takes the example of an Inuit trying to catch a seal. According to him, such a scene shouldn't be shot by alternating shots of the hunter and shots of the game. In such an unpredictable situation – as no one knows what the final result of the hunt will be – editing is considered as disrupting spatial reality and, therefore, seen as a deceptive trick destroying the sequence's ambiguity.

In order to avoid interfering with the harmony of the text and to protect the energy and rhythm of the actors within a scene, directors have thought of shooting whole pieces of script in sequence shots. Those sequences are composed of one continuous unedited shot, using only the movements of the camera, the changes in depth of field and the entries and exits of characters. In his 1953 adaptation of *Julius Caesar*, Joseph Mankiewicz, fearing to disrupt the fluidity and the emotional dimension of scenes, frequently films the actors' confrontation, as well as their monologues, within the same shot.[53] To organize the sequences, these directors base their work less on editing and more on camerawork. Yet, it would be inaccurate to think that the momentary absence of editing necessarily means the suppression of cinematic narration. The use of a camera, with the effects and focuses that it can accomplish, seems to mark the first step in the separation between filmed theatre and cinematic art.

CAMERAWORK AND NARRATION

In her 1953 book *Feeling and Form*, Susanne Langer argues that the phase of framing can make the film closer to a narrative than a dramatic presentation – even before editing.[54] In his 1964 work *Logique du cinéma*, André Laffay establishes a link between camera focusing and the narrative process: he invents the notion of a 'virtual narrator' – called 'le Grand Imagier' ('The Great Image-Maker') – who would not only turn the 'pages' of the film for the spectators, but who would also draw their attention to special details of

---

[52] André Bazin, *What is Cinema?*, trans. Hugh Gray (Berkeley and Los Angeles: University of California Press, 1967), p. 50.
[53] See Neil Sinyard, *Filming Literature: The Art of Screen Adaptation* (London and Sydney: Croom Helm, 1986), p. 4.
[54] See Susanne Langer, *Feeling and Form* (New York: Scribner's, 1953), p. 411.

the action.[55] Then, in 1968, Scholes and Kellogg suggest that film 'is a form of narrative rather than dramatic art because it does not present a story directly, without narration, but always through the medium of a controlled point of view, the eye of the camera, which sharpens or blurs focus, closes in or draws off'.[56] Camera movements and changes in focus seem to be the first gestures of the cinematic narrator, creating a first distinction between theatre and cinema. In Zeffirelli's *Romeo and Juliet*, at the end of the balcony scene, the camera shows in close-up the two lovers' hands reaching for each other, before zooming out slowly to disclose the whole situation: Juliet is up on her balcony while Romeo is back on the ground. Instead of presenting a close shot of the hands followed by a long shot of the two lovers apart, Zeffirelli uses a progressive zoom out, thus emphasizing how difficult and painful it is for the lovers to part. Making the camera move or zoom appears to represent a substitute for editing.

Sequence shot, movement and focusing

It seems that moving the camera is already a source of exterior narration, introducing different levels of narrative knowledge. When the camera is held behind a character, it shows what he or she sees, creating an internal focus, or more precisely an 'ocularization' to cite François Jost's concept.[57] Then, as it moves and acquires another shooting angle, the camera may shift to the subjective or semi-subjective[58] vision of another character. A director can, therefore, use many camera effects to introduce a certain form of narration without cutting the rhythm of the Shakespeare text. From theatre to cinema, focus shifts from a status which is mostly external to a status which oscillates between external and internal, between objectivity and subjectivity. In his 1948 *Hamlet*, Laurence Olivier had already chosen to resort frequently to continuous shots. The progressive unveiling of the action was introduced with camera moves but also with changes in the focus of the lens: Olivier could thus shift the object of attention at will without the discontinuity of editing. In his own adaptation of *Hamlet*, Branagh applies this technique to the closet scene. Gertrude and Hamlet are seen in profile in the foreground. The Ghost appears suddenly in the background, full face in the middle of the screen. It is out of focus but quickly becomes

---

[55] See Albert Laffay, *Logique du cinéma* (Paris: Masson, 1964), pp. 80–2.
[56] Kellogg and Scholes, *Nature of Narrative*, p. 280.
[57] See François Jost, *L'œil-caméra. Entre film et roman* (Presses Universitaires de Lyon, 1987), pp. 27–8.
[58] In a semi-subjective shot, the camera films both the character and his or her point of view. The spectator watches the character (usually seen from behind) in the act of watching.

sharp. That change reveals the Ghost, but loses the mother and the son into blurredness. Even though the family is shown in the same shot, it is nevertheless separated on two levels, foreground and background. The aesthetic effect reinforces the divided situation of the family. According to Branagh, action filmed in one unbroken shot 'allows the characters to interact [and] to retain a certain idea of theatre'.[59] Nevertheless, if Branagh's use of long takes helps to protect stage acting, emotional crescendos and the unity of a scene, it retreats from theatrical art by the very mobility of the camera, which guides the audience's gaze. By showing the spectators several events seen through a multiplicity of viewpoints in the course of a single shot, the sequence-shot can be read as the sum of successive editing effects. In Branagh's adaptations, long whirling moves put the audience right into the heart of the action and the group of characters. By giving the impression of sharing confidences, these circular movements regularly put the public into an intrusive, almost voyeuristic situation. According to Pierre Berthomieu in his book *Kenneth Branagh* (1998), 'Branagh meets . . . the Hollywood narrative aesthetic, in which the exploration of space allows the signifying groups of characters to be arranged. Camera movements . . . select . . . narrative information, move from one group-theme to another group-theme.'[60] These curves, therefore, participate in advancing the plot by bringing a character, an object or an action useful to the story into the camera field at the right moment.[61] In *Hamlet*, the camera moves are adapted to the labyrinthine setting, losing and finding the characters in the palace maze. During long shots which are used to film soliloquies, the arrival of Rosencrantz and Guildenstern, the nunnery scene in which Hamlet drags Ophelia down the hall, or the confrontation with Claudius prior to Hamlet's exile, the camera turns around the action and then gets closer to an individual as if to capture his or her thoughts. The rotation ends in a forward move to intercept emotions at a particular moment. This travelling strangles space, enclosing the character and often signalling reflection and introspection. It is notably used to film King Henry V's night meditations, Claudius's confession and Ophelia's lament for her father's death.

If the actor sometimes enters the frame by himself and shows up voluntarily, he can also try to avoid us. In Akira Kurosawa's *Throne of Blood*, a free

---

[59] Quoted in French by Pierre Berthomieu, *Kenneth Branagh* (Paris: Jean-Michel Place, 1998), p. 202. My translation.

[60] *Ibid.*, pp. 98–9. My translation.

[61] Branagh himself establishes a link between circular movement in a continuous shot and the idea of a written narration: 'It is as if you turned the pages of a book. You had forgotten a character for a few seconds, then he comes back.' Quoted in French by Berthomieu, *Kenneth Branagh*, p. 203. My translation.

adaptation of *Macbeth*, the audience only sees Washizu (Macbeth) in the camera field when his wife advises him to kill the king and rise to power. Washizu's wife is not revealed during the whole speech. The image is that of Washizu, but the sound comes from his spouse. It is as if her voice has turned into a voice-over belonging to Washizu's mind and conscience. By concealing the ambitious wife from the screen at this particular moment, Kurosawa highlights her voicing of her husband's most intimate and unavowed thoughts. To fetch the wine that she will use to drug the guards, Lady Washizu disappears again from the screen into a pitch dark room. She becomes, metaphorically, the incarnation of evil itself. At the time of the actual killing, she is finally the entire focus of attention while the victim is hidden from view. Instead of showing the murder, Kurosawa imposes the sight of the murderer only, putting the stress on the very act that will lead to remorse rather than on a voyeuristic image of the killing.

Olivier's *Richard III* begins with a court celebration filled with joyful music. There is no trace of Richard himself. With a long tracking shot, the camera has to go and find him lurking behind a door, inside the throne room. Richard finally appears as a black exclamation mark in the colourful set, and walks towards the front of the screen. As soon as Olivier's version starts, crossing a threshold means entering Richard's realm. At the end of the wooing scene, Anne disappears quietly through a door in the wall behind her. Being won, Anne symbolically crosses the boundary that leads her into Richard's domination.

In Branagh's adaptations, Henry V is a character who keeps coming in and going out of the field willingly. When the Chorus describes the king in the most laudatory terms on the night before the battle, Henry's face in profile enters the field suddenly, imposing itself on our vision. In contrast, Hamlet's first appearance takes place in the mode of denial. During the first court scene, Hamlet refuses to show himself. The audience does not see him until his first cue. The camera must go and seek him out with a tracking shot to the far side of the room, forcing him to face the court's gaze as well as ours.

Unveiling and narration

By progressively revealing the people, the set or the action, the moves and effects of the lens add a time dimension to space. As opposed to the theatre, in which the stage is wholly perceived at every moment, cinema can disclose elements little by little to compose the action. Film shifts from a spatial, whole vision to a breaking of space in the course of time. This gradual unveiling brings a new time dimension and introduces a narrative unfolding within the very act of showing. The camera movements offer a reading itinerary, impose a gaze on the audience, and reveal an exterior enunciation. The notion of editing can be found not only in the succession of shots but also *inside* the shots. The films shift from director Sergei Eisenstein's idea of editing, in which different shots are linked together, to that described by André Bazin in his book *What is Cinema?*, in which the continuous shot becomes a window opened onto a world containing its own succession of actions.[62]

With *Titus* in 2000, Taymor sets a new trend as she often works with the mode of change in continuity. For example, after receiving Titus's arrows bearing messages to the gods, an agitated Saturninus runs through the hallways of the palace, wearing only a bathrobe. His moving down the corridors is followed with both camera motion and cuts until he reaches a large door. Taymor then cuts to a shot inside the Senate. When Saturninus briskly opens the door, he bursts into the Senate with a new costume on. He no longer wears a bathrobe but a grey, formal suit. He then begins to rant in front of the Roman senators. The transition is thus achieved without the energy and movement being broken. The audience rarely realizes that a change of costume has been made. Taymor edits, but preserves an impression of continuity as if she were filming a sequence-shot. The same kind of 'similar-in-change' effect happens just a bit later on in the movie. A dissolve leads the spectators from Saturninus pacing back and forth in a palace room, to Lucius also pacing back and forth in a tent in Gothic territory. The two movements are co-ordinated so that the second seems to extend the first. Again, Taymor constructs the transition with editing, but maintains a sense of theatrical continuity through the preservation of rhythm and energy.

Slow-motion and quick-motion

Framing is a phase which not only adds focus but also allows some control of time. Even before the stage of editing, it is indeed possible to introduce a gap between the length of the story and that of narration, especially through slow-motion. This effect is introduced during the shooting of the film. It calls for a high-speed camera that facilitates the shooting of more images per second. When the film unwinds at normal speed, the action then seems to unfold more slowly.

[62] See Bazin, *What is Cinema?*, p. 166.

Branagh was the first film director to extensively appropriate slow-motion in Shakespeare adaptations. This effect can be frequently found in key moments of his other films, such as the apocalyptic finale in *Dead Again*, the creature's attack at the Sea of Ice in *Mary Shelley's Frankenstein*, and the cheerful reunion that concludes *Peter's Friends*. Slow-motion brings power, producing a lyrical and passionate pause. For Branagh, it helps 'to insist, to add colour. It is an extra stroke of brush which underlines a scene or draws attention to one element.'[63] Consequently, this effect appears not only as a technique that masters time, but also as a process of focusing. In *Henry V*, the use of slow-motion turns the battle of Agincourt into a dream-like sequence verging on nightmare.[64] Slow-motion adds power to the combatants' blows and, by dilating time, underlines the soldiers' heroism and physical effort. But it can also stress the futility of action. When Henry hears the long howl of pain coming from the pages being slaughtered, he starts running to save them. His desperate rush is filmed in slow-motion, stressing the king's inability to stop the course of tragic events.

In Taymor's *Titus*, when a mutilated Lavinia is discovered by Marcus in the swamps, she opens her mouth in slow-motion and lets a flow of blood fall. Marcus's reaction is filmed in close-up, also in slow-motion. The reduced speed produces an effect of contemplation, of emotional emphasis. During the climatic sequence of the banquet, Taymor goes so far as to freeze time with the Time-Slice camera-array system, used notably by the Wachowski brothers in their 1999 film *The Matrix*. After Saturninus has slaughtered Titus by thrusting a candelabra into his chest, and Lucius has forced Saturninus to swallow a spoon, the camera turns around the scene while the action is frozen. Lucius's son watches his father suddenly pull a gun and shoot Saturninus in the head, while everything else still doesn't move. In an *American Cinematographer* interview, Taymor commented on that particular moment:

I decided that if I was going to use it [this system], I should do it to highlight the final act [of violence] that the child sees. I think in that regard, it worked as the climax of the film . . . We shot that sequence without the effect as well, but I think you need to stop that moment to highlight the way we create art out of violence, or masterpieces out of torture.[65]

---

[63] Quoted in French by Berthomieu, *Kenneth Branagh*, p. 203. My translation.
[64] It is to be noted that, in Branagh's films, slow-motion often signals a transition to dreams or memories. In *Hamlet*, Branagh shows the murder of Old Hamlet in a slow-motion flashback.
[65] Interviewed by Stephen Pizzello, 'From Stage to Screen', *American Cinematographer*, bonus on the DVD of Taymor's *Titus*, Twentieth Century Fox Home Entertainment, 2000.

Taymor asserts the emphatic outcome of the freezing of time, as well as the paradox that surrounds every piece of art whose subject is horror. The audience is meant to share the child's viewpoint and contemplate the aesthetics of violence.

In 1991, Lorne Buchman concluded in his book *Still in Movement* that Shakespeare film directors did not take advantage enough of all the narrative possibilities of cinema as they ignored some temporal alternatives:

> Unlike the manner with which [films] develop qualities of space that are distinctly cinematic, [they] rarely accentuate the equivalents of time. To date, there are relatively few flashbacks in Shakespeare films, few instances of the expansion or reduction of time when not already part of Shakespeare's scripts, . . . little use of slow or fast motion, lapsed time, or high-speed photography.[66]

Until recently, directors indeed made little use of the ellipsis, flashback, quick- or slow-motion. It seems as if Branagh changed that habit. His screen adaptations very often include formal work on time. Through a narrative aesthetic, he reshapes Shakespeare's plays, creates story reminders and causal links that bring narrative, spatial and temporal logic. Through the focus in space and the control of time that it implies, narration draws an itinerary of the gaze, imposing a trajectory within Shakespeare plays. Since *Henry V* in 1989, other directors have introduced extensive time effects in their adaptations. Baz Luhrmann uses quick-motion to emphasize the comic and neurotic aspects of Juliet's mother, who is presented as being perennially hurried or disoriented in *William Shakespeare's Romeo + Juliet* (1996). Trevor Nunn, in his film production of *Twelfth Night* (1996), adds short flashbacks when Viola recalls the shipwreck in which she lost her brother. Richard Loncraine films Richard III plunging in slow-motion into the flames of hell at the end of the 1996 movie. Taymor's *Titus* (2000) slows or freezes time to contemplate violence or horror, notably in her 'Penny Arcade Nightmares'.[67] This space and time reorganization is now typical of the narrative adaptations of Shakespeare. It induces an empirical effect, providing viewers with the feeling that the film experience is life-like in terms of physical space and chronological time. Though time is generally considered linear, our actual experience of it involves more complex, anachronic processes. Our current actions are guided by future goals as well as memories of past events, while the same period of time may seem

---

[66] See Buchman, *Still in Movement*, p. 107.
[67] See Lisa S. Starks, 'Cinema of Cruelty', in *The Reel Shakespeare*, ed. Lisa S. Starks and Courtney Lehmann (London: Associated University Presses, 2002), pp. 121–42.

to stretch out for hours or to pass by almost unnoticed.[68] Cinematic flash-backs, flashforwards, ellipses or freezes participate in this realistic rendering of our perception of time, enhancing the impression that the diegesis is happening 'for real'. This poses the ideological problem of the transformation of the original plays' reflexive and metatheatrical aspects in such a realistic cinematic world.

[68] See Pam Morris, *Realism* (London: Routledge, 2003), pp. 107–9.

CHAPTER 3

Masking film construction: towards a 'real' world

This third chapter examines how most film directors elaborate, from Shakespeare plays, classical fictions in which semiotic elements are combined to create a realistic, melodramatic world.

Classical cinema usually favours plots in which characters are psychologically coherent and events can be explained in terms of natural/logical causation. According to Kristin Thompson in *Classical Hollywood Cinema*, the basic principles of a classical film would be the story as the basis of the film, the technique as an 'indiscernible thread', the audience as controlled and comprehending, and complete closure as the end of all.[1] This chafes against the tradition of the Elizabethan stage that disclosed theatrical illusion through metatheatrical devices. In Shakespeare's time, actors directly addressed the audience during monologues or asides. Mirror constructions, such as plays within plays, added a second level of dramatic action, while a Chorus, a Prologue or an Epilogue could alienate the spectators from the action. Metatheatrical discourse constantly blurred the frontier between reality and fiction, revealing the mechanisms of theatrical production.

Mainly based on film semiotics and psychoanalysis, this chapter argues that, unlike theatre, the medium of cinema tends to tell a realistic fiction in which narrative construction prevails over the disclosure of enunciation. In this chapter, the function of music is also examined, not only in its more or less redundant connections with the Shakespeare text, but also as a means to create or disclose filmic illusion.

THEATRE AND CINEMA: FROM ALIENATION TO IDENTIFICATION

Theatre, 'semiotization' and alienation

Theatre seems naturally inclined to establish a distance between the audience and the play. Complete illusion is difficult to create because of the

[1] David Bordwell, Janet Staiger and Kristin Thompson, *The Classical Hollywood Cinema* (London: Routledge, 1985), p. 195.

actual presence of the players on stage. This presence in the flesh requires a strong and active will from the spectator to abstract the actors and to institute the illusion of a fiction. The characters are more objects of opposition than objects of identification.[2] Stage fictions would only give a weak impression of reality because theatre is much too real. As the actors are present in the same time and space as the spectators, exhibitionism is necessarily coupled with voyeurism. The actors give their consent to be observed and the spectators can be seen by the actors. To mark the distance between real people in the same space, theatre has resorted to conventions. Characters belong to codified types, and each object is at the same time signified and signifier, which means that it can represent different things during the performance of the play. A seat can be used as a mere chair in one scene, then become a throne in another, connoting power and monarchy. For example, in the first scene of *Henry IV part 1* directed by Michael Attenborough for the Royal Shakespeare Company in 2000, King Henry IV appears sitting on a throne, but this throne soon becomes a chair supporting a drunk Falstaff during the following scene. The signification of the object can thus go beyond a utilitarian function. This 'semiotization'[3] of the object is much less frequent in the cinema where the construction of a realistic world imposes on the object a definite and unchanging function. Unlike theatre, cinema presents the natural tendency to tell stories and hide the marks of enunciation.

Cinema, virtuality and realism

Even if the spectators perceive film images as a show occurring 'live', a movie is a recorded event, which is experienced after some delay. One of the particularities of the film is to topple everything it nominates into an accomplished time. The actors played their parts in the present during the shooting and, each time the film is shown, this 'past present' works in the present mode again. If in the theatre the action is performed, in the cinema it is reported.[4] The film, therefore, presents itself as a closed sequence of events, as a fictional narrative with a beginning and an end, produced by a telling authority. This narrative is inclined to conceal its enunciation by virtue of the medium. What is perceived is not the object itself but its

---

[2] See André Bazin, *What is Cinema?*, trans. Hugh Gray (Berkeley and Los Angeles: University of California Press, 1967), p. 99.
[3] See Keir Elam, *The Semiotics of Theatre and Drama* (New York, London: Methuen, 1980), p. 8; p. 12.
[4] See Christian Metz, 'The Imaginary Signifier', in *Film and Theory: An Anthology*, ed. Robert Stam and Toby Miller (Oxford: Blackwell, 2000), p. 423.

shadow. The film unwinds from the distance (like a play on stage), but also in the absence (unlike a play on stage). The screen completely segregates the film and the audience. Real life can never interfere with the reported action. The presence of actors being only ghost-like, their perception as fictional characters is made much easier for the spectators, who do not have to make any effort to abstract them. Through this bodily absence, cinema encourages a form of voyeurism that is no longer coupled with exhibitionism. The spectators can contemplate the action on screen without being seen and without any consent of the actors. This lack of assent would explain an old principle of classical cinema, which is to forbid the actor to look at the camera. By refusing to look at the lens, the actor denies both the existence of a recording device and the presence of the spectator, who can remain an unacknowledged, secret voyeur. Director Trevor Nunn believes that:

The camera requires work of actors that is quite fundamentally untheatrical and unstylized. It requires actors to be as truthful as is conceivably possible. The camera is associated with eavesdropping on the real event. Consequently, what is said in front of the camera needs to convey to the cinema audience the sense that it has not been written, that the language of the screen is being invented by the character in the situation spontaneously at that moment. We must not be aware of the writer.[5]

Nunn clearly states that cinema is prone to hide the marks of its enunciation, to conceal discourse under the unfolding of events. In a 1998 interview, he explains how much realism was essential to his vision of his 1996 adaptation of *Twelfth Night*:

For *Twelfth Night*, I delighted in embracing that capacity for verisimilitude. It was wonderful to be able to have Olivia's household as a place where you could imagine how strong that father's influence had been, how stricken the household was with the unexpected death of the brother, . . . and therefore the house had become dependent on Malvolio . . . So there's a whole set of circumstances which can be presented only because of cinematic verisimilitude that provide layers of, first of all, credibility and, finally, of tragic meaning to Malvolio's story.[6]

Nunn establishes a close relationship between aesthetics and interpretation, between the realism of environment and the verisimilitude of context. Cinema allows a credible world to be created where each situation is the consequence of a series of precise events, where realistic environment

---

[5] Interviewed by Gary Crowdus in 'Shakespeare in the Cinema: a Film Directors' Symposium, with Peter Brook, Sir Peter Hall, Richard Loncraine, Baz Luhrmann, Oliver Parker, Roman Polanski and Franco Zeffirelli', *Cineaste* 24.1 (1998), 50.

[6] *Ibid.*, 52.

reflects and conditions the characters' feelings at the same time. The director stresses the characters' personal history, favouring a psychological and individualizing approach. This naturalistic tendency of cinema encourages the impression of a world in which the actor and the set are on the same level of reality. Some film scholars even deny the very notion of set in the cinema. According to them, by definition, a set is not on the same level of reality as the actors, but should surround them like a frame.[7] In the cinema, as the distance between the film and the audience is already established by an impassable screen, the players can go beyond the stage archetypes and act in the mode of individualization. For example, during the shooting of the 1996 *Hamlet*, Branagh intensively rehearsed even minor characters to give them the look of veteran serving persons at the court.[8] Branagh applies the principles of verisimilitude and psychological coherence that govern film narrative and particularly Hollywood movies. In her 2000 adaptation of *Titus*, Taymor uses editing to construct realistic personalities. In Act iii, scene i, after his hand has been cut, Titus roars and laments close to Lavinia. Taymor comments:

This scene was the most difficult for Anthony Hopkins to shoot. He was constantly wavering between repressing his emotions and letting them explode . . . We took two days to shoot it because the actor would go from one extreme to another purposely. So these are cuts from many takes . . . We juxtaposed this rage with the compassion and control before and after . . . This is something that an actor could probably never do on a stage.[9]

Instead of favouring a continuous, theatrical form of acting, Taymor composes a discontinued scene out of different takes, thus giving the impression that the actor moves from one state to another effortlessly, as if he was really living Titus's experience. Though artificial in its nature, editing allows a realistic personality to be created out of several performances separated in time.

Cinema, desire and ideology

By stimulating perception through many pictorial and sound signifiers but immediately overturning this perception in the absence, cinema works, much more than theatre, on realism and undisclosed illusion. The physical

---

[7] See Metz, *Essais sur la signification au cinéma*, vol. 2 (Paris: Klincksieck, 1981), p. 54; p. 67.
[8] Information given by Russell Jackson in a personal discussion, 12 January 1998.
[9] From Taymor's commentary on the DVD of *Titus*, Twentieth Century Fox Home Entertainment, 2000.

absence of the signifier makes the film inaccessible and infinitely desirable at the same time. This absence of signifier maybe explains why the cinematic medium lends itself well to romantic stories, which themselves contain a longing for what is not present here and now. These mechanics of lack and desire are reflected not only in the nature of the medium but also in film aesthetic.

Editing and camera moves, by progressively revealing the action, create an enunciative mode which operates alternately on concealment and revelation. According to André Bazin, in his book, *What is Cinema?*, the screen would not be a frame, but a mask which would allow the audience to see only one part of the action.[10] In Metz's theory, the screen becomes a mask only revealing parts of the diegetic world (i.e. what is represented), as well as a frame surrounding the representation (since the screen is a limited surface).[11] This tension between absence and presence arouses desire as the spectators generally want to see what is being hidden from them. It can also be used as a major aesthetic tool to create suspense or dramatic irony, since part of the action might be hidden from the on-screen character but revealed to the audience. Any screen adaptation of a Shakespeare play notably involves the introduction of this tension between hidden and disclosed action. In 1969, when the director Tony Richardson chose to adapt his theatre production of *Hamlet* on screen, he decided to shoot most scenes in the theatre where the stage performance had taken place. But his adaptation does not look like filmed theatre at all since it is entirely built on the editing of close shots. By avoiding long shots that could reveal the limits of stage space, the film denies any frontier to the dramatic action and turns a centripetal show into a centrifugal fiction. The analogy that the spectator then perceives between the shots and the real space makes him forget the presence of an 'off-camera' (or 'off-frame') – that is the location where the technical apparatus necessary to the making of the film can be found. The camera field is imagined as belonging to a larger diegetic space which would include it. Here appears the notion of 'off-screen' (or 'off-field') that can be defined as a group of elements which are not included in the field but exist, nevertheless, for the spectator. The off-screen space can be constructed in several ways: through the characters' entrances and exits, through a gaze, a gesture or a word addressed by a character (who is seen on screen) to another (who is not seen but whose presence is imagined). In the cinema, the notion of 'off-screen' comes to replace the notion of 'backstage' and, unlike the latter, extends the space of representation in the

---

[10] See Bazin, *What is Cinema?*, p. 105. [11] See Metz, *Essais sur la signification au cinéma*, vol. 2, p. 23.

spectator's imagination instead of restricting it. If the off-screen remains invisible for the spectators, it nevertheless exists in their imagination as belonging completely to the diegetic world. This kind of adaptation thus encourages the development of a realistic diegesis in which illusion is not revealed.

However, even if a film gives greater importance to diegesis, it remains a piece of discourse, assuming a speaker and a hearer, embodying beliefs and values, and governed by the ideological struggles that constitute the historical and social realities at the moment of production.[12] The film's effectiveness resides precisely in its skill at erasing the marks of its enunciation and, therefore, the presence of a discourse. However, this concealment has profound ideological consequences. It is useful here to recall the definition offered by Althusser for the term 'ideology': 'ideology is a system (with its own logic and rigor) of representations (images, myths, ideas or concepts, depending on the case) endowed with a historical existence and a role within a given society'.[13] If any ideology aims at establishing, justifying and/or legitimating structures of power, dominant ideology has the particularity of being considered obvious and natural. The impression of reality given by the aesthetic of Hollywood cinema intensifies this feeling of evidence, reinforcing the ideology conveyed by the actions and the situations in the movie.[14] In Hollywood films, the camera seems to record events that really took (or take) place in front of it. Director Julie Taymor establishes a strong difference between the spectator's perception in the theatre and in the cinema: 'you know you're in a theater and you know that what's up on stage is an imaginative creation. It's not like a film where you're like a "Peeping Tom", peering into what looks like a real situation.'[15] To some extent, a film can offer the illusion of being as real, if not more real, than life itself. Director Kenneth Branagh gives a revealing answer in an interview in 1993 for Canal +. The journalist was playing a word association game and, to the words 'real life', Branagh replied immediately, 'movies'.[16]

By giving the spectators the feeling that they can master time and space and can occupy a central place in a vanishing point, the Hollywood aesthetic

[12] See Michel Foucault, *Madness and Civilisation*, trans. Richard Howard (London: Random House, 1965) and *The Archeology of Knowledge*, trans. Alan Sheridan (London: Tavistock Publications, 1973).
[13] Louis Althusser, *For Marx*, trans. Allen Lane (Harmondsworth: Penguin Books, 1969), p. 231.
[14] See Jean-Patrick Lebel, *Cinéma et idéologie* (Paris: Editions Sociales, 1971), p. 16.
[15] Interviewed by Joel Snyder. <http://arts.endow.gov/explore/Taymor/Taymor.html> Accessed 3 June 2002.
[16] In an interview with Isabelle Giordano, *Le journal du cinéma*, Canal +, 1993 Cannes Festival. Personal archive.

conveys an ideology of certainty and of the familiar. It is often based on ellipsis in order to give greater importance to the intense moments and deny the repetitive aspects of everyday life. For example, in the 1996 *William Shakespeare's Romeo + Juliet*, Baz Luhrmann constructs Romeo's return from exile as an episodic sequence, showing successively the car starting off in the desert, arriving in town and being tracked down by helicopters. The end of the sequence puts the emphasis on time with a close-up on a watch, and with a following close shot on Friar Lawrence waking up in haste and apprehension. In the same way, when, in his 1989 *Henry V*, Branagh feels the need to add episodes which are absent from the original play – such as the painful march to Calais – he eventually creates a sequence in which only the most impressive and epic moments of the march are shown. The soldiers are seen crossing rivers, or falling into the mud with exhaustion.

This spatial and temporal control leads to a loss of ambiguity as it guides the spectator's perception and interpretation. Such an aesthetic builds a world where everything is more or less foreseeable, where emotion and catharsis rule, where every event has a meaning and where lives are turned into destinies. According to Jean-Louis Baudry, in his 1978 book *L'effet cinéma*, by creating 'a phantasmatisation of the subject, cinema efficiently contributes to the upholding of idealism'.[17] The spectators are, in fact, put in the same dominant and narcissistic position as in their dreams or fantasies, though in the cinema they attend the daydreaming of other people – the director, the set-designer, the screen-writer, the lighting engineer and so on. According to George W. Linden, 'A film is a dream whose gesture is not ours.'[18] The fact that film resembles fantasy may explain why the spectators can have a very strong reaction of love (or hate) for a movie if they recognize (or not) their own mental images in the materialized images on the screen.

Cinema and denial

The darkness of the auditorium and the physical stillness also lead to an artificial regression of the subjects (who find themselves back in their mother's safe womb)[19] and reproduce the conditions of Oedipal identification: the spectators successively identify themselves with the different characters

---

[17] Jean-Louis Baudry, *L'effet cinéma* (Paris: Editions Albatros, 1978), p. 25. My translation from French.
[18] George Linden, *Reflections on the Screen* (Belmont: Wadsworth, 1970), p. 180.
[19] Baudry, *L'effet cinéma*, p. 38.

according to the scenes, exactly as they supposedly used to alternate periods of love and hate for their parents. The phenomena of identification increase the emotional involvement of the spectators, who find themselves plunged into the delusion of the cinematic fiction.

When we attend a theatre performance or a film, a process of denial takes place. We know that the show is a mere fiction, but one part of ourselves tends to deny this fact and believes in the illusion. This process could be summed up by the sentence: 'I know this is false, but everything seems so true all the same.'[20] In the theatre, the natural alienation induced by the physical presence of the actors generally forces us to stop at the first part of the sentence: 'I know this is false.' In the cinema, on the other hand, identification and emotional involvement make us tend less towards incredulity and more towards the belief in the realistic illusion: '. . . but everything seems so true all the same'. The spectator is, therefore, more inclined to be conquered by the ideology of the film. In order to avoid this passive absorption of ideology, a film should perhaps attempt to reveal the fact that it is only a manufactured product and that its diegesis is only simulated. Revealing the enunciative marks would tend to restore certain vigilance in the audience by disclosing the presence of a discourse, i.e. by showing the presence of a speaker within the filmic utterance and by consciously acknowledging the listener/viewer.

But most directors clearly favour diegesis over discourse, narration over enunciation. The exposure of discourse remains outside the films, in what Genette calls an 'epitext', i.e. elements such as interviews, publicity announcements, reviews, and any other authorial/editorial communication.[21] In the case of Shakespeare films, this 'epitext' often includes documentaries on the shooting ('making of'), interviews granted by the artists to the media, and published screenplays in which the director's intentions are revealed. The DVD edition of Baz Luhrmann's *Romeo + Juliet* is typical of this trend. The film itself is supplemented by a commentary by Baz Luhrmann and his collaborators, a documentary entitled 'Go Behind the Scenes with Baz Luhrmann', cast and crew interviews, music videos and screenplay comparison excerpts. Luhrmann also edited the screenplay (alongside the original text) including his notes and comments, and showing stills from the film.[22] In a similar manner, the DVD of Taymor's *Titus* contains a commentary by the director, scene-specific commentary

---

[20] See Metz, 'The Imaginary Signifier', 429–33.
[21] See Gérard Genette, *Paratexts: Thresholds of Interpretation*, trans. Jane E. Lewin (Cambridge University Press, 1997), pp. 407–8.
[22] Baz Luhrmann and Craig Pearce, *Romeo and Juliet* (London: Hodder Children's Books: 1997).

by Anthony Hopkins and Harry J. Lennix, a Q & A session with Taymor, a 'Making of' documentary, a costume gallery and Elliot Goldenthal's isolated filmscore. *Titus: The Illustrated Screenplay* has been published, allowing Taymor to share her thoughts, feelings and experiences on the making of the movie.[23] But this tendency to expose the discourse underlying the films and the making of the films is not limited to recent productions. The release of older movies on DVD has provided the opportunity to accompany them with features aiming at 'plucking the heart out of their mysteries'. The DVD of Laurence Olivier's *Henry V* (Criterion Collection) includes a commentary by film historian Bruce Eder, stills galleries of *Book of Hours* photos and production photos. Even Welles's *Othello* has been newly released on DVD with a 22-minute featurette called 'Restoring *Othello*'. These 'epitexts' somehow aim at establishing the films' authorial intentions, indicating how the films should be 'properly' interpreted. Therefore, instead of deconstructing the films from within, this particular unveiling of what goes on behind the scenes controls and channels the audience's reception, emphasizing the correctness of the authorial point of view. This specific disclosure of discourse uses fetishist processes that actually celebrate the making of illusion within the film, thus participating in the fascination with the 'star-system'. Branagh's 1996 adaptation of *Hamlet* is especially surrounded with 'epitexts' of various kinds. The film is accompanied by three documentaries on the making of the movie,[24] by a screenplay and a diary relating almost day by day the events during the shooting.[25] Moreover, in some ways, the film *In The Bleak Midwinter*, which Branagh wrote and directed in 1995, also reveals the director's intentions in the 1996 adaptation. Treated in the mode of comedy and burlesque, *In The Bleak Midwinter* dramatizes the project of amateur actors attempting to mount a performance of *Hamlet* in a small village. Branagh said in a 1997 interview: 'When people ask, "Why do *Hamlet*?" I say all the answers are contained in *Bleak Midwinter*.'[26] He considers this comedy as carrying the discourse which underlies *Hamlet* one year later. *In The Bleak Midwinter* seems, in fact, to be a way to purge Branagh's film of *Hamlet* from every parodical and

[23] Julie Taymor, *Titus: The Illustrated Screenplay* (New York: Newmarket Press: 2000).
[24] *The Readiness is All: The Making of 'Hamlet'* (Author Patrick Reams, A BBC Education Production, 1997), *To Cut or Not To Cut: The Making of 'Hamlet'* (Authors: Jane Dickson, Jill Poppy and Ian Wall, Film Education BBC2, 1997) and *To Be on Camera: A History with 'Hamlet'* (included in the special widescreen video edition (Atlanta, GA: Warner Home Video, 2000)).
[25] See Russell Jackson, 'Diary', in *'Hamlet' by William Shakespeare: Screenplay, Introduction and Film Diary*, Kenneth Branagh (London: Chatto & Windus, 1996), pp. 179–213.
[26] Quoted by David Gritten, 'The Film's the Thing', *The Daily Telegraph*, 11 January 1997, A1.

metadramatic element, in order to insist even more on diegetic illusion in the latter.[27]

VISIBLE OR INVISIBLE ENUNCIATION

Soliloquies

Soliloquy is a stage convention for which it is difficult to find a realistic equivalent. Through a soliloquy, the actor speaks to the public and meditates on the character's supposed psychological and moral situation. According to Mary Z. Maher in her book, *Modern Hamlets and Their Soliloquies*, there would be two ways of staging a soliloquy in the theatre: 'the actor can move toward the audience or the actor can allow the audience to move toward him'.[28] In the latter case, the actor meditates and speaks to himself without making contact with the spectators. Alternatively, the actor can communicate directly with the public in a quasi-metatheatrical awareness. The soliloquy can thus lead to a breaking of illusion and establish a direct connection with the public. According to Maher, these 'direct-address soliloquies are perceived as more persuasive and objective, cooler and more rational than internalized soliloquies'.[29] However, in the cinema presenting a soliloquy becomes problematic as it means a long vocal sequence delivered by one single person, which is far from normative in the cinema. Soliloquies challenge realism, and compromise the alternation of viewpoints since there is no exchange any longer. To solve these two problems, directors of Shakespeare films have treated soliloquies with the mode of interior voice, or turned them into verbal and/or visual dialogues. If the soliloquy uses a voice-over, the character is filmed while he does not speak but thinks. The character's lips do not move but the spectators learn what he thinks as if they had penetrated his brain. We hear the words of the character but we do not see him utter them: sound and image occupy distinct spaces. With this technique based on a major filmic convention, the cinema imitates the way we listen to our own conscience. The soliloquy goes from a vocal to a more mental field here. In fact, the direction of the monologue 'To be, or not to be' (III.i.55) in Laurence Olivier's 1948 *Hamlet* makes the audience almost visually enter the brain of the Danish prince: the camera quickly

[27] For a deeper analysis of this point, see Emma Smith's article, ' "Either for Tragedy, Comedy": Attitudes to *Hamlet* in Kenneth Branagh's *In The Bleak Midwinter* and *Hamlet*', in *Shakespeare, Film, Fin de Siècle*, ed. Mark Thornton Burnett and Ramona Wray (London: Macmillan, 2000), pp. 137–46.

[28] Mary Z. Maher, *Modern Hamlets and Their Soliloquies* (Iowa University Press, 1992), p. xiv.

[29] *Ibid.*, p. xxvi.

moves onto the back of Hamlet's head to sound its twists and turns, while he utters the beginning of the speech with an interior voice. The voice-over literally becomes the voice of the mind.

In Grigori Kozintsev's 1964 *Hamlet*, most soliloquies are also delivered in voice-over. In his book of 1935, *What Happens in Hamlet*, John Dover Wilson makes the assumption that the soliloquy 'O, what a rogue and peasant slave am I!' (II.ii.550) would only be a recapitulation of all the feelings Hamlet has experienced while listening to the First Player's speech on Pyrrhus and Hecuba. According to John Dover Wilson: 'Though the soliloquy is actually uttered after the players have gone out, it is in effect a dramatic reflection of what has already taken place.'[30] Kozintsev, by filming in 1964 the soliloquy in voice-over while the First Player is still delivering his text, therefore follows this critical line: the director presents the soliloquy as Hamlet's live process of thinking. The cinema can actually show the two events occurring simultaneously – the action of the Player, and Hamlet's thoughts born from that action – instead of presenting them successively. The use of voice-over allows the creation of two distinct sound spaces at the same time: one is real and the other mental. In his 1967 book, *Time and Conscience*, Kozintsev justifies the use of voice-over for Hamlet's soliloquies: 'We hear the words of his thoughts, but the sleuth who clings to the door hears nothing. He has nothing to write in his report. Hamlet thinks. There is nothing more dangerous.'[31] Interior voice isolates Hamlet from the courtiers. Even if Claudius surrounds his nephew with spies and courtiers, he cannot stop him from thinking. Kozintsev, therefore, uses voice-over to call to mind the fact that thoughts and inner freedom are a formidable force in the battle against corruption, oppression and the court's culture of covert spying. This choice of direction no doubt has its roots in the fact that Kozintsev was a dissident in the Soviet system. Hamlet's thoughts are presented as pregnantly dangerous and pointedly subversive.

In his version of *Macbeth* (1971), Roman Polanski prefers to alternate the two techniques – voice-over and loud voice – and provides the example of a subtle transition from verbal to mental over the course of a single soliloquy. Polanski rewrites the 'Vaulting ambition' soliloquy (I.vii.27) by transforming it into a quasi dialogue between Macbeth and himself.

If Laurence Olivier uses voice-over for the nocturnal soliloquy 'Upon the King!' (IV.i.230) in *Henry V*, Branagh does not use this technique in his own version of the play. His Henry speaks to himself aloud. Branagh thus mines

---

[30] John Dover Wilson, *What Happens in Hamlet* (Cambridge University Press, 1964), p. 142.
[31] Grigori Kozintsev, *Shakespeare: Time and Conscience* (London: Dobson, 1967), p. 250.

an aspect of prayer from the speech, which anticipates his plea to God in the following soliloquy 'O God of battles, steel my soldiers' hearts' (IV.i.288–9). This device also emphasizes the fact that, in this speech, Henry continues to present a defence against Soldier Williams who questioned the rightness of war in the previous scene. Nothing is better indeed than a speech uttered *aloud* to defend and justify oneself. In fact, Branagh uses the technique of voice-over only rarely when he shoots soliloquies. He prefers to present them as energetic flows, as essentially vocal events.

During a soliloquy on stage, the character is supposed to be alone, which necessarily involves an absence of exchange. Yet, unlike the theatre, which is a medium based on action, cinema seems to be built more upon reaction. The film medium naturally calls for inserted shots showing the different reactions of the characters. When editing soliloquies, some directors prefer to emphasize the visual aspects and include a succession of different shots. They wish to bring some cinematic rhythm to a scene that should, supposedly, be static. This technique is used extensively in Richard Loncraine's *Richard III*. Richard begins his first soliloquy 'Now is the winter of our discontent' (i.i.i) while he is not alone but in a public place – the royal court. He even uses a microphone in order to be heard by everyone. Loncraine takes advantage of that scene to insert several reaction shots of the courtiers enjoying the beginning of the speech. He thus introduces those shots of action/reaction which are often needed by the cinematic enunciation. Orson Welles goes even further with his treatment of some soliloquies, notably those of Falstaff in *Chimes at Midnight*. Not only is the visual flow cut, but so is the verbal one: Welles cuts the soliloquies into pieces and transforms them into dialogues, even creating imaginary characters and giving them soliloquy verses as cues. It is also the case in *Othello*, in which not a single soliloquy of Iago is left intact. Welles either transforms the monologues into dialogues, or cuts them and regularly places some sentences in the course of the film. Hence, some lines of Iago's soliloquy after Cassio's disgrace become part of a dialogue between Iago and Roderigo. Welles does not go against the filmic illusion and, like Richard Loncraine's *Richard III*, he also introduces the reaction shots needed by narrative cinema.

Franco Zeffirelli does not transform monologues into dialogues like Welles, but he applies the same technique of shooting the soliloquies with many action/reaction shots. In his 1990 adaptation of *Hamlet*, during the soliloquy 'O that this too too sallied flesh would melt' (1.ii.129), Zeffirelli inserts some shots of Claudius and Gertrude kissing in the courtyard. Those shots are diegetic shots as they belong to the story of the film. In fact,

Hamlet's sentences seem to spring out in direct reaction to these inserted images. The soliloquy emerges as a reply to what Hamlet sees outside. Zeffirelli thus establishes less a verbal dialogue than a visual one. In his 1996 screen adaptation of *Twelfth Night*, Trevor Nunn does not hesitate either to introduce reactions, but he inserts extradiegetic shots that do not chronologically belong to the sequence. Viola's monologue, which happens just after Malvolio has given her the ring, is regularly interrupted by comical shots of Olivia revealing her loving feelings, though she is not physically present during the scene.

Nowadays, the cinema has learned to deal with soliloquies so well that some directors do not hesitate to transform Shakespeare dialogues into monologues. In *Prospero's Books*, shot in 1990, Peter Greenaway gives John Gielgud nearly all the other characters' lines, thus turning the play, in effect, into one very long monologue. But this trend can also be found in films shot in a more classical and narrative mode. In Baz Luhrmann's 1996 *Romeo + Juliet*, Romeo first appears alone in the movie, composing some poems in voice-over. The director rewrites what Romeo usually says to his cousin Benvolio ('O heavy lightness, serious vanity, / Misshapen chaos of well-seeming forms' 1.i.178–9) and creates a little soliloquy, adding a particularly romantic dimension to the character, one that is tuned in to the perfect image of the James Dean-like solitary and rebellious adolescent.

Film directors have, therefore, reconstructed the soliloquy in many ways in order to accommodate it within the movie medium. They have transformed it into a verbal or visual dialogue, and even sometimes into a verbal *as well as* visual dialogue. But Kenneth Branagh has chosen another method of adaptation. Unlike Loncraine, Nunn, Welles and Zeffirelli, Branagh does not cut the soliloquies, visually or verbally. He treats them in one continuous and sustained shot. He remains coherent with his presentation of the monologue as an energetic flow, as an inner journey. Every monologue in his *Hamlet* is shot in one single take, without any visual or verbal dialogue. In a TV documentary on the making of the film, Branagh stated:

We tried with most of the soliloquies to let them play in one take, in one sustained shot. I thought it would be easier for the audience to understand if the actor, from line to line, was, like in the theatre. Following one thought into the other. I was concerned that cutting also cuts the sense of it as well. I often find that it's through having a run at it rather than doing it in bits that you can really maintain the overall sense of what Hamlet is saying.[32]

[32] Interviewed in *To Cut Or Not To Cut: The Making of Hamlet*, a documentary by Jane Dickson, Jill Poppy and Ian Wall about the making of Branagh's *Hamlet*, for Film Education (BBC2), 1997. Personal archive.

When Branagh films soliloquies, he resolutely remains theatrical. Voice is as important as image. Moreover, he does not use any literal illustrations of the words as he sometimes does elsewhere in his movies. His monologues prefer the relative simplicity of visual correlative. Hence, a small model theatre appears in the field of the camera during the soliloquy of 'O, what a rogue and peasant slave am I!' (ii.ii.550), as a simple visual embodiment of Hamlet's plan to stage a play and catch the conscience of the king. Symbolically, theatre conquers cinematic space. In Branagh's handling of the soliloquies, the monologues become a series of physical as well as emotional events that the characters go through listening to their own voice: an inner journey which the character talks himself through.

Camera angles and realistic connotations

In his 1977 book, *Initiation à la sémiologie du récit en images*, Alain Bergala writes of 'diegetisation of enunciation' – when a film hides its discourse of construction under the story it tells. The film then tries to 'make diegesis look natural' and to 'diegetise enunciation'.[33] Discourse would disappear beneath a narrative which would present a zero-degree enunciation, in a story where events seem to be told by themselves.[34] The film is shaped to give the impression of a natural world, and enunciative discourse is drowned within this world. This aesthetic finds a fervent supporter in André Bazin. To reiterate, this film theorist advocates the sequence shot rather than editing to remain faithful to reality. If there is editing, it must be as discreet as possible to conceal the discontinuity that it generates since, according to Bazin, 'Whatever the film, its aim is to give us the illusion of being present at real events unfolding before us as in everyday reality.'[35] It is possible to talk about 'transparency' when the film's only function is to tell a story while hiding its very filmic nature. In this specific aesthetic, the passage from one shot to another as well as the camera movements inside these shots are justified as much as possible by the logic of the story. The impression of continuity is obtained with what are called 'continuity cuts', which can be defined as every change in shot where elements of continuity are preserved on each side of the cut. The change is thus erased in itself. Continuity cuts can be motivated by gazes (with shots/counter-shots, for

---

[33] See Alain Bergala, *Initiation à la sémiologie du récit en images* (Les cahiers de l'audiovisuel, Ligue Française de l'Enseignement et de l'Education Permanente, [1977]), p. 39.
[34] See Bordwell *et al.*, *Classical Hollywood Cinema*, pp. 24–5.
[35] André Bazin, *Orson Welles: A Critical Review*, trans. Jonathan Rosenbaum (London: Elm Tree Books/Hamish Hamilton, 1978), p. 77.

example), gestures (with 'action cutting' – a gesture starts in one shot, then ends in another) or movements (with 'matching cutting' – the transition is facilitated by the continuity of a character's movement). Camera moves are generally accompanying tracking shots, following characters or anticipating their displacement. Editing, camera moves and positions then do not appear any longer 'as the relatively arbitrary doing of enunciation but as a logical, plausible, natural and almost necessary effect of the diegetic world itself'.[36] As far as Bazin is concerned, invisible editing is required to evoke this diegetization of enunciation. For him, in this type of editing, 'the mind of the spectator quite naturally accept[s] the viewpoints of the director which are justified by the geography of the action or the shifting emphasis of dramatic interest'.[37] Consequently, though enunciation still exists within this cinematic aesthetic, it finds itself concealed by (and under) narration.

This invisible construction works on a system of connotations governed by shooting angles, camera movements, editing and music. The style and expression of the director come to superimpose themselves on the mere denotation of images and sounds. In the majority of Shakespeare adaptations, these connotations participate in the construction of a natural world where the form is always in adequacy with the situations in the film.

Shooting angles call for our kinaesthetic memory – that is, our unconscious muscular recollections. The spectator, according to this formulation, relates certain positions of the camera to the parental authority that was experienced in childhood.[38] In a high-angle shot, the camera films the subject from above. The character will look smaller and more vulnerable. That is how Horatio, Barnardo and Marcellus are presented in the first scene of Branagh's *Hamlet* when they try to escape the ghost that chases them. In Baz Luhrmann's *Romeo + Juliet*, Romeo is also seen from above after his killing of Tybalt. As he cries 'I am fortune's fool!' (III.i.136), the camera rises, leaving him stranded and helpless in the rain. In the 1944 *Henry V*, Laurence Olivier also used high-angle backwards moves to film Henry's war speeches. These shots are meant to accommodate vocal expansiveness, but they also make the king seem weaker within the picture. According to Anthony Davies in his 1988 book, *Filming Shakespeare's Plays*, 'In moving to this position, the camera's implicit statement is to stress Henry's relative smallness.'[39] Through

[36] Bergala, *Initiation*, p. 46. My translation from French.	[37] Bazin, *What is Cinema?*, p. 24.
[38] See Robert Edmonds, *The Sights and Sounds of Cinema and Television: How the Aesthetic Experience Influences Our Feelings* (New York, London: Teachers College Press, 1992), p. 18.
[39] Anthony Davies, *Filming Shakespeare's Plays* (Cambridge University Press, 1988), p. 28.

the high-angle shots, Olivier emphasizes Henry's inferiority against the numerous French enemies, while romantically colouring the speeches with sympathy for the hero–king's brave determination.

By contrast, in the low-angle shot, the camera is located beneath the subject, filming it from the ground. Directors will very often film characters in low-angle shot when they wish to make them imposing. In Orson Welles's 1948 *Macbeth*, for example, angles are used in such a way. Kenneth S. Rothwell has cogently noticed that 'Macbeth . . . is often photographed from a low angle to give him the image of overpowering authority.'[40] In Branagh's 1989 *Henry V*, the camera is also situated very close to the ground when it shows the mysterious and commanding figure of King Henry V entering the throne room. Later in the film, the French army posted on top of a hill before the Agincourt charge is framed in low-angle shot. While there are no more than four or five soldiers in the camera field, this choice of shooting angle imparts power to the army.

In the 1965 film, *Chimes at Midnight*, Orson Welles alternates between low and high angles to connote power and fragility successively. John Gielgud as King Henry IV is very often filmed from the ground, suggesting grandeur and dignity. Hal is generally seen in the background, below the king, symbolically trying to show his father that he can be up to the demands of royalty. When Falstaff stands in for Henry IV in jest, he is also filmed in low-angle shot on his throne, while Hal is again seen from above. The conventions of fatherly authority and filial submission are respected even during play-acting. But when it is Hal's turn to substitute for his father, he delivers his flow of insults against Falstaff in a low-angle shot, thus acquiring a kingly, threatening position. The same angle is repeated at the end of the film when Hal is properly crowned king in the cathedral. As Hal is replaced by Henry V, the low-angle shots become extreme, even showing the cathedral's vaulted ceiling at the same time as the king rejects Falstaff. The camerawork thus emphasizes the transformation into a religiously conscious character, one invested by a new, theologically aware mission. By contrast, Falstaff is shown in extreme high-angle shots, reflecting his pathetic and tragic stage.

The method of filming the characters in relation to one another within one shot is also extremely meaningful. In Welles's 1948 film, Macbeth is sitting on his throne while Lady Macbeth is far away from him. As Kenneth S. Rothwell again convincingly comments, 'the wide-angle lens, by distorting the connection between the man and woman, underscores their spiritual

---

[40] Kenneth S. Rothwell, 'Shakespeare for the Art Houses', *Cineaste* 24.1 (1998), 29.

isolation'.[41] At the beginning of the nunnery scene in Branagh's *Hamlet*, the prince approaches Ophelia and kisses her tenderly. She interrupts the kiss and pushes him back slightly. The camera then shows Hamlet standing to the left of the screen, and Ophelia to the right. In the centre, a long corridor opens up, appearing to separate the two lovers. The camera creates a specific gulf between the two characters, as well as a more general atmosphere of misunderstanding and treason.

Film shooting, therefore, brings connotation and interpretation to mere images. Editing helps to play on the rhythm of the film – that is, the interior movement achieved with the respective length of shots. While theatre inevitably presents a constant visual flow, film directors often play on the speed of shot succession, adapting it to the diegetic situation. According to Béla Balazs, 'the dramatic rhythm of the story is transposed into visual picture-rhythm and the external, formal rhythm steps up the speed of the internal drama'.[42] In other words, the quicker the succession of shots is, the more it connotes an intense diegetic situation. In Branagh's *Henry V*, the feverish rhythm of editing appears during the battle of Agincourt, recalling the way Orson Welles presented the battle of Shrewsbury in *Chimes at Midnight* (1965): the rapid succession of shots mirrors the violence of the fights.[43] In Luhrmann's *Romeo + Juliet*, the fights between Capulets and Montagues are also filmed with an increase in the number of shots, reflecting the vagaries that aggression and confusion bring to its heated participants.

Melodramatic cinema

In this system of filmic connotations, music is perhaps the semiotic element which contributes most to the diegetization of enunciation. According to Claudia Gorbman, author of the book *Unheard Melodies: Narrative Film Music*, 'Fundamentally, the classical Hollywood film is melodrama – a drama with music.'[44] As far as music is concerned, many Shakespeare movies are situated in the tradition of Hollywood classical cinema, itself in line with the melodramas staged during the Victorian period. Orchestral and lyrical, Hollywood film music is generally inspired by the tonal and romantic music which was fashionable at the end of the nineteenth century. When this kind of music is mixed with Shakespeare texts, questions of

[41] *Ibid.*
[42] Béla Balazs, *Theory of the Film*, trans. Edith Bone (New York: Dover Publications, 1970), p. 129.
[43] See Lorne Buchman, *Still in Movement: Shakespeare on Screen* (Oxford University Press, 1991), p. 41.
[44] Claudia Gorbman, *Unheard Melodies: Narrative Film Music* (Bloomington: Indiana University Press, 1987), p. 7.

semiotic interactions are raised. However, the familiar discourse about the redundancy of music and text will be included in a more general discourse on the creation and the disclosure of illusion.

The frequent use of music in Anglo-Saxon cinema has often been related to the presence of music and songs in Shakespeare's plays, as opposed to the tradition of classical theatre which would have influenced continental cinema, generally less prone to use music.[45] This theory forgets an essential difference between the music present in Shakespeare's plays and film music. Shakespeare uses music as an apparent means of transition, dramatic pause or progress. Music remains on the fringe of dialogue and is often followed by some characters' comments. The interludes in which songs are performed or instruments are played do not operate in the background, but are openly presented as musical, almost autonomous moments. In Hollywood cinema, on the contrary, music is mixed with dialogue and merged into it. It does not proclaim itself as an apparent musical moment, but operates in the shadow, forming one body with the events in the film. Historically, the Hollywood musical style was chosen to favour the association between music and the other semiotic elements of the film. The first techniques of synchronized sound that appeared in 1926 did not aim to synchronize images and words, but to reinforce this intertwining between images and music, thus suppressing the need for an orchestra to play during the projection. Cinema, therefore, very soon favoured the romantic, instrumental recitative because it worked well along with the images and dialogues, participating in the construction of the illusion of a real world. The Hollywood classical pattern thus presents two quasi-paradoxical features: music is used extensively, but it operates in the background; it is an essential element of the film, but it mustn't be noticed. Music can even anticipate events by arriving slightly ahead of images. It then comes to suppress the fear that everyone feels faced with uncertainty and unpredictability. It puts the spectator in a situation of omniscience, and participates in the ideology of an organized world where everything is predestined and everything can be explained.[46]

The scores which composer Patrick Doyle writes for Kenneth Branagh's Shakespeare films are inscribed in such a pattern, as acknowledged by the composer himself: 'the music shouldn't prevail over . . . drama. It stays in the background, it helps the film. As much as possible, it shouldn't invade the images.'[47] Doyle's melodies follow the outline of the words,

[45] See Michel Chion, *La musique au cinéma* (Paris: Fayard, 1995), p. 33.
[46] See Anne-Marie Bidaud, *Hollywood et le Rêve américain: cinéma et idéologie aux Etats-Unis* (Paris, Milan and Barcelona: Masson, 1994), p. 199.
[47] In an interview by Bruno Talouarn, 'Interview avec Patrick Doyle', *Main Title*, June 1993, 15. My translation from French.

underline actions and create atmospheres. They clarify situations, construct the mood of a sequence and the feelings experienced by the characters. Music participates in a deliberate guiding of the meaning and emotions, as confirmed by the composer's words: 'Shakespeare is a strange language and the music can help an audience which is unfamiliar with it grasp the significance of the lines. It can tell you when to be scared or when to be moved.'[48] This massive use of a lyrical and *recitativo* style as an emotional guide consequently turns Shakespeare's plays into melodramas where nothing is left unexplained, where everything is made explicit.

In Taymor's *Titus*, composer Elliot Goldenthal writes a warm and humane melody – played by cors anglais – when Andronicus meets his daughter for the first time after his homecoming from the war. This melody is then played by a saxophone as soon as the intimate scene gives way to the arrival of Saturninus and Bassanius. An imitation of mid-fifties jazz punctuates the succession of cars, horses and carts, reflecting a sense of modernism and change in the air. As the apparently insane Saturninus is made emperor of Rome, Goldenthal retreats to more orchestral sounds to underline the dangers of the situation. The sudden, gigantic operatic music for the coronation emphasizes the fact that Saturninus could bring trouble to the empire.

Film music can underline what happens on the screen, often through the technique of 'Mickey-Mousing', which means following exactly the rhythm of the action.[49] At the end of Laurence Olivier's 1955 *Richard III*, the death of Richard is accompanied by Mickey-Mousing music (composed by Sir William Walton) which follows every single spasm of the final agony. In Taymor's *Titus*, when the eponymous character is walking down the street gathering his family and friends to shoot arrows at the gods, the exaggerated music presents him as a parody of a general, a pathetic, comical, almost cartoonish figure. The music punctuates every jerky, military movement of his arms, as in a silent movie.

Film music generally works on recurrent themes, giving a magnified, symbolic and subjective value to events. Musical themes come directly from the Wagnerian rules in terms of leitmotivs. A theme is associated with a particular character, action, situation or emotion, reappearing throughout the film to create reminders or nostalgic effects. The score with motifs – that

---

[48] Patrick Doyle, 'Music', in *Hamlet* (presentation notes), Random Century Audiobooks, RTC in association with BBC Radio Drama, RC100, 1992.

[49] The expression 'Mickey-Mousing' comes from the extensive use of this technique in Walt Disney's animated pictures.

is, a score including themes whose diegetic associations do not change – then contributes to the clarity of dramatic structures.

Goldenthal's score for *Titus* is constructed around three major themes which are more associated with situations than characters. A first theme is linked to vengeance, a second theme is related to asking for pity and a third theme reflects mercy. The theme of vengeance first arises when Tamora sees the disembowelled parts of her eldest son being burnt during the rites of 'irreligious piety' (I.i.130), and reappears each time Tamora and Titus are face to face, looking at each other through imaginary fire. The theme of asking for pity appears when Tamora begs Titus to spare the life of her son, when Lavinia pleads Tamora not to leave her in the cruel hands of Chiron and Demetrius, when Titus asks for the life of his two sons on the paved road and, finally, when Aaron begs Lucius to save his baby son. The theme of pity therefore binds all the main characters together. They are all placed in a position of pleading for pity at some point or another. The theme of mercy arises as Marcus discovers a mutilated Lavinia in the swamps. A hollow sound with bass flutes in low register reflects the hole that appears when she opens her mouth and reveals a stream of blood instead of a tongue. Later, the theme surfaces as Lucius's boy offers a pair of wooden hands to Lavinia. A viola da gamba and soprano voices replace the bass flutes to give a sense of hope and compassion. For Goldenthal, the mercy theme alludes to a kind of burgeoning Christianity, as opposed to Titus and Tamora's world of paganism.[50] The theme emerges again when Titus learns to read the signs of his daughter, reaching a humanity that he had almost lost. One last time, the theme appears when Titus breaks the neck of his dishonoured daughter, thus presenting this killing as an act of charity and mercy.

In Doyle's score for Branagh's *Henry V*, the *Non nobis* theme can be found in several moments of the film to evoke the waste of war. It first starts up during the credits, and is taken up again when the king recalls, for the first time, the victims of war in front of the French ambassador: 'for many a thousand widows / Shall this his mock mock out of their dear husbands' (I.ii.284–5). During the battle of Agincourt, the music begins as martial with drums, but is quickly transformed into an elegy following the *Non nobis* tune, mourning for the English and French dead soldiers at the same time. Even before the famous march which terminates the battle, the *Non nobis* theme is presented as an anthem for the dead. The peace negotiations themselves also are haunted by this melody when the dead characters appear

[50] In Goldenthal's commentary on the DVD of *Titus* (Twentieth Century Fox Home Entertainment, 2000).

one last time in a flashback. In Branagh's *Hamlet*, the score is more divided. Doyle composed three main themes: a nostalgic but non-gloomy melody for Ophelia; a feverish canon played by a string quartet to reflect Claudius's dark and tormented soul; and a musical motif for Hamlet, which, according to Doyle, had to mirror both the character's heroic and desperate actions:

Behind the glamour, there is tragedy. So the music had to be heroic, with a degree of melancholy, with inevitability in it but not depressing inevitability. Positive inevitability. Like a man climbing a mountain knowing he is not going to get to the summit, but he tries and tries until he gets to within five metres, before he dies.[51]

Music thus participates in the interpretation of the play. By adding emotional depth, it gives the spectators the impression that they are experiencing the action along with the characters, allowing them to relate more easily to the scenes by working in the mode of effusion and emotional outburst.

Music: from redundancy to synergy

This musical profusion is generally accused of imitating what takes place on the screen, and therefore of being redundant. Anne Souriau offers two definitions for the term 'redundancy'. The first is pejorative: 'an element of speech which uselessly doubles another; by extension, an abundance of emphatic and superfluous words'.[52] The second one is neutral: 'In the theory of information, redundancy is an element loaded with the same information as another element; it works as a safety device if the other element is not received.'[53] In both cases, the notion of redundancy supposes an autonomy of semiotic elements, which would overlap and communicate the same message twice.

However, to speak of musical redundancy in the cinema is to forget that the semiotic elements that compose the art of cinema do not operate in an autonomous way. It is often wrongly believed that an image or a text creates a meaning independently from music, and that the latter would carry a redundant message to the already present meaning. It is assumed that the last semiotic element is superfluous without realizing that it contributes to the construction of the meaning as a whole. According to the theory of added value, as elaborated by Michel Chion in his 1995 book, *La*

[51] Sarah Hatchuel, 'Making Melodies for Branagh's Films: an Interview with Patrick Doyle', *Shakespeare* 2.1 (Winter 1998), 13.
[52] Anne Souriau, 'Redondance', in *Vocabulaire d'esthétique*, ed. Etienne Souriau (Paris: Presses Universitaires de France, 1990), p. 1209. My translation from French.
[53] *Ibid.*

musique au cinéma, there is actually a back-and-forth move between image and music.[54] Image and text are influenced by music which, in return, is affected by them. There is never a unique and necessary relation between a sequence and its music. Words and music, images and music, would operate synergistically. They are sources of meaning only in the time and space of their combination. It would, then, be wrong to think that music 'accompanies' a film since it is part of it. According to Michel Chion, a film is a semiotic, interdependent ensemble without any dominant elements, which music 'co-irrigates' and 'co-structures'.[55] If, in Shakespeare's theatre, words give birth to dramatic action, in the cinema they become mere components of this action.[56] To consider film music in itself is to overlook the fact that it is part of a whole, that it collaborates with the cinematic work by inserting itself in a network of semiotic relations. Associating music with a film means both to abandon and exploit artistic as well as dramatic possibilities, since each musical choice brings out different textual or visual details. Music has a narrative role: one musical punctuation is enough to draw the audience's attention to one detail of the image or dialogue, to one turning point of the script or to a particular editing effect. A musical attack called a 'stinger' can signal some dramatic tension or sudden revelation.[57] For example, in Branagh's *Hamlet*, when Polonius talks about the prince's madness with the king and queen, Patrick Doyle introduces a stinger to signal the discreet arrival of Hamlet. This brief musical moment guides the audience's vision to the top of the screen, to the upper gallery from which Hamlet turns an ironic and mocking gaze on the situation. Music here acquires a focusing role and represents a substitute for editing which could have shown the prince's entrance in close-up. In Taymor's *Titus*, Elliot Goldenthal uses musical attacks for the start of violent acts. A stinger, for instance, signals the beginning of the fight between Tamora's wild sons and Aaron, who wants to protect his newborn heir. Another one marks Aaron's unexpected murder of the nurse who attended Tamora's childbirth, or the sudden arrest of Demetrius and Chiron disguised as Rape and Murder in Titus's house.

According to Claudia Gorbman, discourses of musical parallel and contrast should not be used to analyse film sequences either. These two notions, which establish a distinction between music that imitates and music that works in opposition to the other elements of the film, again suppose an

---

[54] See Chion, *La musique au cinéma*, p. 205.   [55] *Ibid.*, p. 215.
[56] See Metz, *Essais sur la signification au cinéma*, vol. 2, p. 53.
[57] See Gorbman, *Unheard Melodies*, p. 88, and Chion, *La musique au cinéma*, p. 125.

autonomy of the semiotic elements.[58] Another terminology is required to describe the different types of music used in the cinema. Michel Chion proposes to distinguish empathic from anempathic music.[59] Empathic music supports the feeling created by the scene (or experienced by the characters), whereas anempathic music exhibits its indifference towards the action in the film. The typical example would be to hear joyful music while images of murder are shown on the screen.

Oliver Parker's 1995 *Othello* works in the mode of empathy towards Desdemona and Othello. For their death and, later, for their funerals at sea, Charlie Mole composed highly romantic music which both idealizes the love relationship and pities its sorrowful ending. In this adaptation, it is as if Desdemona and Othello were presented as 'star-cross'd lovers'. As they are plunged into the sea, the lovers are reunited in death, the melodious music soaring to nostalgic heights, turning their lives into destinies. By contrast, the end of Orson Welles's 1952 version features dark, mysterious and atonal music. Instead of finishing with accents of passion, the music composed by Alberto Barberis and Angelo Lavagnino emphasizes nothingness, emptiness and the pointlessness of those events. Welles's *Othello* does not appear as a tragedy of love, but puts the stress on Iago's unmotivated evil and Othello's guilty weakness.

The original score for Richard Loncraine's 1995 *Richard III*, composed by Trevor Jones, oscillates between empathic and anempathic music. The soundtrack often features music that does not sympathize with the characters' woeful situations. As Richard leaves a stranded Lady Anne in the mortuary room after the wooing scene, he struts off accompanied by upbeat jazz music. A Swing version of the song *Sitting On Top of the World* also commences as Richard falls into hellish fire at the end of the film. With such anempathic music, death is presented with derision, as if the film was winking at an audience that is expected to see cataclysmic fatalism as funny rather than tragic.

Elliot Goldenthal's score for *Titus* generally works in phase with the characters' feelings, but sometimes, as in Loncraine's *Richard III*, it also alienates the spectators from the tragic situation, revelling in black humour. As Aaron carries the hand of Titus that he has just severed, the music is loud and jazzy, not sympathizing with the atrocity of the situation, but emphasizing Aaron's exhilaration and inviting the audience to see the events

---

[58] Gorbman, *Unheard Melodies*, pp. 14–15.
[59] See Michel Chion, *Audio-Vision: Sound on Screen*, ed. and trans. Claudia Gorbman (New York: Columbia University Press, 1994), pp. 8–9.

from an ironic distance. But the most notable example of anempathic music takes place at the end of the film, after Titus has cooked two pies using the blood and flesh of Tamora's sons. Carlo Buti's joyful Italian song *Vivere* ('Living') starts while the screen images, by showing the two pies smoking at the window, emphasize atrocious death. It continues as Titus serves the human food to the revellers who eat it with delight. The positive-sounding music clashes with the horror of an unaware mother devouring her children. The *Vivere* song brings irony and distance, emphasizing the most grotesque aspects of the situation.

By contrast, Branagh's films never present anempathic music. They express the determination never to make the world of fiction, and therefore the spectator, indifferent to the dramatic events. Doyle's music is always in phase with the main characters' emotions. Even its absence reveals itself to be empathic. During the monologue 'O that this too too sallied flesh would melt' (1.ii.129), Doyle plays on the contrast between the loud fanfare accompanying the leaving of the court and Hamlet's voice ringing in the new silence. The cinematic presentation, therefore, opposes the very public pomp of a mendacious government with the sincere thoughts of a troubled young man. Director Grigori Kozintsev treats the same sequence differently. In his 1964 adaptation, Hamlet is not alone, but is surrounded by a throng of courtiers talking. The soliloquy can be heard in voice-over while cheerful, classical music is played in the background. Kozintsev thus uses an anempathic tune to insist on Hamlet's loneliness in a world of social hypocrisy that ignores his suffering.

If Patrick Doyle's music only works on the empathic register, it nevertheless can take two distinct forms if its very origin is considered. Branagh's films present both diegetic music – which arises from the story – and extradiegetic (nondiegetic) music, which has an imaginary source, exterior to the world of fiction.

Music, diegesis and illusion

Extradiegetic music is a matter of pure convention. It constitutes an exception within Hollywood classical cinema, in which everything is to belong to diegesis in order to elaborate a fictive, realistic universe. According to David Bordwell, 'the use of non-diegetic music itself signals the narration's awareness of facing an audience, for the music exists solely for the spectator's benefit'.[60] However, paradoxically, instead of unveiling illusion by

---

[60] Bordwell *et al.*, *Classical Hollywood Cinema*, p. 34.

being exterior to the fiction, it participates in the invisibility of enunciation, and, furthermore, plunges the spectator into diegesis. If, in the theatre,
music links certain scenes together, extradiegetic music in the cinema not
only links the scenes but also the shots together. It has, indeed, a sutur-
ing function, making the cuts less obvious and creating the impression
of a continuous unfolding. By reinforcing the hypnotic nature of cinema,
extradiegetic music makes the spectator less aware of the frame, technical construction and filmic articulations, contributing to hide enunciation
under fiction. Episodic sequences frequently present extradiegetic music.
The latter helps the audience to accept the quicker or slower passage of
time. In Branagh's adaptation of *Henry V*, the painful march to Calais,
presented in episodes, is wrapped up with music that sympathizes with the
soldiers' efforts and softens the discontinuity born from film cutting and
editing.

In the scenes in slow-motion, music creates a bubble where actions are
freed from fleeting time. In Luhrmann's *Romeo + Juliet*, slow, melancholic
music can be heard when Romeo is writing poems and walking in slow-
motion, thus presenting him as the ultimate romantic figure. Music and
slow-motion also come together when the lovers kiss under water, giving
the impression of a love both out of time and out of reach. The scene of
the party at Capulet's mansion uses slow-motion to reflect, in subjective
camera, the disorienting effects of the drugs taken by Romeo. The sequence
is notably infused with quick-beat diegetic music, putting the stress on
the power of drugs to create another impression of reality and time. In
Branagh's *Henry V*, several moments of the battle are shot in slow-motion.
Slow-motion creates a time suspension, especially when real noises cannot
be heard any longer. Diegetic noises are replaced by the musical theme of
the *Non nobis* and muffled sounds. Only the heartrending neigh of horses,
the muted noise of the bodies falling in the mud and Exeter's iron weapon
crashing down in a ghostly sound can be heard. An 'out-of-time' moment
is created, one that escapes from chronological continuity. Music brings
a dream-like aspect that contributes to the fading of disbelief within the
spectator. The battle of Agincourt becomes a quasi-eternal fight, a never-
ending tumult that symbolizes every other armed conflict. Extradiegetic
music helps to transcend the characters' individual stories and turn them
into heroic destinies with universal consonances.

In Branagh's Shakespeare films, extradiegetic music often extends
diegetic music which is anchored in the very story of the film. The nocturnal theme of Henry V for the 'Upon the King!' (IV.i.230) speech is
just the extradiegetic extension of a diegetic melody played on a pipe by

one of the soldiers. The large-scale, orchestrated music of the *Non nobis* at the end of the battle begins with the singing of the soldier, Court, inside the story itself. The long song-and-dance scene which ends *Much Ado About Nothing* starts with the characters singing and playing their own instruments. In *Hamlet*, the theme of Ophelia continues, outside diegesis, the girl's nostalgic singing. These criss-crossings between diegetic and extradiegetic music transform Shakespeare films into kinds of musicals. This cinematic genre, in which characters start singing within the action of the film, and then are taken over by an imaginary orchestra, often present metafilmic aspects through gazes at the camera and the artificial nature of the dancing and singing numbers. In his adaptation of *Love's Labour's Lost*, directed in 1999 as a musical, Branagh played with revealing the illusion of the sets during the musical numbers: the King of Navarre and his three followers soar into the air, and the character of Don Armado takes the moon down with a kick. However, in *Henry V, Much Ado About Nothing* and *Hamlet*, the back-and-forth movement between diegetic and extradiegetic music does not aim at unveiling illusion in any way. As Doyle comments on the orchestral prolongation in these three films: 'it seemed a natural way to do it. Someone sets an atmosphere then the underscore takes up on that and extends it.'[61] While the songs in Shakespeare's plays are apparent and prominent moments, in the cinema they often become introductions to empathic music which operates in the shadow. Consequently, if Doyle's music contributes to drowning film-making within a natural-looking universe, it also ends up turning manifest, musical moments into preludes to lyrical and emotional crescendos. To a certain extent, the same also applies to the score of Luhrmann's *Romeo + Juliet*. The first meeting of the two lovers on each side of the fish tank happens while the romantic song *Kissing You* is performed by a solo artist at Capulet's party. The love theme thus starts as a diegetic, apparent moment. However, it soon becomes a recurrent, extradiegetic melody, emerging during every romantic scene – the kissing in the lift, the exchange of vows in the swimming pool and the wedding night.

Max Reinhardt and William Dieterle's 1935 film of *A Midsummer Night's Dream* includes so much diegetic and extradiegetic music that it could be considered a kind of musical. As in Doyle's scores, extradiegetic music often begins within the story itself. Mendelssohn's wedding march starts being played by a goblin blowing into a flower shaped like a trumpet, then continues as a full, orchestral sound whose source remains outside the

---

[61] Hatchuel, 'Making Melodies for Branagh's Films', 12.

diegetic world. Moreover, each time Puck pours the magical flower juice onto the characters' eyes and whispers the enchanting charm, there is such intermingling between Puck's voice and the score, that it is impossible to tell whether he accompanies the score with his singing or whether the score follows his musical scansion of the text. Puck often acts as if, unlike the other characters, he is able to hear the extradiegetic music inside the world of the story.

In his score for Taymor's *Titus*, Goldenthal alternates between diegetic and extradiegetic music mainly to emphasize contrast between two successive scenes. One example can be found in the transition between the darkness of the mausoleum in which Titus forbids burial for the son he himself killed, and the festive mood of Saturninus's Palace. The score goes suddenly from the gloom of strings and cors anglais with an extradiegetic source to a loud band playing jazz-inspired music for the celebration of Tamora and Saturninus's wedding, music obviously belonging to the world of the story. Another musical contrast takes place after Titus's hand has been cut off. Empathic and discreet string music underscores Titus's speech of rage and sorrow to Lavinia, only to be followed by anempathic, diegetic circus music when messengers come to deliver the heads of Titus's sons.

In a 1992 article, Mark Fortier criticizes the emotional effects induced by images and music: he finds them mechanistic and manipulative.[62] The spectator seems, very often, to have no choice – but can only be moved by the story. Branagh confirms this idea of 'manipulation' in an interview given to the French newspaper, *Le Monde*, in 1998: 'In the theatre, spectators always keep their distance. With the film, I wanted to grab them and say: "Look, you have to participate, you can't stand back."'[63] As a reaction, scholars are often opposed to what they consider an ideological trap. But criticizing the creation of emotion often betrays a denial of the nature of the cinematic experience. The very act of going to the cinema already implies a certain kind of surrender to a particular vision of the world. To watch a cinematic fiction is to enter a new universe, to agree to look at the world through a different gaze. By exposing the manipulation of emotions through the medium of cinema, these critics refuse to accept a world that the spectators have not themselves conceived. However, a film can cause our everyday vision to evolve, particularly because it allows us to compare our own vision with that of the film. Like every work of art, a film can

[62] See Mark Fortier, 'Speculations on *2 Henry IV*, Theatre Historiography, the Strait Gate of History, and Kenneth Branagh', *Journal of Dramatic Theory and Criticism* 7 (Fall 1992), 45–69.

[63] Quoted by Thomas Sotinel, 'Prendre les spectateurs au collet: entretien avec Kenneth Branagh', *Le Monde (Dossier et Documents Littéraires)*, issue 19, April 1998, 4.

renew our perception of things, often dulled by time and habit, and make us enter a different, hitherto unknown imaginary world.

Through the specific use of shots, editing and, above all, music, many Shakespeare films insert themselves in the Hollywood classical tradition. Discourse is generally erased behind the story, and a quasi-hypnotized spectator is immersed into a fictive world that never seems to be questioned. Yet, it is possible to wonder whether, with some cinematic constructions, Shakespeare adaptations wouldn't be able to let enunciation pierce through the narrative. Can cinema present metacinematic figures that would be equivalent to Shakespearean meta-theatre?

CHAPTER 4

Reflexive constructions: from meta-theatre to meta-cinema?

In the theatre, there is a broad spectrum of ways to present Shakespeare's plays, from the illusions of the realistic pictorial stage to Bertolt Brecht's epic theatre, depleted of realistic effects and calling attention to the medium. This chapter will attempt to answer the following questions: is it possible for screen adaptations to adopt the devices of Brechtian presentation? Can the cinema reflect the *mises-en-abyme* (i.e. embedded structures and mirror constructions) that can be found in Shakespeare's plays? Can films defamiliarize the spectators with a play so that they can reach an alienated state of critical distance?

Brecht wished for plays to move away from conducted plots in favour of an anti-illusionist succession of independent events.[1] In this view, the relationships linking the scenes with one another should be more important than the relationships between them and the ending. Epic theatre is structured episodically with highly contrasted scenes and without finality, giving rise to alienation and implying variability. Alienation is also created through dramaturgical devices such as asides, choruses, commenting figures, prologues and epilogues, and the exposure of theatrical machinery to the spectators. The aim is to avoid the audience's identification with the characters on stage, and to encourage distance and criticism. The actors are revealed as actors, the props as props, the sets as sets. According to Manfred Pfister in his 1991 book *The Theory and Analysis of Drama*, 'This emphasises the difference between the reality of the objects and the objects they represent, and imbues them with epic mediating qualities.'[2] Props are presented as semiotic elements, thus preventing them from becoming part of a realistic world.

In the cinema, enunciation can be marked by commentative and reflexive constructions such as voice-over, gazes or speeches addressed to the

---

[1] See Manfred Pfister, *The Theory and Analysis of Drama* (Cambridge University Press, 1991), pp. 69–70.
[2] *Ibid.*, p. 84.

camera, films-within-the-film or flashbacks – which may be considered films-within-the-film since they are partially autonomous.[3] Using these cinematic devices, Shakespeare screen adaptations have often tried to reproduce the metadramatic discourse of the original plays and allow the viewers a direct access to the mechanisms of film-making. For example, gazes or speeches addressed to the camera can be compared to the theatrical convention of asides; screens-within-screens offer equivalents to plays-within-plays; revealing the presence of the camera can be likened to showing what happens backstage. Yet, this chapter will argue that, whatever film directors may do, the very nature of the cinematic experience forbids any radical exposure of illusion: enunciation generally dissolves into narration. This chapter will reveal a dialectic that would govern film illusion, involving not only the aesthetic of cinema but also the spectator's own perception of movies.

ALIENATION THROUGH SETTING

Michèle Willems, in her 1994 article, 'Verbal–visual, verbal–pictorial or textual–televisual? Reflexions on the BBC Shakespeare Series', has identified the similarities and the differences between theatre performance and film depiction:

Superficially, the cinema, television and theatre all appear to rely on the layering of signs to communicate with their publics. Viewer and audience alike must apprehend a variety of signs simultaneously: aural signs such as words spoken by actors, music and other sounds; visual signs such as costumes, setting, lighting and sometimes special effects. But there the similarity ends, because the respective importance and status of these signs vary enormously from one medium to the next. On the stage all the other signs are subordinated to speech (in monologue, dialogue or aside), while on the screen words are secondary: the dialogue follows the image.[4]

In order to offer a commentary on the move from theatre to film, some directors have chosen to disturb this semiotic hierarchy. They base their adaptation(s) more on the analogies existing between stage and screen than on their differences. Their *mises-en-scène* include allusions to the work's dramatic origin, alternating a style inspired by stage conventions and a

[3] See Christian Metz, *L'énonciation impersonnelle ou le site du film* (Paris: Klincksieck, 1991), p. 108.
[4] Michèle Willems, 'Verbal–visual, verbal–pictorial or textual–televisual? Reflections on the BBC Shakespeare Series', in *Shakespeare and the Moving Image*, ed. Anthony Davies and Stanley Wells (Cambridge University Press, 1994), p. 70.

cinematic one. Realism, therefore, gives way to a dialogue between the medium of film and that of theatre.

The start of Branagh's 1993 *Much Ado About Nothing* works on a move from artifice to realism. The first image that the audience sees is a painted landscape. The camera then moves slowly to discover the real scenery, respecting the contiguity of the two spaces as it slides to the left. The author of the painting (Leonato) is disclosed, as the camera tracks away to reveal a luxuriant Italian landscape. From artificial to real countryside, the shot constructs through continuity an image of perfection. It is as if some magical transition had given birth to a heavenly dreamland.

Laurence Olivier's 1944 film, *Henry V*, oscillating between artifice and realism, is famous for disclosing the conditions of theatrical and filmic production. According to Kenneth S. Rothwell, 'It [the film] consciously bridges the gap between theatre and film, and in the act of interrogating the idea of making a Shakespeare play into a film through a virtuoso display of cinematic codes self-reflexively valorizes it.'[5] The film introduces a framing device, opening at the Globe theatre in Shakespeare's time. The centrifugal experience of the cinema only begins when the Chorus mentions the departure of the English army. But the interpolations remain at first very stylized, far away from the usual realism of cinema. The distorted perspectives, inspired by medieval illuminated manuscripts, point out the artificiality of the sets. Only the battle of Agincourt drives the viewer into realism. This alternation of theatrical, stylized and realistic direction produces a commentary upon the medium for which the play was written and that for which it has been adapted. Adrian Noble uses a similar technique of adaptation in his 1996 movie *A Midsummer Night's Dream*, alternating theatrical and cinematic direction. The actors often move about on artificial and stagey sets. Oberon opens doors that open on nothing except a forest of light bulbs, symbolically representing the absence of spatial markers in an unknown location. The lovers are metaphorically lost in a maze of empty space. This theatrical imagery is mixed with explicit references to cinematic works. For example, the umbrellas flying in the sky are strongly reminiscent of Robert Stevenson's *Mary Poppins* (1964) and the passing of a bicycle in front of the moon clearly recalls Steven Spielberg's *E. T. The Extra-Terrestrial* (1982). Each style brings the other into focus when a change occurs, thus becoming a source of reflexive commentary.

In another adaptation of *A Midsummer Night's Dream*, this time directed by Peter Hall in 1969, the setting participates in a quasi-Brechtian alienation.

[5] Kenneth S. Rothwell, *A History of Shakespeare on Screen* (Cambridge University Press, 1999), p. 54.

One of the first shots shows the audience an English mansion with the name 'Athens' superimposed over it. This discrepancy between the name of the Greek town and the actual space used for the film forces the spectators to abandon their previous expectations and helps to defamiliarize them with the play. In addition, the film works aesthetically on an alternation between film realism and theatre-related artifice. The environment of wood, mud and bad weather brings extreme naturalism, while the bright lights in the deep forest at night and the fairy characters with their green make-up import surrealistic elements, much more in tone with theatre formalism and stage conventions. In the 1992 *As You Like It*, director Christine Edzard also plays with theatre conventions inside the film itself. The Forest of Arden becomes waste ground in East London where those rejected from capitalist society reside. The gap between the textual references to nature and the environment of concrete and steel that the audience sees on screen thus challenges the very principle of cinematic verisimilitude.[6]

In *Looking for Richard* (1996), Al Pacino films the main scenes from *Richard III* and adds several commentaries composed of stage rehearsals and interviews with scholars, actors and people in the street. The film carries an interesting reflection on the transition from a stage play to a film adaptation since it deals with two processes at the same time – the staging of a theatre production and its transfer onto film. Pacino starts shooting the scenes as filmed theatre, in a relatively static manner, in a space where the artificiality of the set is ostensible. But his camera always frees itself eventually, turning around the actors and concentrating on their faces and emotions. The centripetal stage gives way to a centrifugal cinematic locus as soon as the camera field participates in hiding the limits of the acting space. In other words, as soon as Pacino's camera concentrates on the actors and avoids filming the stage apparatus around them, the theatre *mise-en-scène* starts resembling a cinematic one.

Branagh's 1996 adaptation of *Hamlet* can also be considered as a reflection on the move from stage to screen, as a dialogue between their respective conventions. In his choice of certain sets, Branagh often adopts the conventions of a theatre performance. After his killing of Polonius, Hamlet is chased through the palace. He runs through room after room, effortlessly opening false doors. The camera follows him in profile, in a fast travelling shot, as if the walls of the castle have been removed purposely for the artificial eye to follow the action in just such a manner. In fact, we

---

[6] See Amelia Mariette's essay, 'Urban Dystopia: Reapproaching Christine Edzard's *As You Like It*', in *Shakespeare, Film, Fin de Siècle*, ed. Mark Thornton Burnett and Ramona Wray (London: Macmillan, 2000), pp. 73–88.

are made suddenly aware that none of the walls in the castle is real and all the approved ways of moving from room to room are false, merely an appearance. This scene reminds us that the castle is actually a set – as the camera travels outside the illusionary 'fourth wall' of each of the rooms, as the walls become insubstantial and obviously constructed for the purpose of film-making.

In this film, the major part of the action takes place in the huge throne room. This closed and rectangular space displays centripetal and theatrical features, with its side tiers, its upper galleries and its suspended balconies. The characters enter and exit through secret doors located on each side of the room. According to Anny Crunelle, 'There is a definite sense of back-stage activity in the side rooms behind the State Hall's mirrored doors.'[7] The throne room also turns literally into a theatre during the 'Mouse-trap' sequence.[8] Hamlet, taking the role of the performance commentator, keeps moving from the actors' space to that of the spectators, blurring the boundaries between the two. The show invades the audience as the exchanges between Polonius, Claudius, Gertrude, Ophelia and Hamlet become as interesting for the courtiers as the Players' speeches. The throne room, at the same time used as a stage space and a spying space, introduces meta-theatre on the screen. However, if Branagh here intends a reflection on the metadramatic aspects that are present in the original play, he does not disclose the cinematic apparatus by, for example, filming himself in the process of directing the real actors on the film set. Since 'The Mousetrap' becomes a play-within-the-film and not a film-within-the-film, the subject of performance does not correspond any longer to the very means of per-formance. To call attention to the cinematic medium and reveal traces of enunciation, specific metacinematic devices are needed.

DUPLICATING THE FIGURE OF THE DIRECTOR AND/OR SPECTATOR

One way of drawing attention to the medium is to insert a directorial or authorial figure into the production itself. This figure will mirror the creator of the work of art. In epic theatre, Brecht advocates the use of prologues and epilogues delivered by a person outside the dramatic action as a 'stylised personification of the author himself'.[9] This allows for a

---

[7] See Anny Crunelle, 'All the World's a Screen: Transcoding in Branagh's *Hamlet*', *Shakespeare Yearbook* 8 (1997), 365.

[8] *Ibid.*, 358.   [9] Pfister, *Theory and Analysis of Drama*, p. 74.

comment that distances the spectators from the show and points to its material construction.

Screen adaptations of Shakespeare can highlight prologues and epilogues that are already present in the original plays, or they can introduce other (often interpolated) devices in which viewers witness a fictional counterpart of the director in the act of creating or presenting the production.

Jean-Luc Godard's 1987 experimental appropriation of *King Lear* is highly deconstructionist and metacinematic in form. Woody Allen, who plays the character of the Fool, is filmed in the act of manipulating celluloid strip on a Moviola, as if he was editing the movie itself. This scene interestingly places the Fool as a participant in the film's creation. It also emphasizes the very substance with which the film is made, and thus draws attention to the fact that a movie is a materially constructed product. Cinema is, here, subtextually compared to the immaterial form of live performance.

In Branagh's 1989 *Henry V*, the Chorus's appearances always occur in a metafilmic mode. They coincide precisely with purely cinematic moments that would be extremely difficult to produce on stage – the beginning of the battle of Agincourt, or the introduction of the treacherous nobles on the cliff top at Southampton.[10] From the very first scene, the Chorus does not walk on a stage (as in the Olivier 1944 version) but in a deserted movie studio, where cameras, props, sets and projectors are stored. Rothwell remarks that 'What is mostly a realistic film ironically begins with a touch of Brechtian alienation in its meta-cinematic concern with the mechanics of making a movie.'[11] By showing the audience the film's 'backstage', the Chorus introduces a reflection on the very making of the movie.

In Peter Greenaway's *Prospero's Books* (1992), aesthetic discontinuity forces each member of the audience to create a highly personal movie through ceaseless construction and deconstruction of meaning. Prospero the Magician (played by John Gielgud) is presented as a director shaping the whole dramatic action. For the most part, his voice is given to all the characters in the film, except to Miranda, whose voice is sometimes her own, sometimes combined with her father's. This vocal omnipresence alienates the characters, turning the play into a new experience and obliging the audience to listen to the words even more carefully in order to decipher who is speaking what. Prospero is regularly seen in the process of

[10] For a comparison between Olivier's Chorus and Branagh's Chorus, see the two following articles: Robert F. Willson, '*Henry V*: Branagh's and Olivier's Choruses', *Shakespeare on Film Newsletter* 14.2 (April 1990), 1–2; Derek Royal, 'Shakespeare's Kingly Mirror: Figuring the Chorus in Olivier's and Branagh's *Henry V*', *Literature/Film Quarterly* 25.2 (1997), 104–10.

[11] Rothwell, *History of Shakespeare on Screen*, p. 247.

writing books, notably the very play of *The Tempest*, which is self-reflexively added to the First Folio at the end of the film. He is presented literally as the author of the work in which he appears, and therefore as responsible for his own existence as a character. Prospero seems to stand for both the author of the play and the director who adapted it: he mirrors Shakespeare writing *The Tempest* and Greenaway giving a voice to all the characters on screen.

Michael Almereyda's 2000 film of *Hamlet* certainly abounds in self-conscious, metacinematic figures who represent duplications of the directorial figure.[12] Like Prospero in Greenaway's film, Hamlet is at the same time character, author and director: until the 'Mousetrap' sequence, he is always filming everything with a Pixel camera, mixing different documents into amateur films and video-recording himself when he utters his thoughts aloud. For Courtney Lehmann, 'this quintessentially post-modern Hamlet seems to operate under the assumption that by playing back these primal scenes, he can edit and, ultimately, master them, as he zooms in on particular frames – freezing and manipulating them in time and space'.[13] But as he is filmed watching family videos from a happier past, this Hamlet is also a counterpart of the audience in the cinema. Whereas the original play features a Hamlet who is passionate about theatre and plays, this 2000 Hamlet is an ardent lover of films and videotapes. Instead of mounting a stage production to 'catch the conscience of the King', he edits a film out of various materials.

Christine Edzard's 2001 *The Children's Midsummer Night's Dream* opens with a shot of children in a theatre, ready to see and hear a play. The first shot, therefore, focuses on the spectators, mirroring the audience in the cinema. The opening scene is performed by puppets, while the action is overlooked by the crowd of young spectators. Edzard creates a double level of spectatorship – the children watching the scene and the audience in the cinema watching a show being watched. This double gaze disappears when the children themselves take over the story and start playing each character. However, at the end of the film, the gaze is reversed: the puppets (impersonating Egeus, Theseus and Hippolyta) look at the children giving a performance of 'Pyramus and Thisbe'. Those who were watched have become the watchers. Edzard defamiliarizes us with the play by having children

[12] See Agnieszka Rasmus, 'Michael Almereyda's *Hamlet*: the Film is the Thing . . .? Metatheatre vs. Metacinema', <www.geocities.com/britgrad/2001/rasmus.html> Accessed 8 July 2003.
[13] Courtney Lehmann, *Shakespeare Remains: Theater to Film, Early Modern to Postmodern* (Ithaca, NY, and London: Cornell University Press, 2002), p. 98.

speak the lines but also through this regular awareness of several levels of spectatorship.

Adrian Noble's *A Midsummer Night's Dream* (1996) and Julie Taymor's *Titus* (2000) both cast the same actor (Osheen Jones) as a boy to duplicate a directorial figure and to represent the viewers themselves inside the film. Unlike Greenaway or Almereyda's films, the directorial counterpart is, this time, an exterior interpolated creation, and not a character from the original play. In Noble's *Dream*, the Boy is clearly given a director's role. He is first responsible for the whole story – he literally dreams it; he plays inside a toy theatre with a puppet in the shape of Titania (here obviously designated as a fictional character); he creates soap bubbles in which fairies materialize; and he opens the curtain before the performance of 'Pyramus and Thisbe'. This interpolated character thus gives rise to a reflection on creation and manipulation. However, beside this role of creator, he also remains a figure of spectatorship. He often reacts very violently to Oberon's tricks or apparitions, reflecting the audience's emotional responses. More importantly, the Boy dreams at the beginning of the film that he is looking through a keyhole, witnessing the first dialogue between Theseus and Hippolyta. At this very moment, the Boy is symbolically looking at the primal scene. He appears as a mirror reflection of all the viewers in the cinema who voyeuristically gaze at people who cannot see them.

Titus also starts with the interpolation of a boy, this time playing at war with dolls and food on a large table. The incredible explosion of violence that this child creates finds a direct echo at the end of the film, when so many murders take place around the table of Titus's banquet. This first scene featuring a boy making his dolls fight and kill one another amid the food thus appears as a metaphor for the whole movie, but also stands for the film-maker directing actors. The alienating figure of the Boy then becomes more and more involved in the story. He moves from the status of mere observer (in which he reduplicates the audience inside the film) to active participant (when he movingly finds wooden hands for Lavinia) and eventually to a real character in the story (when he is given the lines of Young Lucius).

In the examples of Noble's *Dream* and Taymor's *Titus*, introducing the Boy figure means creating a new framing, another level of fiction. Noble's version is not only presented as the probable midsummer's fantasies of four young Athenians – it is a boy's dream of a dream. In the same way, *Titus* is framed by the child's destiny. At the start, it is almost as if the Boy's game of violence suddenly materializes on a grand scale. By contrast, the end comes as a bearer of hope: the Boy is carried away towards the horizon as though the cycle of hatred could be stopped for ever.

REVEALING THE ACTOR AS AN ACTOR

Brecht was against the immersion of the actor's own personality into the character, which is one of the typical features of realistic theatre. He favoured a style of acting that let the actor's self shine through the part:

> This principle – that the actor actually appears on stage in a double role, as Laughton and as Galileo; that the showman Laughton does not disappear in the Galileo whom he is showing . . . comes to mean simply that the tangible, matter-of-fact process is no longer hidden behind a veil; that Laughton is actually there, standing on the stage and showing us what he imagines Galileo to have been.[14]

For Brecht, making it clear that every character is played by an actor is one way of disclosing the social and material conditions of theatre production. In a play, actors can reveal their presence by stepping out of their roles to comment on the dramatic action from an outside, distanced viewpoint. Revealing the actor as an actor is a device often used by Shakespeare, notably in *A Midsummer Night's Dream*. At the end of the play, the character of Robin Goodfellow steps out of his *dramatis persona* of Puck and comments on the whole show. He invites the audience to consider the play as a simple dream, thus suggesting a complete reassessment of the action and creating a distance from it. The second level of fiction, in which Peter Quince and his company of actors mount a production of 'Pyramus and Thisbe', allows for a regular disclosure of the acting conditions. The amateur players want to avoid frightening their future audience, and come up with the idea of writing prologues before each alarming situation. These prologues are meant to inform the spectators that Pyramus or the Lion are not what they seem to be, but are simply played by actors: 'for the more better assurance, tell them that I Pyramus am not Pyramus, but Bottom the weaver. This will put them out of fear' (iii.i.19–22). The amateur actors intend to disrupt the viewers' suspension of disbelief by revealing their own status as human beings, thus destroying the illusion of fiction. Nevertheless, this revealing of the actors as actors takes place on the second level of fiction. Bottom admits that he is playing Pyramus, but the actor playing Bottom does not disclose his identity under the part. The first level of fiction is only threatened indirectly, since the audience will relate the rehearsals for 'Pyramus

---

[14] Bertolt Brecht, *Brecht on Theatre*, ed. and trans. John Willet (London: Eyre Methuen, 1964), p. 194.

and Thisbe' to the real-life preparation of the play *A Midsummer Night's Dream*.

Shakespeare films have found some ways of reflecting this acting disclosure. They either resort to purely theatrical devices that question film realism, or take advantage of the cinematic medium to create new techniques showing the woman or man beneath the role.

Noble's 1996 *A Midsummer Night's Dream* and Edzard's 1992 *As You Like It* draw attention to the actors in a way directly inspired by the stage – the doubling of parts. Noble's adaptation features the same actress cast as Titania and Hippolyta as well as the same actors for Oberon and Theseus and for Puck and Philostrate. In Edzard's film, Orlando and Oliver are played by the same actor (Andrew Tiernan), while Don Henderson is cast as both of the Dukes, and Roger Hammond both as LeBeau and Corin. The doubling of parts obviously shows that the characters are only performed, that they are constructed by actors who can take on different parts and personalities. Paradoxically, it is through playing several characters in the same show that actors can start shining through their parts.

In Al Pacino's adaptation of *Richard III* (*Looking For Richard*, 1996), alienation operates through the disclosure of acting. Pacino manages to be at turns King Richard within a sometimes realistic diegesis, an actor playing Richard who upsets the creation of a fictive universe, and himself in search of the 'truth' of the part. When the character of Richard woos Lady Anne in a more or less realistic sequence, the diegesis is brutally interrupted by a surprising, extradiegetic shot of Pacino-the-actor uttering a loud ironic 'Ha!' commenting on Richard's hypocrisy and reflecting his double nature. It is as if the actor's subtext and research on the character were explicitly revealed. Later in the film, when Richard is finally killed, the audience is denied a sight of the corpse. As soon as the weapon falls on Richard, the film moves away from the battlefield, propelling us out of diegesis. The man whom we suddenly see lying on the ground in a New York street is not Richard played by Pacino, but Pacino himself, mimicking a dying man and laughing in the arms of his real-life friend. The death of Richard is, therefore, literal as much as symbolic. With Richard dead, the man beneath the role comes back to life. This alienating shock of a sudden return to reality presents the whole film as an illusion. By alternating processes of fictive construction and deconstruction, Pacino makes a movie that includes its own 'making of' and an explicit discourse on its subtext.

Olivier's 1944 *Henry V* starts with actors backstage, busy with the final preparations for their production of *Henry V* at the Globe theatre. The character of the king is first presented as a mere player clearing his throat before he steps on stage and starts a commanding delivery of his lines. Olivier reveals a player under the role of Henry, encouraging us to see the character of the king as a histrionic Machiavellian.[15] However, Olivier never reveals his own self beneath the part of Henry V. There is no shot offering us a sight of Olivier himself before or after playing the royal role. Part of the illusion thus remains untouched. By contrast, illusion is disrupted in a more radical way in the 1912 film of *Richard III*, partly directed by James Keane and featuring Frederick Warde, a famous stage actor of the time, in the eponymous role. Rothwell notices that, at the end of the film, 'illusions then turn back into reality as the film ends by showing Frederick Warde himself, now in the mufti of a tweed jacket, as he appeared long ago live in the theatre, bowing and smiling graciously to his adoring fans'.[16] This time, the actor is completely revealed under his part. With the final bow at the end of the film the actor pretends to be seen by the cinema audience as if the spectators were in a theatre auditorium. The actor's exhibitionism and acceptance that he is being watched is reintroduced, bringing an alienating element of theatre onto the screen. Film theorist Tom Gunning has argued that the early 'cinema of attractions' generally established a visual contact with the spectators, with actors smiling at the camera or bowing to an assumed audience, as they wished 'to rupture a self-enclosed fictional world for a chance to solicit the attention of the spectator'.[17] This 'rupturing' effect became an underground device in some *avant-garde* films. In the cinema, revealing the actor as an actor often seems, therefore, to lead to the disclosure of the camera apparatus.

LOOKING AT THE CAMERA

In the theatre, asides or addresses establish a direct communication between the actors and the spectators, disrupting the illusion of a realistic world existing independently from the audience. A film can also reveal its enunciation through gazes and speeches addressed to the camera, thus reproducing the theatrical convention of asides. Making the viewer conscious of the camera deviates from the logocentric Hollywood ideology that tries to hide the very mechanism of artistic creation by forbidding any actor to ever look

---

[15] See Michael Manheim, 'The English History Play on Screen', *Shakespeare and the Moving Image*, ed. Anthony Davies and Stanley Wells (Cambridge University Press, 1994), p. 123.

[16] Rothwell, *History of Shakespeare on Screen*, p. 20.

[17] Tom Gunning, 'The Cinema of Attractions: Early Film, its Spectator and the Avant-Garde', in *Early Cinema: Space, Frame, Narrative*, ed. T. Elsaesser and A. Barker (London: British Film Institute, 1990), p. 57.

at the camera. In Hollywood films, the actor is often there to fascinate the spectators, not to call them out. Therefore, during a soliloquy on screen, when a character stares at the spectators and speaks directly to them, he or she causes a shock. The members of the audience, who may have forgotten that they were watching a film as they fully experienced excarnation, are forced to realize the presence of a trick – the camera. The centrifugal experience of the cinema can then be likened to the centripetal experience of the theatre. The spectators are reminded of their own bodies and voyeuristic positions. The gaze to the camera introduces a reversal that betrays and underlines the technical apparatus.

In relatively avant-gardist screen adaptations such as Peter Hall's and Adrian Noble's versions of *A Midsummer Night's Dream* or Tony Richardson's *Hamlet*, the monologues are regularly filmed with the actors facing the camera. In Taymor's *Titus*, Tamora, Titus and Aaron speak to the lens too. There is no clear distinction between characters who would be allowed to share their thoughts with the public, and those who would not. Through this major stage convention, the characters bring the spectators into their psyche while alienating them from the fiction.

By contrast, if we except the treatment of Choruses, Shakespeare films shot in a more realistic mode restrict this technique to the 'baddies'. Only the characters who are linked to Hell – like Iago or Richard III – have been allowed to circumvent the filmic convention, look at the camera and provoke us to participate in their plots. This creates a high complicity between the audience and the scheming characters. Hollywood ideology remains protected, as formal transgression only comes with a transgression within the story: the traditional aesthetic of film is questioned only by a character who is himself on the fringe. In Oliver Parker's 1995 *Othello*, Iago speaks directly to the lens. He makes the spectators participate in his plot, calling them to witness. Iago becomes not only a director of the action in the play, manipulating the characters in the story, but also a director of the images, playing with the camera and instigating the fade-outs himself by covering the lens with his hand. Laurence Olivier, playing the title role in his 1955 film of *Richard III*, also talks to the camera in the first scene, to deliver 'Now is the winter of our discontent' (1.i.1). In Richard Loncraine's 1996 *Richard III*, Ian McKellen acts as if he saw the reflection of the camera or of the spectator in a mirror. He then turns around and starts talking directly to the audience in the cinema. Even when he finally falls into the flames at the end, he is still looking at the camera, creating an ironic distance between us and the show. What is also striking is that, at this very moment, Richmond, who used to be presented as a brave and good man, starts looking at the camera. Now that Richard is dead, it is his turn to gaze at the audience. The film's ending is, therefore, highly problematic. Since Richmond has acquired Richard's ability to acknowledge the audience's presence, we are encouraged to wonder if Richard's hypocrisy and cruelty are not going to be passed on to him as well. With this final aesthetic twist, Manichaeism gives way to a blurring of good and evil.[18]

MIRRORS AND MIRROR EFFECTS

The presence of mirrors in the field of the camera is a recurrent metacinematic figure as it creates a frame-within-a-frame, and complicates the relationship between the spectator and the screen. The screen is considered as a kind of mirror by film theorists since what is perceived on it is not really the objects or persons themselves, but their ghost-like double.[19]

Loncraine's 1995 *Richard III* plays with this similarity between screen and mirror. It is in a mirror that Richard discovers an important fact: spectators are watching him. He first looks at himself casually, and he suddenly realizes that something else is reflected in the mirror – an audience. From this critical moment of recognition, he will not stop looking at us and talking to us. This film, therefore, questions the very nature of cinema, presenting a situation beyond the watertight separation between the space of the story and the space of the audience. It is as if the screen is turned into a real mirror in which the spectators' reflections are seen by the main character inside diegesis.

Kenneth Branagh also uses mirrors to create effects of frames-within-the-frame and to introduce analogies between the actors on film and the spectators in the cinema. In the film of *Hamlet*, the palace of Elsinore is turned into a world of mirrors. Thirty two-way mirrors are placed on each side of the vast throne room, hiding as many secret rooms, and literally (as well as metaphorically) reflecting the paranoia of a narcissistic and opulent world. Hamlet delivers the soliloquy 'To be, or not to be' (iii.i.55) in front of one of these two-way mirrors while Claudius is spying on the other side. In a talk given at Yale University on 8 November 1997, Branagh said that his first intention had been to develop an extreme multiplicity of the reflections:

---

[18] See James N. Loehlin, '"Top of the World, Ma": *Richard III* and Cinematic Convention', in *Shakespeare, the Movie*, ed. Lynda E. Boose and Richard Burt (London: Routledge, 1997), p. 76.

[19] See Christian Metz, 'The Imaginary Signifier', in *Film and Theory: An Anthology*, ed. Robert Stam and Toby Miller (Oxford: Blackwell, 2000), p. 410.

There's a shot in *Citizen Kane* where Orson Welles walks by a mirror, appears to walk by, and then a minute later, he does walk by in actual fact . . . An infinite number of Orson Welleses are walking across the mirror. And I think that's what I wanted with the 'To be, or not to be' soliloquy.

Branagh eventually chose a simpler solution. The camera slowly moves forward onto the prince's reflection that finally invades the whole visual field. This shot creates a blurring between Hamlet's image and that of his double, while reflecting the audience's own situation, looking at the show on the mirror-screen. Claudius is also in the same position as the public in the cinema as he is protected by a screen, voyeuristically observing someone who cannot see him.

In Grigori Kozintsev's 1964 *Hamlet*, Claudius's confession is filmed entirely while the character is looking at himself in a mirror. This introspective scene is turned into a metadramatic moment in which looking at the fault that has been committed becomes gazing at the reflection in the mirror. Claudius transfers his guilt onto a shadow, onto a quasi-other, and cannot receive absolution. A very similar device can be found in Almereyda's 2000 *Hamlet*. The end of Hamlet's soliloquy, 'How all occasions do inform against me' (IV.iv.32), takes place in front of a mirror, in the toilets of a plane. From the sentence 'Rightly to be great / Is not to stir without great argument' (IV.iv.53–4), he carefully gazes at the mirror, as if hypnotized by his reflection. He seems to be talking to another version of himself, one who could be brave and heroic enough to take action against his uncle. During this specific resolution-making soliloquy, the mirror, as a source of likeness and otherness at the same time, allows Hamlet to reconstruct another self and to decide that, from now on, his 'thoughts be bloody, or be nothing worth!' (IV.iv.66).

Dieterle and Reinhardt's 1935 *A Midsummer Night's Dream* does not feature mirrors as such, but rather mirror *effects* in the form of mimics and sound echoes. Puck, played as an infuriating brat, keeps imitating the characters' gestures or repeating their words. Having awakened from her nightmare and found herself all alone, Hermia runs in the woods calling for Lysander. Above in a tree, Puck is observing her and starts imitating her calls and cries. With this echo, Puck creates a distance between the audience and a character thus made ridiculous and harder to identify with. Emotion and sorrow are merged with comical alienation. When all the lovers are lost in the forest, Puck actively impersonates each of them, repeating sentences that they uttered earlier in the film. Again, the sequence works on the notions of echo and repetition. Puck presents himself as an alienating double of each of the four lovers. When they finally all wake up in the morning, they laugh at their behaviour and parody their earlier quarrels, teasingly and light-heartedly mimicking their nocturnal fights. This time, they do not need Puck to laugh at them any more – they now laugh at themselves. It is their turn to distance themselves from their past actions and joke about them.

UNCOMMON CAMERAWORK

In films, ordinary camerawork (in terms of framing, camera movements and editing) is most often felt as non-camerawork. The viewers identify with the camera's gaze (without which no filmic experience would be possible), but they are almost unconscious of this fact. It takes uncommon camerawork to make the spectators more aware of their identification with the camera's viewpoint, alienating them, even for a short while, from the fiction.[20]

Director Orson Welles regularly reveals cinematic enunciation through specific camera angles. His extreme high- and low-angle shots are very noticeable as they are not linked to any gaze inside the story. In other words, no character is, for example, lying on the floor to justify a low-angle shot. The vision of the camera is disconnected from any human point of view. Such angles, then, work to reveal the pure act of an omniscient filmic narrator. The unusual angles alert the spectators, making them more conscious of their viewing position.

In Branagh's adaptations, enunciation is made visible through specific camera movements and angles. The long, obvious circular moves point out their own enunciation by attracting the spectators' eye onto their very trajectory. High-angle shots are often alien to the human gaze, as when the camera overhangs Fortinbras's soldiers carrying Hamlet's corpse away. Laurence Olivier's *Hamlet* includes the same device just before the soliloquy, 'To be, or not to be'. The camera tracks rapidly up the stairs of the tower, then towards Hamlet as if to enter his skull. The audience could legitimately wonder whose viewpoint this shot represents. Would it be the Ghost's? Would it belong to any dangerous spy ready to kill Hamlet from behind? But when the next shot shows the prince facing the camera in mid-shot, there is no one behind him. No danger is lurking. The previous shot was just an 'objective' one, which did not belong to any character inside diegesis. Those shots clearly reveal the intrusion of a superior narrative authority and exhibit their own construction to the viewers.

[20] *Ibid.*, pp. 417–18.

To reveal the presence of the camera in *Looking For Richard*, Al Pacino uses filters placed in front of the lens to absorb some colour radiations and create specific colour effects. During the final battle, the image goes from natural colours to a dominant red, thus underlining the prism of the lens. The red filter intensifies the bloody aspect of the fights while creating a dream-like effect and generating a distance between the viewers and the spectacle of war. In Zeffirelli's *The Taming of the Shrew* (1966), a similar technique can be found. The camera lens is covered with ochre and sepia-tinted filters, giving an artificial touch to the colours and bringing a fairy-tale look to the whole film.[21] These non-natural colours added to the obviously painted scenery of Padua at times disrupt the illusion of a realistic environment.

Peter Hall's *A Midsummer Night's Dream* (1969) and Peter Brook's *King Lear* (1971) are alike in the strategies of alienation integrated into their film-making – they both feature deliberately amateur camerawork, calling attention to the technical apparatus behind the shots. Hall's *Dream* is often filmed with a hand-held camera, giving rise to jumpy, unsteady images. In *King Lear*, Brook also uses a hand-held camera, one that films grainy-textured images and that often remains out of focus. Displaying numerous reflexive devices such as discontinuities, ostensible zoom effects, abrupt editing and static frames (with silent-screen titles) announcing new sequences, Brook's film is designed to engender discomfort rather than comfort in viewers' minds.[22] Baz Luhrmann's 1996 *Romeo + Juliet* applies some of these techniques to a more mainstream production. With a multitude of whip pans, express zooming, extreme close-ups and stylized slow-motions, Luhrmann's camerawork is made highly noticeable. But if the Brook and Hall style aims at minimalism and alienation to emphasize verbal delivery and encourage critical distance, Luhrmann's technical bravura seems, now and then, to take priority over meaning. In one instance, alienating camerawork leads to a concentration on the text; in the other, it displays a fascination with colourful, visual extravaganza.

THE FILM-WITHIN-THE-FILM AND THE
SCREEN-WITHIN-THE-SCREEN

In a play, inserting a second fictional level duplicates the conditions of performance. With a play-within-the-play, a fictional on-stage audience

---

[21] See Michael Pursell, 'Zeffirelli's Shakespeare: the Visual Realization of Tone and Theme', *Literature/Film Quarterly* 8.4 (1980), 210–18.
[22] See Rothwell, *History of Shakespeare on Screen*, p. 151.

mirrors the real audience in the auditorium, and fictional actors and directors stand as equivalents for their real-life counterparts in the actual production of the play. According to the drama theorist, Manfred Pfister,
'The play within the play refers implicitly to the theatrical medium itself,
thereby exposing it and distancing it from the real audience.'[23] Film
directors have come up with more or less comparable devices to duplicate the conditions of cinema inside a movie. These devices can take
two main forms – films-within-the-film and screens-within-the-screen. In
a film-within-the-film, the boundaries of the first level of fiction disappear. The included film erases the material limits of the including film,
which is almost forgotten for a while. This is generally the case with
flashbacks, flashforwards and quick inserts from another time or space
dimension. In a screen-within-the-screen, the filmic conditions are repro-
duced within the boundaries of the main action. Several frames can thus
be seen in the same shot, as when a character is filmed watching a film
on a TV set. At times, a screen-within-the-screen may turn into a film-
within-the-film (if, for example, the camera zooms on the TV set to show
only the included film), or the other way round. The two forms of cinematic framing are not fixed and can evolve in time, even within the same
shot.

Peter Greenaway's 1991 *Prospero's Books* is made up of images carefully
composed to look like Renaissance paintings and juxtaposed without much
of a narrative logic, in a very Brechtian way. Diegesis is constantly interrupted by comments in voice-over, speeches and gazes directly addressed to
the audience and, above all, by *mises-en-abyme* of the screen. Naked bodies
regularly hold a golden frame outlining the main action, and fictional characters look at animated pictures, mirroring the situation of the real viewers
in the cinema. By creating parallel spaces, screens-within-the-screen rein-
troduce the very notion of backstage inside film itself. Greenaway is, maybe,
the director who has gone the furthest in his search for filmic equivalents
to Shakespearean metatheatrical elements. However, it is still possible to
find embedded filmic structures in more conventional, less experimental
Shakespeare films.

In Branagh's 1996 *Hamlet*, flashbacks, as well as visual inclusions during
some speeches, act as films-within-the-film. According to Anny Crunelle,
'the many silent flashbacks . . . are Branagh's cinematic equivalent of
Shakespeare's dramatic inserts'.[24] If 'The Mousetrap' and the Player King's
speech represent two embedded constructions in the original play, Branagh

[23] Pfister, *Theory and Analysis of Drama*, p. 229.   [24] Crunelle, 'All the World's a Screen', 360.

treats them differently when he adapts them to the screen. In the former case, the play-within-the-play becomes a play-within-the-film, losing its function of medium reduplication. In the latter case, the Player's speech-within-the-play is turned into a film-within-the-film. When the Player starts describing the murder of Priam by Pyrrhus, a visual insert shows the destruction of Troy and the death of the old man. This device suppresses the metatheatrical effect but creates a metafilmic one. This reflexivity can also be found in the repetition of images within the movie itself. For example, the sequence that starts the second half (after the 'Intermission') is an episodic flashback of images already seen in the first half. Claudius's speech about the succession of 'sorrows' (IV.v.75–96) is visually complemented by a kind of summary of the previous episodes. Branagh's adaptation of *Hamlet*, therefore, presents a powerful reflexivity as the flow of images ends up 'feeding' on itself.

In Pacino's 1996 *Looking For Richard*, Richard's dream before the battle displays the same kind of reflexivity recycling the film's own material. Almost subliminal flashes feature images and sounds that have previously been seen and heard and, more originally, that will be seen and heard later in the film during the battle. Flashbacks (showing, in a distorted way, the people hurt or killed by Richard's plots) and flashforwards (showing Richard's own future death) are mixed together to produce a dream-like, metacinematic effect.

In Baz Luhrmann's 1996 *Romeo + Juliet*, the opening chorus and the Prince's final speech are replaced by the framing device of a television news broadcast. The first and last words of the play are mediated through a TV journalist: the dramatic action is reduced to mundane fodder for newsreels. The TV set, floating in a non-realistic vacuum space in the middle of the cinema screen, gives rise to a *mise-en-abyme* of the film medium. The embedded structure, especially when the television monitor becomes smaller and slowly shifts away, is even more obvious when the movie is watched on video on another TV set. Even inside the story itself, the framing motif is recurrent. Romeo is first seen alone, sitting on the stage of an open-air theatre. The huge rectangular structure of the theatre clearly reflects the shape of the cinema screen. This particular frame is, therefore, made self-reflexive twice – in its metatheatrical nature as well as in its metafilmic shape. A bit later in the scene, Romeo delivers his line 'O me, what fray was here?' as a direct response to watching a news replay that shows yet another fight between the two families. After the extradiegetic frame, TV monitors seem to invade the diegetic space as well, mirroring a media-obsessed society.

To a certain extent, this could also apply to Almereyda's 2000 *Hamlet* in which screen reduplications proliferate. As in Luhrmann's adaptation, a news anchor on an internal TV screen ends the film. Helped by a highly metacinematic teleprompter, the journalist reads an epilogue-like speech announcing the rise of the new King of Denmark, composed of lines delivered in the original play by the First Player, Fortinbras and the English Ambassador. Symbolically, lines belonging to characters are taken over by the TV news. Everything happens as though Shakespeare's text has been swallowed and appropriated by the media-driven world. During the course of the film, other internal screens can be spotted. Various surveillance monitors are placed in Claudius's building, while Hamlet often plays videotapes on a TV set and edits his own films on a computer. Screen duplications involving Hamlet's amateur recordings generally appear in two ways. They are either narcissistic when the prince films himself during his soliloquies and then replays images of himself several times in a row, or nostalgic when Hamlet plays old tapes of his parents and Ophelia.

Almereyda's screens-within-the-screen actively participate in diegesis, motivating some of Hamlet's crucial decisions. A Tibetan monk, talking on TV about the necessity not only 'to be' but also 'to inter-be' with family, friends and nature, may have spurred Hamlet's soliloquy, 'To be, or not to be' (which is delivered in the metafilmic environment of a video shop). In this adaptation, the First Player, whose speech about Hecuba prompts Hamlet to take action, is replaced by a film actor, famous for representing rebellious youth – James Dean, acting in a black-and-white movie that Hamlet watches at night. Later on, we also catch a glimpse of Shakespearean actor, Forbes-Robertson, holding Yorick's skull in his 1913 screen version of *Hamlet*. This filmic quote not only situates Almereyda's film within the tradition of *Hamlet* on screen, but also creates a weird, unfamiliar diegesis, since Hamlet lives in a world where his story is known and has already been adapted on film.

Almereyda's metafilmic crux lies in the transformation of the play-within-the-play into a film-within-the-film. 'The Mousetrap' is not a play performed by visiting players any more, but an amateur film directed (or rather edited) by Hamlet himself and projected in front of the court in a private cinema room. Michael Almereyda comments on his choice: 'The film within the film answers what Shakespeare called for in the play, in that a mirror is being held up to nature: the audience of the movie is watching an audience watch a movie. It's a hall of mirrors.'[25]

[25] Cynthia Fuchs, 'Looking Around Corners. Interview with Michael Almereyda', <http://www.popmatters.com/film/interviews/almereyda-michael.html> Accessed 2 March 2003.

Hamlet composes a pseudo *avant-garde* video, a collage of heterogeneous excerpts from soap-operas, soft porn and metaphorical animated pictures. A scene actually shows us Hamlet rent the numerous videotapes that will serve as raw material. In a very original aesthetic twist, meta-cinema itself is, therefore, made self-reflexive, as the film-within-the-film is not a pure, original creation, but a metafilmic patchwork made of other films. When Hamlet's work starts unwinding before our eyes and the fictional audience's, a very defamiliarizing title appears on the screen: 'The Mousetrap: a tragedy by Hamlet Prince of Denmark'. Hamlet's authorship gives rise to a comical as well as distancing reversal in terms. Used as we are to 'the tragedy *of* Hamlet Prince of Denmark', the new title using 'by' comes as a small alienating shock. It appears as an ironic reminder that this Hamlet, though he seems to think of himself as the ultimate author, is himself the eponymous character of a tragedy written by a playwright and adapted by a film-maker.

FILM QUOTES

Calling upon the spectators' cinematic culture by appropriating a recognizable movie genre, including references to well-known films or casting famous actors may contribute to presenting the film as a constructed object. References to other films create a post-modern intertext that connects the work to other diegetic worlds.[26] By using filmic codes[27] that the audience associates with a specific genre, such as war movie, western or epic, the director creates a reflexive adaptation that contains in itself a series of films belonging to the same genre. These familiar effects of *mise-en-scène* become aesthetic as well as cultural marks of enunciation. They tend to call attention to the medium by creating a line of 'films-within-the-film'. But this time, the *mise-en-abyme* is no longer applied to filmic apparatus, but to the diegesis and aesthetic specific to each film genre. Casting well-known actors can also contribute to the creation of an intertext revealing the film as a cinematic product. As Keith A. Reader writes: 'The very concept of the film *star* is an intertextual one, relying as it does on correspondences of similarity and difference from one film to the next, and sometimes too

---

[26] I use the concept of intertextuality as it is defined by Gérard Genette: 'a relationship of copresence between two texts' and 'the actual presence of one text within another' in *Palimpsests: Literature in the Second Degree*, trans. Channa Newman and Claude Doubinsky (Lincoln and London: University of Nebraska Press, 1997), pp. 1–2.

[27] See Lawrence Guntner and Peter Drexler, 'Recycled Film Codes and the Study of Shakespeare on Film', *Deutsche Shakespeare* (1993), 31–40.

on supposed resemblances between on and off-screen personae.'[28] As the presence of a famous actor in a film recalls characters that were previously acted, the 'star' will usually bring a kind of instability, multiplicity and virtuality to the part.[29] The trend towards casting renowned film actors in screen adaptations of Shakespeare started early. Svend Gade's *Hamlet* (1920) features Asta Nielsen, one of the most famous actresses in Europe at the time, as the protagonist. Reinhardt's 1935 *A Midsummer Night's Dream* casts movie stars such as James Cagney (Bottom), Mickey Rooney (Puck) and Olivia de Havilland (Hermia), while placing itself in the traditions of both Gothic cinema (exemplified by F. W. Murnau's 1921 *Nosferatu*) and the 1930s Hollywood musical.

Laurence Olivier's *Henry V*, filmed during World War II, borrows from the Hollywood western, a genre that fits well the patriotic response that the director wanted to evoke. As in a western, the film is a straightforward story with relatively caricatured characters, a clear demarcation between good and evil, and horsemen rather than infantrymen. Olivier uses long panning and travelling shots to produce an impression of wide open spaces, like the plains of the Far West. With alternating cuts of the two charging armies, the editing directly calls to mind the Indians and Cavalry of a western. Even the duel between Henry and the Dauphin recalls a final confrontation between two cowboys. This particular genre is again quoted by Olivier in his 1955 *Richard III*. At the end of the battle of Shrewbury, Richard is spatially lost in a long shot, emphasizing his vulnerability and isolation. From above a hill in the background, Richmond's soldiers emerge one by one, in the mode of Indians appearing progressively at the top of a Wild West narrow pass. At this moment, William Walton's music also adopts the sonority typical of western scores. The final rush towards Richard is filmed as a blood-thirsty attack, almost like hounds on a quarry. *Richard III*'s specific appropriation of the Hollywood western genre therefore represents an interesting ideological volte-face: the figures that are rewritten as Indians represent the good side, one that chases a tyrant from power.

By contrast, Olivier's *Hamlet* does not use elements from the western, but borrows from German Expressionist films (such as Robert Wiene's 1921 *The Cabinet of Dr Caligari*) with its expressive camerawork, chiaroscuro lighting and endless stairs and corridors producing a claustrophobic ambience. The film also draws from the offshoots of German Expressionism, i.e. American

---

[28] Keith A. Reader, 'Literature/Cinema/Television: Intertextuality in Jean Renoir's *Le testament du Docteur Cordelier*', in *Intertextuality: Theories and Practices*, ed. Michael Worton and Judith Still (Manchester and New York: Manchester University Press, 1990), p. 176.

[29] See Metz, *L'énonciation impersonnelle*, p. 90.

film noir and the 1940s detective stories, in its use of deep-focus shots, black-and-white rather than colour and melancholic narrative voice-over at the start of the film. According to Guntner and Drexler, in their 1993 article, 'Recycled Film Codes and the Study of Shakespeare on Film':

> The atmosphere in Olivier's Elsinore would remind his 1940s audience of the abandoned American inner city at night; Olivier's alienated Hamlet would evoke memories of Humphrey Bogart or Dick Powell as Philip Marlowe or Sam Spade, who also try to solve bizarre murder cases in a murky and threatening world in which the real and the unreal, good and evil, intersect.[30]

Setting Shakespeare's text into a particular film genre has, therefore, some strong ideological consequences. If Olivier's use of western codes emphasizes a straightforward, heroic and patriotic reading of *Henry V*, the recycling of *film noir* into *Hamlet* stresses, on the contrary, ambivalence and ambiguity.

The Shakespeare films of the nineties onwards perpetuate this trend of film quoting, all the more so since they emerged in a nostalgic, post-modern era in which most artistic creations recycle achievements from the past, pay homage to them or make fun of them. Loncraine's 1995 *Richard III* recycles the codes of gangster films[31] as well as those from World War II movies. The battle of Bosworth is presented in a very realistic interpolation, where agitated editing reflects the chaotic situation of civil war. As his jeep remains stuck in the mud, Richard cannot escape, and thus exclaims 'A horse! A horse! my kingdom for a horse!' (v.iv.7–8). What could have sounded anachronistic in a context of cars and tanks is explained and made natural. By recycling war movies, this diegetic environment offers an unfamiliar, distancing view of the famous line. Loncraine's battle sequence originally combines realism with alienation. In the 1995 *Othello*, Oliver Parker casts Laurence Fishburne as the Moor, thus bringing into the part echoes of his past role as Ike Turner (Tina Turner's brutal husband) in *What's Love Got to Do With It* (1993). Choosing this actor for the part, according to Stephen Buhler, 'fetishize[s] Othello as the black aggressor of racist – and popular – stereotype'.[32] Through role association, the film encourages the audience to see Othello, from the start, as the potential murderer of his wife. This is emphasized in the interpolated sequence of

[30] Guntner and Drexler, 'Recycled Film Codes', 34.
[31] See Loehlin's 1997 article '"Top of the World, Ma": *Richard III* and Cinematic Convention', which analyses how Loncraine recycles the codes of gangster movies, in particular those starring James Cagney.
[32] Stephen Buhler, *Shakespeare in the Cinema: Ocular Proof* (Albany: State University of New York Press, 2002), p. 26.

the wedding night, which is shot in the mode of hunting: before their love-making, Othello moves menacingly towards Desdemona, while she, almost frightened, retreats from him. Viewers' expectations are, at this moment, guided through the intertextual quote of Fishburne's past film: love is linked to violence, passion to aggression.

Almereyda's *Hamlet* and Taymor's *Titus*, both released in 2000, both cast a highly connoted actor in the title role – Ethan Hawke as Hamlet and Anthony Hopkins as Titus. Ethan Hawke got his breakthrough part in Peter Weir's 1989 film, *Dead Poets Society*, as Todd Anderson, a shy, hesitating, uneasy student, tormented by his lack of confidence and his need for parental love. A decade later, Hawke still carries with him traces of this part in his screen persona and in the viewers' minds. Whereas Zeffirelli's 1990 *Hamlet* presents a more virile and resolute prince through Mel Gibson's roles in action-packed movies,[33] Almereyda's *Hamlet* is virtually imbued with a *Dead Poets Society* intertext. Hawke's Hamlet is very much like Todd in his introverted discomfort, tormented nervousness, continual hesitations and desperate longing for parental recognition. For her adaptation of *Titus*, Julie Taymor cast Anthony Hopkins in the title role. In Shakespeare's play, the eponymous character kills the sons of his enemy Tamora, makes meat pies of them and then serves them to their mother and her allies. In this context of anthropophagy, Anthony Hopkins as Titus imports echoes of his world-famous role of Dr Hannibal Lecter in Jonathan Demme's 1992 film, *The Silence of the Lambs*. Since he played this psychiatrist turned human-flesh-fixated serial-killer, Hopkins's leering screen persona has represented the fascination/repulsion of human eating human in the public consciousness. Hopkins's prominent role of Hannibal Lecter immediately instils the character of Titus with an expected, ambiguous personality. The spectators are immediately encouraged to think of Titus as intelligent and mad, manipulative and manipulated, capable of the most horrible acts and of the most elaborate schemes. What can almost be called type-casting embeds a very familiar movie into an unfamiliar play. It creates immediate complicity with the audience, while recalling another cinematic work in an ostensible metafilmic quote.

Kenneth Branagh is probably the director who has gone the furthest in his appropriation of cinematic codes and conventions. As Samuel Crowl argues: 'Branagh is a product of the post-modern moment dominated by a sense of belatedness – a sense that originality is exhausted and that only parody and

---

[33] See Harry Keyishian, 'Shakespeare and Movie Genre: the Case of *Hamlet*', in *The Cambridge Companion to Shakespeare on Film*, ed. Russell Jackson (Cambridge University Press, 2000), pp. 77–8.

pastiche and intertextual echo remain . . . Branagh is a reconstructionist – an artist who creates out of the bits and shards of the post-modern moment.'[34] Branagh's Shakespeare adaptations have all reformulated a high number of past works, more or less ostensibly. In a 1993 interview, Branagh stated:

When making . . . *Henry V*, I've been influenced by a number of movies. I seem to know a lot of war movies, a lot of battle movies. I remember bits of Orson Welles's film, *Chimes at Midnight* and Kurosawa's *Ran* as also being very influential. Everything, from *The Great Escape* through *The Longest Day*. A whole pile of stuff that I can't coherently reference. Ideas stolen from everywhere.[35]

In the critical response to Branagh's 1989 *Henry V*, the whole film or some specific moments from it were commented on in references to other films. With its muddy ground, transcended pains and manly friendships, the film recalls Vietnam movies such as Oliver Stone's *Platoon* (1986). Chris Fitter notices that 'the structure . . . owes much . . . to Vietnam movies of the 1980s, particularly its moral ambiguity: war is hell but it heroizes'.[36] The Southampton treason scene occurs in a secluded place, in an atmosphere of claustrophobia. The scene starts with a shot of the doors being locked up. Kenneth S. Rothwell comments:

[Henry's] wrath and fearful assault on the hapless traitors are reminiscent of the post-prandial entertainment at a Hollywood version of a Mafia dinner party. He and Exeter take everything but a baseball bat to his erstwhile friends.[37]

Rothwell may allude to a scene from Brian de Palma's *The Untouchables* (1987) in which Robert De Niro as Al Capone takes a baseball bat and breaks open the skull of a traitor. The dark image of Henry V with his cape coming in like a threatening and mysterious figure has been compared many times to Darth Vader in George Lucas's *Star Wars* (1977). For Deborah Cartmell, 'the inhuman black masked figure inevitably recalls Darth Vader in *Star Wars*'.[38] Michael Pursell even perceives an armoured Exeter threatening the French king as another Robocop or Terminator, 'a killing machine praying for war'.[39] In its glorification of male bonding – Henry and Falstaff in the

---

[34] Samuel Crowl, *Shakespeare at the Cineplex: The Kenneth Branagh Era* (Athens, OH: Ohio University Press, 2003), p. 28.

[35] John Naughton, 'The Return of The Magnificent Eight?', *Premiere*, September 1993, 63.

[36] In Chris Fitter, 'A Tale of Two Branaghs: *Henry V*, Ideology, and the Mekong Agincourt', in *Shakespeare Left and Right*, ed. Ivo Kamps (New York, London: Routledge, 1991), p. 270.

[37] Kenneth S. Rothwell, 'Kenneth Branagh's *Henry V*: the Gilt [Guilt] in the Crown Re-Examined', *Comparative Drama* 24 (1990), 175.

[38] Deborah Cartmell, 'The *Henry V* Flashback: Kenneth Branagh's Shakespeare', in *Pulping Fictions: Consuming Culture across the Literature/Media Divide*, ed. Deborah Cartmell, I. Q. Hunter, Heidi Kaye and Imelda Whelehan (London and Chicago: Pluto, 1996), pp. 73–83.

[39] Michael Pursell, 'Playing the Game: Branagh's *Henry V*', *Literature/Film Quarterly* 20 (1992), 270.

old days, Henry held up by Exeter after the siege of Harfleur, Henry weeping in Fluellen's arms after the battle – Branagh's *Henry V* also takes us back to the John Wayne westerns such as Howard Hawks's *Rio Bravo* (1958), where this theme is prevalent. Moreover, the king's irruption during the Harfleur siege on a white rearing horse, like the Lone Ranger, is another traditional mark of the genre. The Hollywood western works on some founding myths of the American dream: the myth of the Earth of abundance, of a classless society, of the 'self-made' and 'common' man.[40] In such an ideological context, the battle of Agincourt becomes a quest for the Promised Land, and the king becomes a man who knows how to be a hero and mix with simple soldiers at the same time.[41]

An allusion to the western genre is also apparent in Branagh's 1993 *Much Ado About Nothing*. When the soldiers return from war on galloping horses for the big overture, their number (seven) as well as their arrangement (all lined up) make them look like John Sturges's *The Magnificent Seven*. However, the film is mainly shot with the codes of musical comedies. According to Pierre Berthomieu, 'The movement of love, the pure eroticism of the bodies, the kinetics of the groups: Branagh's prologue is truly a *musical . . . Much Ado About Nothing . . .* sends us back . . . to Robert Wise's *The Sound Of Music*.'[42] Even the final dance through the patios refers to a scene from *The Sound Of Music* in which the children and Maria dance in the garden. Explicit allusions to Stanley Donen's *Singin' In The Rain* have also been noticed. Benedick, believing in Beatrice's love, plunges into water. Samuel Crowl speaks of 'Branagh's Gene Kelly-like splashing in the fountain'.[43] Gene Kelly's character, in love, sings 'I'm ready for love' in pouring rain. Benedick, ready just the same, joins in.

The 1996 *Hamlet* is a hybrid film, appropriating a multiplicity of genres and quoting, deliberately or not, a lot of films. For Iska Alter, 'Branagh has filled *Hamlet* with proliferating remembrances of films past, Shakespearean and otherwise.'[44] The film is an epic thriller, a war movie and a horror film all at once, with bloody close-ups, heart-breaking screams and speedy

[40] See Anne-Marie Bidaud, *Hollywood et le Rêve américain: cinéma et idéologie aux Etats-Unis* (Paris, Milan and Barcelona: Masson, 1994), p. 15.
[41] In his article 'Branagh's Iconoclasm: Warriors for the Working Day', Paul Rathburn writes: 'His [Branagh's] is an icon of the heroism of the common man', *Shakespeare on Film Newsletter* 15.2 (April 1991), 16.
[42] Pierre Berthomieu, *Kenneth Branagh: traînes de feu, rosées de sang* (Paris: Jean-Michel Place, 1998), p. 32. My translation from French.
[43] In Samuel Crowl, '*Much Ado About Nothing*', *Shakespeare Bulletin* (Summer 1993), 40.
[44] Iska Alter, '"To See or Not To See": Interpolations, Extended Scenes, and Musical Accompaniment in Kenneth Branagh's *Hamlet*', in *Stage Directions in 'Hamlet': New Essays and New Directions*, ed. Hardin L. Aasand (Cranbury, London and Mississauga: Associated University Presses, 2003), p. 165.

chases through the corridors of Elsinore. The ending recalls the adventure movies of the 1940s and 50s: Hamlet and Laertes fight like musketeers with sword assaults and secret thrusts, taking the lead in turns. When Hamlet eventually throws his sword like a javelin towards Claudius and jumps down through the hall to finish off his uncle, the film reproduces the great final moments in Errol Flynn movies. But, above all, Branagh's *Hamlet* follows the tradition of Hollywood epic and spectacle. *Hamlet* is an epic film by virtue of its cast, length, scope, landscapes, extras, sets and even its 'Intermission'. It is easy to establish a parallel between the scene of 'My thoughts be bloody or be nothing worth' and the sequence in *Gone With The Wind* (1939) in which Scarlett O'Hara asserts her new resolution ('As God is my witness, I'll never be hungry again!'). The camera moves backwards in the same way until the heroic character is lost in an infinite space – Scarlett under the Tara tree, Hamlet in a snowy landscape where, in the distance, Fortinbras's army marches past. The army charging on horses in the snowy plains of Russia in David Lean's *Doctor Zhivago* (1965) inspired the charge of Fortinbras's soldiers on Elsinore in *Hamlet*. To make this allusion more obvious, Branagh casts Julie Christie (who played Lara) as Gertrude. By importing well-known actors, Branagh hoped to achieve a popular success for the movie, but these stars also bring with them the echoes of other movies. Through his major roles in William Wyler's *Ben Hur* and Cecil B. De Mille's *The Ten Commandments*, Charlton Heston as the Player King brings even more epic into the Hecuba speech and the vision of a destroyed Troy, while Billy Crystal (as the First Gravedigger) and Robin Williams (as Osric) carry a comic intertext that instantly informs the way the audience receive their respective scenes.

Love's Labour's Lost, released in 2000, goes further than *Much Ado About Nothing* in its appropriation of codes from Hollywood romantic musicals, interpolating some George Gershwin and Cole Porter songs into the original text. The film is directly inspired by the Fred Astaire and Ginger Rogers movies, includes famous numbers like *Shall We Dance, Cheek To Cheek, The Way You Look Tonight,* and presents a synchronized swimming sequence evoking the aquatic ballets of Esther Williams. The artificiality of the sets creates a fairy-tale atmosphere recalling the look of the musicals from the thirties to the fifties. Filmic illusion is shattered when Don Armado kicks the moon out of the set during his number, *I Get A Kick Out Of You.* Branagh sets the film on the eve of an imaginary world war, which gives him the opportunity to import motifs from well-known film romances. When the men and women have to part, the farewell scene takes place at a deserted airport in the mist, a moment very reminiscent of the end of

Casablanca. Then, although Shakespeare's play ends ambiguously, leaving the audience to wonder whether the boys will ever meet the girls again, Branagh adds a sequence showing us the different destinies of the characters during the war, and then reuniting boys and girls at the Liberation. Branagh thus chooses to suppress the ambiguity and ends the film in the restored romantic harmony of a musical.

Branagh's adaptations, therefore, oscillate between the creation of a realistic diegesis and the powerful exhibition of its construction through filmic quotes. This ambivalence is at the root of two kinds of reproach that are often made against Branagh's films. Some critics accuse the director of making Shakespeare's meta-drama disappear into a naturalistic universe without alienating effects. In his 1991 article on Branagh's *Henry V*, Nicolas Saada considers that 'the audience, in front of this display of means, extras, sets and sound effects, can only smile at the Chorus's initial warning "For 'tis your thoughts that now must deck our kings . . .", which is very quickly put back by this spectacular show.'[45] By contrast, other critics accuse Branagh of not respecting the realism of film diegesis and of favouring big effects over plausibility and verisimilitude. For example, H. R. Coursen in his 1997 article, 'Words, Words, Words: Searching for Hamlet', underlines the various inconsistencies of Branagh's *Hamlet*: 'In this wintry landscape, nettles would be the only available foliage. Crow-flowers, long purples and daisies cannot be growing nearby.'[46] Such critics prefer a coherent diegesis, and consider the contrast between the text and the diegetic environment as illogical. By contrast, other scholars, like Jacek Fabiszak, see in this divergence an alienating shock: 'One may also wonder why Branagh chose winter (which clashes with the text), but this seems to be concordant with the epic grandiosity and distancing devices employed in the film.'[47] Branagh seems to place his movies in an in-between. He favours the creation of a realistic and coherent diegesis, but on some occasions he does not hesitate to subordinate the text to a general vision based on code recycling – for example, *Hamlet* as an epic and wintry fresco *à la Doctor Zhivago*. Branagh inserts the play into a specific cinematic genre whatever the consequences may be on the diegetic world. The diegesis is, therefore, turned into a kind of fairy tale in which anything can happen if the situation requires it. Flowers can

---

45 Nicolas Saada, 'Le théâtre apprivoisé', *Les Cahiers du Cinéma*, January 1991, 66. My translation from French.
46 H. R. Coursen, 'Words, Words, Words: Searching for *Hamlet*', *Shakespeare Yearbook* 8 (1997), 320.
47 Jacek Fabiszak, 'Branagh's Use of Elizabethan Stage Conventions in His Production of *Hamlet*', paper given at the conference 'Shakespeare on Screen' organized by the University of Malaga, Benalmadena, 21–4 September 1999.

grow in winter, Hamlet's father can rest in a snowy orchard and Ophelia can drown herself in a frozen river. By producing a clash with the meaning of the text, the big effects of genre give rise to effects that are not necessarily alienating but surely strange and unusual. Nevertheless, Branagh does not introduce intertext and references to other films to produce an irony that would agitate against his adaptations. While recalling our knowledge of previous films, it is meant to work on the first level, for the emotional effect it generates. Paradoxically, embedded filmic structures do not always have alienating effects.

THE LIMITS OF META-CINEMA AND THE PROTECTION OF DIEGESIS

As we have seen, it is certainly possible to notice several reflexive aspects in Shakespeare films, which mirror the various metadramatic structures in the original plays. However, they can never endanger the diegetic world completely. In Branagh's *Henry V*, the character of the Chorus serves as much to create an effect of alienation as to plunge the audience into the fiction. Even if he appears in a metafilmic mode, he invites the audience to enter the fictive story, and eventually becomes a participant of diegesis himself, joining the soldiers' painful marches under the rain. At the beginning of the film, the Chorus speaks directly to the camera, then opens a huge wooden door leading to the world of the fiction: alienation is coupled with a powerful irruption into diegesis.

This frequent use of doors in Shakespeare films could, in fact, be explained by a desire to import metadramatic elements into the films while retaining the impression of reality brought by the diegesis. Olivier's *Richard III* also starts with the opening of a door behind which the Duke of Gloucester is lurking. Through the course of the film, the space behind the door will be symbolic of Richard's evil power. In Taymor's *Titus*, this door motif is taken up again in the gigantic metallic doors of the Senate, which Saturninus keeps opening briskly and angrily. In Noble's *A Midsummer Night's Dream*, doors become symbolic of the forest in which the lovers get lost. They are not ensconced within walls, but stand as autonomous objects, opened and closed at Oberon's will. Generally, doors are metadramatic as they symbolically open on another space highly evocative of a stage or a fictive world. Doors create the reflexive effect of a frame within a frame, but at the same time they can remain frames entirely motivated by the film story. In the same way, shots through keyholes introduce a secondary screen. This is the case, for example, in Branagh's *Henry V* when the faithful nobles at Southampton use the lattice-work of a door to spy discreetly on the three traitors. During a brief shot, the traitors are seen through a diamond-shaped hole. A similar figure takes place in Noble's *A Midsummer Night's Dream* as Theseus and Hippolyta are observed by the Boy through a keyhole. In both cases, the characters are surrounded by a black frame and duplicate their situation as screen actors who are watched in secret by voyeuristic viewers. However, though they point to the film's construction, these shots do not jeopardize narrative development and diegetic logic in any way. They would not prevent a viewer from being immersed in the fiction.

The metafilmic use of mirrors also dissolves into the story and even contributes to the audience's identification with the characters. In fact, when we look at characters looking in a mirror, our gazes on the reflection turn back on the characters who become other ourselves. Our identification with the position that the characters holds in space is thus reinforced.

When directors add flashbacks in their movies, the reflexivity born from such devices does not always jeopardize diegesis either, but facilitates its development, helping to clarify the storyline. Even the emphatic camera moves participate in the narration. They dissolve into the diegesis by bringing into the camera field such characters or actions as are useful to the story. Again, film directors invite the audience to enter the diegetic world through reflexive devices. Adaptations often display elaborated narrative tendencies – very much in line with the Hollywood film style that makes the story more logical and the situations more explicit. Sometimes, enunciation pierces through narration with ostentatious camera moves or reflexive images, but it often finds itself swallowed by the diegesis and by the audience's natural capacity to suspend disbelief. The metacinematic devices are numerous, but often they eventually melt into the stories themselves.

Shots whose source is different from a human gaze and reveal a superior, omniscient narrative authority can also be made diegetic. Spectators themselves may establish a link between the source of a shot and a character's gaze. In his 1997 article, 'Suiting the Word to the Action: Kenneth Branagh's Interpolations in *Hamlet*', David Kennedy Sauer wonders about the origin of certain shots: who observes Elsinore from outside? Who watches Ophelia's face under water? Who sees, from the ceiling, Hamlet's corpse being carried by Fortinbras's soldiers? For Kennedy Sauer, it would be the spectre himself. All those shots would be filmed from the Ghost's viewpoint. The Ghost would be an omniscient character who would spy on the film's action and who would be at the source of these so-called 'objective' shots.[48] The filmic vision actually starts and ends with the spectre: Branagh's *Hamlet* opens on the father's statue and closes on its destruction. Instead of recognizing the existence of an impersonal, enunciative authority, David Kennedy Sauer prefers to link certain 'objective' images to a diegetic point of view. By establishing a connection between a gaze belonging to the story and shots that tend to reveal the presence of filmic apparatus, this article reveals, in fact, that the spectators have a propensity themselves to diegetize the elements that are likely to alienate them from the story and the characters.

One may wonder if meta-cinema can ever match meta-theatre in the exposure of illusion and in the blurring of the line between the show and the audience. Attempts to defictionalize a spectacle seem to be easier on stage than on film. In her thorough study of *In The Bleak Midwinter*, a film directed by Branagh in 1995, Kathy Howlett notices that, by telling a story of actors mounting a production of Hamlet, Branagh 'distinguishes between levels of fictionality inherent in the two acting media'.[49] Howlett focuses on the reflexive and Brechtian aspects of the film, as she states that 'the theatrical spectacle at the film's center . . . continually alerts the audience to the circumstances of its own artifice and production',[50] 'defamiliarizing the audience with the play and . . . revealing the principles of construction upon which theatrical artifice is grounded'.[51] However, though *In The Bleak Midwinter* discloses the conditions of production for a stage performance, it does not reveal the conditions of production for the film itself. As Howlett points out, 'the cinematic spectacle . . . denies the viewer any direct access to its own mechanisms . . . The viewer never witnesses Branagh directing the film, never is cued that the actor who plays Joe Harper is anything other than that character.'[52] Yet, even if Branagh had filmed himself making the film, there would always come a time when the film could not reveal its conditions of birth any further. Even if a director films the camera, he does not reveal the act of this filming.[53] Whatever a film director may do, the actors on screen and the spectators in the cinema necessarily remain apart. Even if filmic illusion is sometimes jeopardized, it eventually remains protected. The frontier between the world of the film and the space of the audience can never be totally fractured. In the last shot of Greenaway's

[48] David Kennedy Sauer, 'Suiting the Word to the Action: Kenneth Branagh's Interpolations in *Hamlet*', *Shakespeare Yearbook* 8 (1997), 341.
[49] Kathy Howlett, *Framing Shakespeare on Screen* (Athens, OH: Ohio University Press, 2000), p. 184.
[50] *Ibid.*, p. 185.   [51] *Ibid.*, p. 198.   [52] *Ibid.*, p.184.
[53] See Metz, *L'énonciation impersonnelle*, p. 30.

Prospero's Books, however much Ariel attempts to force his way through the confines of his screen-prison, he will never reach the viewers. Though he ardently wishes to circumvent the boundaries of cinema, he can only remain caught within the shadowy world of filmic fiction. Meta-cinema is always counteracted by the primordial unreality of the movie medium and the inevitable segregation of spaces between screen and audience.

Meta-cinema would actually combine enunciative disclosure and submersion in the narrative world. A more general dialectic would, in fact, exist between the acts of disclosing and creating illusion, in the cinema as well as in the theatre. The techniques that tend to reveal artificial devices can, paradoxically, also participate in the making of illusion. In a dramatic text, a Chorus or a Prologue can underline stage devices only to immerse us in the fiction even further. In Shakespeare's *Henry V*, the first speech of the Chorus insists on theatrical fabrication and the disclosing of illusion ('Can this cockpit hold / The vasty fields of France?' Prologue, 11–12), while encouraging the audience to imagine a realistic universe ('Think, when we talk of horses, that you see them', Prologue, 26). In the same way, a play-within-the-play seems to both reveal the illusion and make the first level of dramatic fiction more real. In his psychoanalytic study of *Hamlet*, André Green comments on 'The Mousetrap':

[The] arrival of other actors shifts the status of the previous ones. The first actors are confronted with actors playing the parts of actors. The presence of these second-degree players makes us forget that the first ones were actors and brings them a semblance of reality, the illusion of theatre taking refuge in the Players.[54]

Green's remarks on the play-within-the-play could also be applied to the film-within-the-film. The included film, presented as an illusion or a memory in flashback, can serve as much to disclose illusion as to make the including film (the film as such) seem even more real. Two examples will illustrate this. In Branagh's *Hamlet*, quasi-subliminal images make us dive into the prince's criminal thoughts during Claudius's confession scene. For a brief moment, as we see a dagger plunged into Claudius's ear, we believe that Hamlet has committed his murder at last. But the film quickly shows a shot of Hamlet still hesitating to stab. The previous images were just a dream, an illusory insert. In Almereyda's *Hamlet*, Ophelia comes near the swimming pool as her father is reading Hamlet's love letters aloud to Claudius and Gertrude. Tormented by feelings of betrayal and guilt, Ophelia wants to get away from it all. She suddenly jumps into the pool

---

[54] André Green, *'Hamlet' et Hamlet* (Paris: Balland, 1982), p. 84. My translation from French.

in an attempt to drown herself. But the next shot reveals Ophelia still on the edge of the pool: she did not jump. We only visualized her secret wish of committing suicide under water, which will happen for real later in the story. These very short inserts are eminently metafilmic since they mirror (and duplicate) the fictive nature of cinema. Nevertheless, they also enhance the impression of reality given by the main action when the viewer is jolted back into it. In the audience's subtle mechanism of belief/disbelief, if the included film is an illusion, it means that the including film is not, or is somewhat less.[55] Therefore, in the same way as meta-theatre in Shakespeare's plays both discloses illusion and, at times, gives extra reality to the 'master action', meta-cinema combines enunciative disclosure with submersion in the narrative world.

The efficiency of meta-cinema eventually seems to depend on reception – that is to say on the audience's range of expectations and on the ability of each spectator to spot the marks of enunciation in a movie. According to the literary theorist, Tzevtan Todorov, public opinion, whose range of expectations and understandings changes through time, sets what is credible and legitimate in a given genre. Todorov renews the concept of 'verisimilitude'. In opposition to what is considered 'realistic', verisimilitude covers the range of viewers' expectations about what is believable and acceptable for representation. Verisimilitude can involve totally unrealistic (but acceptable) acts such as characters bursting into song during a film musical. What is at stake is coherence with a given genre rather than similarity to the real world.[56] Consequently, metacinematic devices attempting to circumvent realism in Shakespeare films may fall into verisimilitude if the viewers expect these devices within the bounds of the genre. The more metacinematic effects are used in Shakespeare films, the more they will be seen as legitimate and credible. If metacinematic devices become expected and accepted within a given genre, they will also be less disruptive of the fictional diegesis. Viewers will be, therefore, less likely to be alienated from the fiction. The ability of meta-cinema to disrupt realism also seems to depend on each viewer's ability to detect the marks of film enunciation. According to André Gaudreault and François Jost, 'The perception of film enunciation is shared very unequally. It varies according to the spectator.'[57] For one person, the enunciative authority may always seem visible, for another

---

[55] Metz, 'The Imaginary Signifier', p. 430.
[56] See Tzvetan Todorov, *The Poetics of Prose* (Ithaca: Cornell University Press, 1977), p. 87 and Paul Cobley, *Narrative* (London: Routledge, 2001), pp. 244–5.
[57] André Gaudreault and François Jost, *Cinéma et récit II: le récit cinématographique* (Paris: Nathan, 1990), p. 44. My translation from French.

it may never be obvious. It all depends on the more or less detailed and careful reading we make of a film. In an essay entitled 'Representing *King Lear* on Screen: from Metatheatre to "Meta-cinema"', Kenneth S. Rothwell locates reflexive devices in several adaptations of the play. He argues that Peter Brook's 1969 version is eminently metacinematic because of its very ostensible zooms and dissolves, as well as its lack of continuity in terms of editing. He then looks for a cinematic presence in Grigori Kozintsev's 1970 *King Lear*, which is, according to Rothwell, much more discreet:

> Wherein, however, is the film meta-cinematic? How does it show awareness of itself as a work of art? . . . The answer must be that Kozintsev moved very close to that ideal stage of film-making . . . that favours neither the accumulation of detail (*mise-en-scène*) nor the selection of detail (*montage*), but interweaves through skilful editing all elements into a coherent design. The commentary that Kozintsev makes about his film within his film is clandestine, implicit, expressed as much through what is not seen as through what is seen.[58]

In a film that uses few visible filmic techniques, Rothwell still identifies an 'implicit' metafilmic commentary. Every image starts designating its own nature of image when an attentive spectator begins to watch it as such. According to Metz, 'the more the audience is educated, the more the number of neutral images decreases'.[59] Therefore, it should not necessarily be the director's responsibility to make a film that discloses its own illusion. The spectators should also be conscious of the enunciation by picking out the choices that, for example, govern the position of the camera and the changes of shots. 'Educated' viewers become aware of being credulous and incredulous at the same time. They can then enjoy any aesthetic with full knowledge of the facts, deciphering the illusion processes while being plunged into the diegesis. Consequently, it would not be accurate to establish a distinction between Shakespeare screen adaptations that disclose the conditions of their creation and those that constantly foster diegetic illusion. There are only films working on different levels of illusion and which more or less make us forget the origins of their birth.

---

[58] Kenneth S. Rothwell, 'Representing *King Lear* on Screen: from Metatheatre to "Meta-cinema"', in *Shakespeare and the Moving Image*, ed. Anthony Davies and Stanley Wells (Cambridge University Press, 1994), pp. 223–4.

[59] Metz, *L'énonciation impersonnelle*, p. 169. My translation from French.

CHAPTER 5

Screenplay, narration and subtext: the example of Hamlet

In 1997, Kenneth Branagh was nominated for the Academy Award® for the *Best Screenplay Based on Material from Another Medium* for his 1996 adaptation of *Hamlet*. It immediately spurred a debate. Since Branagh used every word of the conflated Shakespeare text, how could his screenwriting work be worthy of such an award? This chapter argues that writing a screenplay for a filmed Shakespeare play involves a complex narrative instigation. The dramatic text becomes coated with a subtext that appropriates quasi-novelistic aspects, alternating between dialogues, narrator interventions and focused narrative. Shakespeare dialogues and monologues become the framework of a written narrative that describes, comments, offers an interpretation or creates interpolations. The screenplay represents an intermediary step between the initial dramatic text and the film itself.

In the case of a theatrical production, the textual additions can be implicit when the choices have not been recorded in a written form, or made explicit if the director records notes in a promptbook. In the case of a Shakespeare film, the decisions in terms of *mise-en-scène* are often made explicit in the published screenplay that accompanies the release of the movie. Regarding the film *Richard III* in which he played the title role, Ian McKellen says: 'We were not making a film of the play, we were making a film of a screenplay from the play.'[1] He thus emphasizes the fact that a film is less faithful to the Shakespeare text than to a first reading of that text. The director's notes that are found in a screenplay can take several forms. They may be a commentary on the action in progress, alter the chronology of the narrative, and/or reveal the illusion underlying the narration. In the latter case, the notes can turn into a metafilmic discourse, unveiling details not only of the action in the movie, but also of the way the action is filmed.

[1] In an interview with Gary Crowdus, 'Shakespeare is up to Date: an Interview with Sir Ian McKellen', *Cineaste* 24.1 (1998), 46.

Shakespeare plays provide very few stage directions. They contrast with plays written in the nineteenth and twentieth centuries by playwrights such as Henrik Ibsen, Arthur Miller or Eugene O'Neill. These plays usually include numerous stage directions that describe precisely the setting as well as the characters' behaviour and emotions. Such dramas are, in a way, accompanied by their own commentary guiding the forthcoming *mises-en-scène*. They seem to carry within themselves the very setting in situation of their dialogues. By contrast, if one excludes the few stage directions generally indicating the characters' entrances and exits, Shakespeare's dramatic texts are mainly composed of dialogues and monologues.[2] Over the centuries, scholars, storywriters and directors have tried, in their own way, to build a frame for the plays. With different enunciative processes, they have constructed discourses around the Shakespeare texts. To identify the nature of the notes offered by film-makers in their screenplays, this chapter will focus on screenplays of *Hamlet*, as some very distinct adaptations are available for study – Laurence Olivier's (1948), Franco Zeffirelli's (1990), Kenneth Branagh's (1996) and Michael Almereyda's (2000). It will compare these screenplays to other forms of discourses, such as the tales adapted from Shakespeare plays, a certain form of Shakespearean criticism, and the theatrical subtext theorized by Constantin Stanislavski and Patrice Pavis. The purpose is to bring to light different ways of 'telling' and then to determine their ideological consequences.

Since the end of the eighteenth century, many writers have rewritten Shakespeare's plays in a narrative prose form. Confronted with the difficulties of this task, they have resorted to different narrative techniques. The first form of narration aims at giving the impression that the reader is attending a performance of the play. It is used particularly in the very first tales drawn from Shakespeare's plays, which were written in 1783 by, as surprising as it may sound, a Frenchman called J. B. Perrin. These *Contes Moraux et Instructifs, à l'usage de la Jeunesse, tirés des Tragédies de Shakespeare* are based on theatre productions of the time, which Perrin attended in London.[3] Mary Macleod also applies this method in her 1902 *Shakespeare Story-Book*. According to Stanley Wells, 'in her narrative passages she makes

[2] The first quarto is slightly more prolific in terms of stage directions than the First Folio. For example, the first quarto of *Hamlet* gives information on the *mise-en-scène* of Ophelia's burial. While the Folio specifies that Laertes leaps into Ophelia's grave – see William Shakespeare, *The Works of William Shakespeare in Reduced Facsimile from the Famous First Folio Edition of 1623* (London: Chatto & Windus, 1876), p. 278 – the first quarto adds that Laertes is soon joined by Hamlet: 'Hamlet leaps in after Laertes' – See Kathleen O. Irace, ed. *The First Quarto of 'Hamlet'* (Cambridge University Press, 1998), p. 88.

[3] See Stanley Wells, 'Tales from Shakespeare', *Proceedings of the British Academy* 73 (1987), 137.

a strong attempt to convey a conception of the play in performance'.[4] She ends the story of *Hamlet* with a flight of angels singing for the hero's death, thus following the example of actor–manager Beerbohm Tree in his production at the turn of the century. Leon Garfield follows the same tradition of storytelling in his 1985 book, *Shakespeare Stories*. In a 1990 article, 'The Problem of Writing Stories From Shakespeare', he expounds his narrative techniques: 'I have tried to produce the plays on the printed page.'[5] By describing actions that could easily be presented on stage, Garfield would like to give the reader less a feeling of reading the stories than of seeing them performed. The passage he writes for the first apparition of the Ghost in *Hamlet* appears as a case in point:

He [Horatio] smiled at his pale companions, who had dragged him up to this cold, dark, windy place with their fantastic tale of –
'Look where it comes again!'
He looked; and his sensible eyes started from his sensible head. All reason fled for in weirdly gleaming armour and with weightless tread, the dead King stalked slowly by! The watchers, huddled in their cloaks, trembled with amazement and dread.
'Speak to it, Horatio!' breathed one, for the apparition seemed to linger.[6]

This excerpt transforms the dramatic text into a realistic narrative, alternating dialogues and focused commentaries by a narrator. The original drama, which works in the mode of 'showing' (in other words, direct presentation of conversations and events, without any narrator) is here transformed into a narrative operating in the mode of 'telling'. It is now presented through the mediation of a narrator who, instead of leaving the spectators to draw their own conclusions from what is seen or heard, comments on the dialogues and situates them in relation to 'what is real', thus creating a specific ideology.[7] This kind of narrative prose seems to work as an 'objective' commentary on the dialogues. It can indicate what is 'true' or not in the characters' speeches presented in inverted commas. By commenting on the characters' actions, motivations and feelings, storywriter Leon Garfield creates a subtext that interprets the subjective viewpoints that are conveyed by dialogues. The writer fills some gaps in the play and plunges the reader into a realistic fiction whose enunciation is not revealed.

---

[4] *Ibid.*, 142.
[5] Leon Garfield, 'The Penny Whistle: the Problem of Writing Stories from Shakespeare', *Essays by Divers Hands* 46 (1990), 97.
[6] Leon Garfield, *Shakespeare Stories* (London: Victor Gollancz, 1985), pp. 169–70.
[7] See Colin MacCabe, 'From Realism and the Cinema: Notes on Some Brechtian Theses' in *Contemporary Film Theory*, ed. Antony Easthope (Harlow: Longman, 1993), p. 54.

The point of view adopted by Garfield is that of a spectator who would watch the action live and would believe in the stage illusion. According to Garfield, 'the best viewpoint to take is that of a deeply attentive audience whose imagination has indeed "turned the accomplishment of many years into an hourglass" and "into a thousand parts divided one man".[8]

This form of narration presents us with the action through a gaze that has been immersed in the story. The narrative prose is meant to make the reader forget that it has been written. Its aim is to become obvious and transparent, almost immaterial. The act of saying (or the enunciative origin) is hidden under what is said to make the diegetic world seem evident and unquestionable. In the narrative prose, things are presented as real, not as another subjective viewpoint. The readers are, therefore, placed in a situation of pure specularity – they are presented with how things look and are. As a consequence, the 'real' can hardly be presented as contradictory and/or ambivalent. The narrative discourse offers interpretation of the dialogues that it surrounds, but is not open itself to interpretation. It is here to tell what 'reality' is and to assess the dialogues in relation to this so-called objective truth.

This narrative technique, therefore, seems consistent with a realistic vision of the plays. It is not surprising that most storywriters who have chosen this narrative technique, such as Perrin, Macleod or Garfield, have been inspired by realistic theatre productions to compose their stories. Perrin used to attend the productions of David Garrick, who was the first actor–manager to establish a watertight separation between the stage and the auditorium, and to use processes of illusion. Macleod was directly influenced by the productions of Henry Irving and Herbert Beerbhom Tree, who, during the Victorian era, led the performances of Shakespeare to heights of unequalled romantic realism. As far as Garfield is concerned, he seems mainly to have been inspired by neo-realistic productions which, in his own words, 'completely captivated'[9] him. This connection made between narration and realism can also be found in the comments of scholars. For example, Stanley Wells describes a production of *Othello* directed by Trevor Nunn in 1989 for the Royal Shakespeare Company by comparing its discourse of *mise-en-scène* with a novel: '[it is] rooted in naturalism; indeed, a fully written account of this production would read like a Victorian novel'.[10]

[8] Garfield, 'The Penny Whistle', 96.
[9] 'It [The production of *The Comedy of Errors*] was . . . so swift and energetic that I was completely captivated by it; and straightaway attempted the re-telling of that particular play', Garfield in 'The Penny Whistle', 97.
[10] Stanley Wells, 'Shakespeare Productions in England in 1989', *Shakespeare Survey* 43 (1991), 195–6.

Realism is here tied to a discourse of *mise-en-scène* that can be read like a novel. This discourse, either explicit in a tale or a screenplay or implicit in a stage production, remains at the source of the debate on a potential narrative presence in the theatre. Pure showing would be in fact limited, as nothing could be shown without a critical apparatus, therefore without being said.[11] Theatre theorist Patrice Pavis specifies in his book *Voix et images de la scène* that: 'To elaborate a *mise-en-scène* always means to publish a reading, to situate oneself in relation to the tradition of interpretation, to display a commentary on the text and on tradition and, therefore, to offer, in view of its realization, a metatextual commentary.'[12]

This metatextual commentary is close to the notion of subtext defined by Pavis in his *Dictionnaire du théâtre* as 'what is not explicitly said in the dramatic text, but comes out from the way the text is interpreted', 'a kind of commentary given by the *mise-en-scène* and the acting of the players'.[13] In a production, this subtext makes the play lose its original opaqueness by presenting an interpretation of it. Performance critic H. R. Coursen uses the notion of *Zeitgeist* to designate the whole subtext in a given production.[14] According to him, the presence of an underlying, interpreting text is inevitable in every performance. The actors and the director must create this subtext to inform the spectators of the characters' psychological states, thus producing a gap between what the dramatic text says and what the stage shows. In fact, it seems that the more realistic the semiotic elements shown in performance are, the more the subtext, if it was written down, would tend towards a particular kind of narrative, the realistic novel. The text that storywriters such as Perrin, Macleod or Garfield weave around the Shakespeare text has similarities to a subtext that has been made explicit, giving birth to a realistic universe that hides the origin of its enunciation. This desire to develop and explain what is left ambiguous in the Shakespeare text seems to have been encouraged by the rise of the novel, a type of narrative that reveals much more about the characters' psychology than an Elizabethan play.[15] At the end of the eighteenth century, a time in which the first Shakespearean tales emerged, the development of the psychological, realistic novel certainly shaped the way in which the directors

[11] Patrice Pavis, 'Ostension', *Dictionnaire du théâtre* (Paris: Editions Sociales, 1980), p. 269.
[12] Patrice Pavis, *Voix et images de la scène: pour une sémiologie de la réception* (Villeneuve d'Ascq: Presses Universitaires de Lille, 1985), p. 261. My translation from French.
[13] Pavis, 'Sous-texte', *Dictionnaire du théâtre*, p. 368. My translation from French.
[14] See H. R. Coursen, *Reading Shakespeare on Stage* (London: Associated University Presses, 1995), pp. 40–1.
[15] See Harold Jenkins, '*Hamlet* Then Till Now', in *Aspects of Hamlet*, ed. Kenneth Muir and Stanley Wells (Cambridge University Press, 1979), p. 22.

and scholars read Shakespeare's plays. According to T. J. B. Spencer in his 1963 article 'The Decline of Hamlet': 'The growth of what can be called the "psychological novel" (that is, the kind of fiction which describes in great detail the states of mind of its characters) profoundly influenced the interpretation of Shakespeare's powers of characterisation.'[16]

In the eighteenth century, Samuel Johnson, just like Goethe, focused on the description of the Shakespeare characters as well as on their inner stories before and during the play. The impression of reality that can be garnered from the feelings told and shown in the plays convinced them that Shakespeare used the same techniques as the authors of psychological novels to create his characters. At the time, it was commonly believed that Shakespeare mastered his characters, creating a consistent personality for them and knowing exactly how each of them would react faced with any situation. One of the critic's goals was then to discover the characters in their completeness from clues scattered in the play.[17] At the beginning of the twentieth century, scholars mainly favoured the study of characters and the construction of a subtext that was as much narrative as explanatory. In his 1904 book, *Shakespearean Tragedy*, A. C. Bradley explores the Shakespeare heroes and specifies what their motivations for action are. In 1935, John Dover Wilson seeks to understand why Hamlet's uncle does not react to the dumb show whereas he responds to 'The Moustrap' a few minutes later. His conclusions lead him to recommend a *mise-en-scène* that almost meets the art of novel. In his book, *What Happens in 'Hamlet'*, he thus describes the reaction of Claudius in front of the play-within-the-play:

Murderer, wife! wife, murderer! second husband, poison! The thing is clear. The plot of the interlude is his life's history. *Hamlet knows all!* Claudius is not safe; anything may happen. He pulls himself to his feet, and, squealing for light, he totters as fast his trembling knees will carry him from the terrible, the threatening room.[18]

Wilson offers here a narrative focused on the character of Claudius, which could easily be found in a tale from the play. *What Happens in 'Hamlet'* provides a thoroughly documented historical context, reveals

---

[16] T. J. B. Spencer, 'The Decline of *Hamlet*' in *'Hamlet': Stratford-upon-Avon Studies 5*, ed. John Russell Brown and Bernard Harris (London: Edward Arnold, 1963), p. 188.

[17] T. J. B. Spencer sums up this way of thinking when he writes: 'Just as Shakespeare himself held a character complete in his mind, so the reader . . . can, by noticing every indication the author gives, also hold the character complete in his mind.' In 'The Decline of *Hamlet*', p. 189.

[18] John Dover Wilson, *What Happens in 'Hamlet'* (Cambridge University Press, 1964), p. 195. Italics by Dover Wilson.

secondary plots, discloses some of the characters' secret motivations, studies their personalities and describes the evolution of their feelings scene by scene.

In composing a written narrative between the dramatic text and its representation on screen, the storywriters and some scholars seem to follow the advice of Russian theatre director Constantin Stanislavski who conceived the theory of subtext. The 'Stanislavski method', launched in the middle of the twentieth century, notably concentrates on the psychology of the role, and consists of seeking in the play how the characters describe themselves or how they are described by the other characters. The aim is to grasp a global and unified image of their personalities and, therefore, to reach the 'truth' of the parts.[19] The characters are considered quasi-real men or women whose psyche must be decoded in order to understand what motivates their actions. The actors must look into themselves for sensual and emotional memories that are linked to what they have to play.[20] They must also imagine a dialogue with other characters and invent realistic (even contradictory) motives of behaviour for the parts.[21] Stanislavski calls 'the score of a role'[22] or 'subtext' this complementary script to the original play which the actors must create in their mind to prepare for their roles. In his 1968 book *Building a Character*, Stanislavski gives the following definition: 'It [The subtext] is the manifest, the inwardly felt expression of a human being in a part, which flows uninterruptedly beneath the words of the text, giving them life and a basis for existing . . . It is the subtext that makes us say the words we do in a play.'[23]

The actor has to 'bring to life what is hidden under the words' of the play.[24] Every physical act or gesture must have, according to Stanislavski, an inner emotional source or motive. The subtext may be a mere description of what is physical and external (such as 'a handshake'), psychologically simple ('a sincere handshake') or complex ('shaking hands to apologize for an insult').[25] In order to find the motive of a part, a verb rather than a noun must be found to describe the action. According to Stanislavski, the actor has 'to fill out what he [the playwright] leaves unsaid' as far as the characters' experiences and personal histories are concerned.[26] By running this subtext in their minds, the actors will create mental pictures that they

---

[19] See Constantin Stanislavski, *Building a Character* (London: Methuen, 1968), *An Actor Prepares* (London: Methuen, 1980) and *Creating a Role* (London: Methuen, 1981). See also the chapter 'Stanislavski's Theoretical System' in *Modern Theories of Performance* by Jane Milling and Graham Ley (Palgrave: New York, 2001), pp. 1–25.

[20] See Stanislavski, *Creating a Role*, p. 9.   [21] *Ibid.*, pp. 36–8.   [22] *Ibid.*, pp. 56–62.

[23] Stanislavski, *Building a Character*, p. 113.   [24] Stanislavski, *An Actor Prepares*, pp. 50–1.

[25] *Ibid.*, pp. 119–20.   [26] *Ibid.*, p. 257.

will try to communicate to one another on stage when they speak.[27] In the case of Shakespearean tales or screenplays, this subtext becomes written and explicit, and can take the form of physical descriptions or psychological comments.

The second technique of narration used by the storytellers of Shakespeare not only describes the live action of the play, but also constructs numerous interpolations and analepses based more or less on information given in the play. In *Tales from Shakespeare, Designed for the use of Young Persons* (1807), Charles and Mary Lamb aim to make the plays more moral, but also to clarify and simplify them. Each tale concentrates on the main plot. The tale of *Hamlet* focuses on the eponymous hero whose feelings are turned into objective realities. For example, Claudius is indeed a despicable man, far from matching his brother's qualities: 'Claudius did no ways resemble her [Gertrude's] late husband in the qualities of his person or his mind, but was as contemptible in outward appearance, as he was unworthy in disposition.'[28] The prose provides a kind of 'objective truth' and ideology that approve of Hamlet's personal interpretation of events.

Despite the great textual reduction they imply, these tales provide many interpreting and/or interpolated passages. Charles and Mary Lamb bring forward interpretations for Hamlet's madness (it is seen as a stratagem aiming at hiding some real distress)[29] and for his procrastination (Claudius would be too well protected, and there would still be some doubts regarding the nature of the Ghost).[30] They also use some of the characters' cues to create interpolations or analepses, thus reorganizing the time-flow of events. The narrative starts before the action of the play begins. We are first informed of Old Hamlet's death, Gertrude's second wedding and the prince's sorrow. After situating the action in its diegetic context, the narrative returns to a description of the live action from the moment when Hamlet meets the Ghost of his father. But from now on, analepses and interpolations are not totally excluded from the narrative. A flashback covers the relation between Hamlet and Ophelia: 'Before Hamlet fell into the melancholy way which has been related, he had dearly loved a fair maid called Ophelia . . . He had sent her letters and rings, and made many tenders of his affections to her.'[31] Dialogues are transformed into narrative interpolated episodes. The pirates' assault and the letter substitution are removed from Hamlet's speech when he returns to Denmark, but are inserted into the narrative while he is in exile: 'Hamlet, suspecting some treachery, in the

[27] Stanislavski, *Building a Character*, p. 119.
[28] See Charles and Mary Lamb, *Tales from Shakespeare* (London and Glasgow: Collins, 1953), p. 215.
[29] *Ibid.*, p. 218.   [30] *Ibid.*, p. 220.   [31] *Ibid.*, p. 219.

night-time secretly got at the letters, and skilfully erasing his own name, he in the stead of it put in the names of those two courtiers . . . Soon after the ship was attacked by pirates, and a sea-fight commenced.'[32]

Charles and Mary Lamb elaborated a narrative technique based on inter-polation, which can be found in other tales, in some Shakespeare scholarship and in various screen adaptations. In *Stories from Shakespeare*, written in 1910, Thomas Carter begins his tale of *Hamlet* as Charles and Mary Lamb did, i.e. before the start of the play. However, instead of focusing on the family plot, he underlines the political context by describing Old Hamlet's victory over Old Fortinbras.[33] In his 1982 book, *'Hamlet' et Hamlet*, literary critic André Green also emphasizes this political context when he seeks to penetrate the original myth of the play. From clues found in the dramatic text, he reconstructs a grounding past to the play, with Old Hamlet and Old Fortinbras as the main characters:

All began . . . with the challenge of [Old] Fortinbras to a younger adversary, [Old] Hamlet The Valiant, whose exploits endangered the reputation of his Nordic neighbour. But . . . Gertrude was also the stake of this duel. Like Claudius later on, King Hamlet did not want to risk his crown and his Queen. He, therefore, preferred to resort to trickery. He bought the services of Polonius who suggested to him the same stratagems that Shakespeare will again use for the duel between the prince of Denmark and Laertes. Fortinbras is beaten . . . Claudius, who is jealous of his brother and does not like war, takes advantage of the king's absences to woo Gertrude who eventually yields. The birth of Hamlet is highly suspicious. Is the prince the son of Hamlet The Valiant or of Claudius The Traitor?[34]

Green's conclusions are presented in the form of a real political and family saga, creating a major past interpolation that conditions a global interpretation of the dramatic text: Prince Hamlet and Laertes would pay with their lives for the past schemes of their fathers.

This very realistic form of narration somehow goes against another tra-dition of writing. The third technique used by writers reveals enunciation within diegesis itself. In Shakespearean tales, this disclosing of illusion can take several forms. In his 1964 book, *Six Stories from Shakespeare*, Francis Brett Young composes a story from *Hamlet* that only features a single view-point. Young draws his inspiration from Hamlet's cue to Horatio before dying ('draw thy breath in pain / To tell my story', v.ii.347–8). He writes all his tale as a flashback, with Horatio as narrator. Horatio gives his version of

---

[32] *Ibid.*, p. 224.
[33] See Thomas Carter, *Stories from Shakespeare*, (London: George G. Harrap, 1913), pp. 75–6.
[34] André Green, *'Hamlet' et Hamlet* (Paris: Balland, 1982), p. 246.

the story, interpreting and commenting on his friend's actions. This focusing remains unchanged throughout the tale and tends to introduce back into the fiction a metadramatic aspect, creating a double level of enunciation – that of the author (Francis Brett Young) and that of the narrator (Horatio). In this case, the storyteller inserts his double within the story itself as a source of *mise-en-abyme*. Other storywriters reveal an enunciative presence by adopting an exterior viewpoint – that of a commentator. In her 1960 book, *Stories from Shakespeare*, Marchette Chute gives her personal opinions on the play before starting the story: 'Hamlet is perhaps the most famous of all Shakespeare's tragedies . . . The story opens in the cold and dark of a winter night in Denmark, while the guard is being changed on the battlements of the royal castle of Elsinore.'[35]

Enunciation is revealed ('The story opens') in the form of an intrusive narrator commenting on the story. This rupturing effect, consisting of the narrating agency revealing itself, takes place in a narrative told in the present tense. With this specific narrative tense, spectators are less plunged into the fiction. This form of narration relates much more to a stage action as if it were described live. It is not reported in the past tense as in Leon Garfield's extremely realistic stories.

In this survey of tales adapted from Shakespeare plays, a certain form of Shakespearean criticism, and the theatrical subtext theorized by Stanislavski and Pavis, three techniques of writing around the Shakespeare text have emerged. The first one consists of describing and commenting on the action as if it was unfolding on stage in real time. The second one begins the narrative before the action of the play has even started, often adopting one of the characters' point of view and using the information given in the play to create interpolations and analepses. Finally, the third technique frequently reveals its own enunciation with the adoption of an exterior viewpoint or the introduction of a double level of enunciation. How do screenplays from Shakespeare plays relate to these techniques? Shakespearean screenplays generally seem to prolong a tendency that is at the same time explanatory and narrative. They offer a dramatic text coated with comments usually aimed at creating a realistic fiction and bringing a psychological consistency to each character. However, screenplays of *Hamlet* display various types of comments, which will be thoroughly analysed now.

First, the screenplays may describe the action that will happen on screen in the finished film. They emphasize the movements, actions and behaviour of the characters. Franco Zeffirelli's script offers the following passages:

[35] Marchette Chute, *Stories from Shakespeare* (London: John Murray, 1972), p. 157.

Gertrude fights back tears and goes to the bed sitting on it. Hamlet stops packing and falls to his knee before her. She holds him, his head upon her breast, a natural, familiar gesture.[36]

Hamlet and Laertes go to a sword rack where they part their personal weapons up. Hamlet turns to Laertes and speaks for all to hear, but his voice is gentle, the words of a comrade.[37]

Zeffirelli's screenplay focuses on the characters' motions in space, as well as on their gestures and expressions. What is noticeable is that Zeffirelli, rather than writing about the emotions of the characters, usually prefers to describe the symptoms of those emotions. Instead of revealing the characters' states of mind with adjectives such as 'sad' or 'happy', Zeffirelli gives an account of how feelings are expressed and communicated: Gertrude is described as 'fighting back tears' and Hamlet as 'speaking with a gentle voice'. Zeffirelli's earlier career as a stage designer seems to have influenced the way he carefully sets a detailed geographical background and architecture for his films. His screenplay of *Hamlet* insists on describing locations and/or situating the characters in specific locations, as the following excerpts show:

Horatio, Marcellus and Bernardo and Francisco come into view and take the stairway up, disappearing into the fog.[38]

Hamlet appears at the top of the steep stairs leading to the battlements, silhouetted against the grey sky.[39]

It is a vaulted room filled to overflowing with scrolls, books and other documents in shelves, in niches, all covered with dust.[40]

There is a sound of footsteps and the three friends arrive at the mouth of the passage . . . Hamlet comes out of a long doorway and sees the Ghost stepping up a winding stair. He follows.[41]

Zeffirelli's subtext that describes the live action is, therefore, relatively limited to outward or visible/audible aspects of the characters, objects and locations. The screenplay mainly comments on the action according to what the film audience will see and hear in the finished film.

Almereyda's screenplay differs from that of Zeffirelli as it concentrates much more on the characters' thoughts and emotions, and less on their movements in a given space. Almereyda exploits several ways of making

---

[36] Christopher Devore and Franco Zeffirelli, 'The Screenplay of *Hamlet* Freely Adapted from William Shakespeare's Tragedy', p. 10. Date of draft: 3 April 1990. Unpublished screenplay. Consulted at the Shakespeare Institute Library, April 2003.
[37] *Ibid.*, p. 111.   [38] *Ibid.*, p. 13.   [39] *Ibid.*, p. 8.   [40] *Ibid.*, p. 39.   [41] *Ibid.*, p. 28.

this inner subtext explicit. Adjectives are used extensively to describe the emotions felt by each character, as in the following extracts:

Laertes is impatient, scarcely listening, preoccupied with his luggage.[42]

Hamlet continues staring at the corpse [of Polonius], his eyes hard, remorseless.[43]

Not only are the characters' actions described, but so are their states of mind while performing those actions. Almereyda's screenplay also includes many comparisons. They aim at offering precise impressions of the characters' exterior aspects or behaviour:

The ghost freezes, abruptly cautious, staring out into the night like a vampire fearing daylight.[44]

The comparisons also give details on the characters' intonation when they speak, as in the following passages:

HAMLET
My uncle!
He says it as if this is what he's expected, what he knows . . . Hamlet looks heartsick, amazed and appalled. His father, we might sense, never spoke to him so directly while alive.[45]

HAMLET
Mother! Mother!
Gertrude looks up. Polonius takes up by the arm, pulling her to her feet. She jerks away from him, but he looks at her squarely, as if to say: Snap out of it.[46]

These two excerpts provide the reader with a subtext based on various techniques – the report of the action ('pulling her to her feet'), the use of emotional adjectives ('heartsick', 'amazed', 'appalled') and, above all, comparisons ('as if . . .') extending the description of the actors' performances. The subtext clearly aims at deciphering the characters' psychology. Almereyda goes as far as giving details about the characters' motivations or secret wishes – their thoughts are made explicit in sentences introducing or following the dialogues:

Hamlet wants to roar a dozen questions, but instead he says, quietly:
HAMLET
I shall in all my best obey you, madam.[47]

This unveiling of secret thoughts undoubtedly recalls Constantin Stanislavski's advice for preparing roles and building characters. The same

---

[42] Michael Almereyda, *William Shakespeare's 'Hamlet': A Screenplay Adaptation* (London: Faber & Faber, 2000), p. 27.
[43] *Ibid.*, p. 80.   [44] *Ibid.*, p. 31.   [45] *Ibid.*   [46] *Ibid.*, p. 77.   [47] *Ibid.*, p. 15.

technique can be found extensively in Kenneth Branagh's screenplays. His autobiography, *Beginning*, includes passages which reveal how much Branagh, like most actors, has been influenced by this method of acting. He describes a class at the Royal Academy of Dramatic Art in 1981, when he was rehearsing for the part of Chebutykin in Chekhov's *Three Sisters*:

> We rehearsed . . . with a director determined to rehearse as Stanislavski might have done . . . She . . . insisted that we 'headlined', or described each line that our character spoke. For instance, if Chebutykin said in the text 'Hello, Natasha', the headline would be 'The doctor greets Natasha warmly'. Then a subtext had to be written: 'The Doctor appears to be greeting Natasha warmly, but in fact only slightly covers up his annoyance with her, whilst appearing to be polite for the others'. As this was done for every single sentence of dialogue, rehearsals entailed *writing a short novel* which was then questioned by the director, who wanted subtextual rewrites every time you discovered something new.[48]

Branagh is gently ironic about the rigour of such a method, but he already recognizes its merits. His screenplays refer above all to this technique of subtext and novelistic creation that enters the characters' mind and tells us about their most intimate feelings and motivations. The screenplay of *Hamlet* offers many kinds of subtext. The first one reminds us of Zeffirelli's focus on the characters' motions in a geographically detailed space, as in this account:

> He [Hamlet] opens the door in a bookcase to let them [Horatio, Barnardo and Marcellus] out, which reveals another exit. He ushers them out and as the door closes he rushes up the steps of his study library. The shelves are crammed with books.[49]

Branagh's subtext puts the stress on the peculiar architecture inside Elsinore: secret doors everywhere enhance an atmosphere of surveillance and paranoia. If Branagh's screenplay follows Zeffirelli's in its description of space and action, it is also similar to Almereyda's in its inclusion of adjectives and comparisons. Adjectives come to qualify the characters' personalities and intonations as often as possible:

> The King begins to speak. Measured, compassionate, intelligent.[50]

Comparisons can also be found to emphasize attitudes and emotions, as in Almereyda's screenplay:

[48] Kenneth Branagh, *Beginning* (London: Chatto & Windus, 1989), p. 64. My italics.
[49] Kenneth Branagh, *'Hamlet' by William Shakespeare: Screenplay, Introduction and Film Diary* (London: Chatto & Windus, 1996), p. 23.
[50] *Ibid.*, p. 11.

The Royal Couple race out like the hungry newlyweds they are.[51]

Hamlet speaks the first phrase with a weariness so intense it's as if he's been wounded.[52]

What is particularly original in Branagh's screenplay and cannot be found in another *Hamlet* script is the creation of a semi-direct speech, a subtext in the form of thoughts as if coming directly from the characters' mind. In the scene in which Barnardo, Horatio and Marcellus come to inform Hamlet of the Ghost's apparition, the subtext makes us alternately enter the minds of the three men and that of Hamlet, in order to follow their respective course of thoughts, doubts and questioning:

HAMLET
Methinks I see my father.
The three men look at each other while the Prince experiences this reverie. Unless, of course, he too . . . Hamlet almost aggressive in his thirst for the information . . . He tries to catch them out. It can't be true . . . But if it was his father, how was he? The pain returns. He is intensely vulnerable.[53]

The first part of this extract focuses on Barnardo, Horatio and Marcellus. Their thoughts are made explicit in 'Unless, of course, he too . . .' This unfinished sentence imitates the process of thinking with its interruption, hesitations and suppositions. It is made clear that the three men are asking themselves if Hamlet's words of 'I see my father' should not be understood literally: maybe he too saw the Ghost. In the second part of the extract, the subtext concentrates on Hamlet. While the sentence 'He tries to catch them out' reveals information on his motivation *à la* Stanislavski, the sentences 'It can't be true' and 'But if it was his father, how was he?' are presented as transcriptions of his inner denial and questioning. In Branagh's screenplay, not only does the subtext describe, qualify or compare the appearance of things, it also dives into the characters' own reflections. This kind of free indirect speech, in which the voice of the narrator becomes 'contaminated' by the speech and perspective of a character, almost creates a dialogue which would compete with the original play if it didn't remain unspoken.

Following Stanislavski's recommendations, Branagh also encourages actors to invent a virtual history or 'backstory' for their characters. In his introduction to the 1993 screenplay of *Much Ado About Nothing*, he stresses the importance of such a method to research the part and communicate it to the public:

---

[51] *Ibid.*, p. 17.   [52] *Ibid.*, p. 60.   [53] *Ibid.*, pp. 19–21.

The audience won't know specifically my off-screen history for Benedick – his upbringing, his family, his likes and dislikes – but I hope that with this history firmly in my mind, they will at least intuit part of it, feel a depth to the character beyond what he says and does.[54]

The actor here reconstructs a previous history and treats the dramatic dialogue as a result of it. Such a history remains implicit. In the film *Much Ado About Nothing*, it is left unseen and off-screen, as it does not give rise to interpolations. The film does not offer any scene disclosing Benedick's childhood or revealing the battles in which he participated before arriving at Leonato's mansion. However, in Shakespeare films, the histories invented to build the characters' personalities do not always remain virtual and implicit. Instead of creating stories from characters' pasts and minds that remain unseen, film directors can show them to the audience. According to Branagh, this second process of adaptation extends the first one, as cinema allows the various stories imagined by the actors to be rendered explicit: 'Cinema offers the possibility of bringing to light something that the actors might have discussed together, on which they agreed and which would have otherwise remained off-stage or off-screen.'[55]

Film directors compose analepses in their screenplays, though these flashbacks revert far less to the past and are less extreme than those speculated by André Green in his book, *Hamlet et 'Hamlet'*. Directors Grigori Kozintsev and Franco Zeffirelli both begin their screen adaptations of *Hamlet* with sequences that are chronologically situated before the start of the original play, very much along the lines of Charles and Mary Lamb's tales. The 1964 film directed by Kozintsev opens with a rider who gallops across the plain at high speed: this is Hamlet returning from Wittenberg to attend his father's funeral. The sequence ends with his arrival at the palace and an embrace with his mother. In 1990, Zeffirelli's film opens with Old Hamlet's funeral. This interpolated sequence highlights a triangular exchange of gazes between Claudius, Hamlet and Gertrude:

Hamlet's eyes come up to look at Claudius, his grief giving way to startled disbelief. Claudius eyes him back [. . .] And now Hamlet turns to his mother. Gertrude trembles slightly and will not look at him. Claudius watches her, and aware of this scrutiny, she lowers her veil back over her face. Hamlet turns to take in the silent congregation. No one moves.[56]

[54] Kenneth Branagh, 'Introduction', in *'Much Ado About Nothing' by William Shakespeare: Screenplay, Introduction and Notes on the Making of the Film* (London: Chatto & Windus, 1993), p. xi.
[55] Quoted in French by Pierre Berthomieu, *Kenneth Branagh* (Paris: Jean-Michel Place, 1998), p. 230. My translation from French.
[56] Devore and Zeffirelli, 'The Screenplay of *Hamlet*', p. 2.

This interpolated scene at once introduces an explicitly Oedipal interpretation, marking out the Queen as a prize between the two men. Zeffirelli
wishes to familiarize the spectators with the diegetic context before moving
on with the action of the original play. But, within the action itself, he does
not hesitate to insert interpolations that replace some of the play's speeches.
For example, Ophelia's report to Polonius on Hamlet's strange visit to her
is turned into a speechless sequence that shows the actual meeting:

> Ophelia is very surprised at this odd and savage vision . . . Hamlet, in his fantastic
> state, is walking slowly toward Ophelia, staring at her sorrowfully . . . Hamlet lets
> her hand go and keeping his eyes on her face, he backs slowly toward the door and
> is gone. Ophelia, confused and frightened, is almost in tears.[57]

Zeffirelli's screenplay favours a visual strategy over a verbal one. Telling is
transformed into showing as often as possible. In those interpolations that
affect the play's time-flow, Zeffirelli's subtext makes the characters' states of
mind much more explicit than it does elsewhere in the script. These passages, almost composed from scratch, give rise to a more prolific, novelistic
creation that specifies not only the characters' actions, but also their emotions. In the given example, Ophelia is described as 'surprised', 'confused
and frightened' while Hamlet stares 'sorrowfully'. It is only in those kinds of
interpolated sequences that Zeffirelli's script displays adjectives giving such
emotional details beyond the mere description of movements or gestures.

Branagh also inserts interpolations into his screenplays. However, these
interpolations work in a very particular way, as they do not reorganize the
unfolding of events. They are always inserted in the very flow of the action,
to illustrate speeches, dive into one character's thoughts or create parallel
narrative lines.[58] Branagh's adaptation of *Hamlet* does feature the funeral
of Old Hamlet, but in contrast to what goes on in Zeffirelli's film, this
interpolation is situated not before the start of the original action, but in
the course of it. It comes to illustrate the speech in which Hamlet invokes
the Ghost of his father:

> Let me not burst in ignorance, but tell
> Why thy canoniz'd bones, hearsed in death,
> Have burst their cerements; why the sepulchre,
> Wherein we saw thee quietly inurn'd,
> Hath op'd his ponderous and marble jaws
> To cast thee up again.　　　　(I.iv.46–51)

---

[57] *Ibid.*, p. 36.
[58] See David Kennedy Sauer, 'Suiting the Word to the Action: Kenneth Branagh's Interpolations
in *Hamlet*', *Shakespeare Yearbook* 8 (1997), 329: 'more often, they [the interpolations] are of an
interpolated time or place intercut into the present moment of the text, usually with a voice-over'.

Images of Old Hamlet in his mausoleum are inserted within the action itself while Hamlet speaks. Branagh's narrative strategy consists of describing and commenting on the action of the play as if it was taking place live, while inserting explicit, realistic interpolations into the course of this action. Branagh's screenplays do not alter the dramatic presentation of events, but create simultaneous perceptions. In a given diegetic time, Branagh presents concomitant actions, or different levels of reality. For this director, it is almost as if the desire to add interpolated sequences within dramatic action was at the core of his motivation for adapting this play to the screen. In his introduction to his screenplay of *Hamlet* he writes: 'I longed to allow audiences to join Fortinbras on the plain in Norway, to be transported, as Hamlet is in his mind's eye, back to Troy and see Priam and Hecuba.'[59]

These words are revelatory of the two dimensions developed by Branagh in his adaptations – the exterior dimension with the creation of centrifugal plots allowing for geographical escape, and the inner dimension which immerses the audience into one character's subjectivity. Lorne Buchman is very close to Branagh's approach when he writes in his 1991 book *Still in Movement*: 'Film presents Shakespeare's world through a "mise-en-scène" that renders the vastness of intimate space as much as the intimacy of a vast exterior.'[60] Beyond interpretation that adds a gloss around the dramatic text, interpolation creates imaginary fictive moments that often put their stamp on the movie to become the most symbolic and memorable moments. The director's subtext then becomes dominant over Shakespeare's text. Instead of the subtext being constructed from the dramatic text, the strategy here consists of either suppressing the text or making the text dependent on the subtext. The gap, therefore, widens between the play and the film, as during Fortinbras's arrival presented as a military *coup d'état*. The written narration created between the two works then takes greater importance (and length) in the screenplay. Branagh's screen version of *Hamlet* presents us with even more interpolated moments than his other Shakespeare adaptations. The reason for this increase in the number of interpolations may be found in Branagh's decision to retain the complete Shakespeare text in his film. Branagh has adapted to the screen a conflation of two existing versions, that of the First Folio and that of the second quarto.[61] As he chose not

[59] Branagh, *'Hamlet'*, p. vii.
[60] Lorne Buchman, *Still in Movement: Shakespeare on Screen* (Oxford University Press, 1991), p. 33.
[61] The starting point of the screenplay was the text from the First Folio edited by Stanley Wells and Gary Taylor (*Oxford Complete Works of William Shakespeare*, Oxford University Press, 1986) to which Branagh added passages from the second quarto found in the appendixes of Wells and Taylor's edition. Some changes were then made (often at the actors' own demand) on the basis of the editions by Harold Jenkins (New Arden Shakespeare, London: Methuen, 1982) and by G. R. Hibbard (Oxford University Press, 1987).

to delete any word from the play, Branagh deprived himself of the textual cut, an important tool that usually allows directors to point up aspects of the play they want to explore and to bring out a strong interpretive line. According to Laurence Olivier, cutting is a necessary process when adapting *Hamlet*:

I had learnt that in dealing with 'Hamlet', the only real way to solve the problem of adaptation for the screen was to be ruthlessly bold in adapting the original play . . . [W]e have taken out altogether Rosencrantz and Guildenstern, and also Fortinbras. This is a radical approach to adaptation, and because it is so much more than mere condensation, I feel that the film 'Hamlet' should be regarded as an 'Essay in *Hamlet*'.[62]

When Laurence Olivier considers his film 'an Essay in *Hamlet*', he emphasizes the fact that a screen version of the play can merely offer a facet of the work. A production can only provide the audience with one version of the play. Branagh had to find new means to communicate his own reading of the text. Much like the cutting recommended by Olivier, the addition of interpolations makes a transition between the play written by Shakespeare and a personal filmic 'essay' possible. Instead of elaborating his personal vision by deleting passages, Branagh chose to develop whole narrative pieces through the use of flashbacks and parallel stories. The screenplay of *Hamlet* thus describes several interpolated images (or whole scenes) that interweave different narrative lines and levels of reality. Instead of concentrating on the hero's own turmoil, the film leads the audience into a centrifugal experience in which the stories of Ophelia and Fortinbras gain importance and contribute to a decentralization of place and time. By constructing an explanatory and explicit discourse, Branagh dilutes or even suppresses dramatic ambiguities and replaces them with narrative and psychological certainties. He seems to apply two methods – that advocated by the actor–managers of the eighteenth century whose aim was to bring solutions to every enigma of the play, and that urged by Stanislavski to play the characters as if they were real persons with a psychological profile both consistent and identifiable.

With these two methods, Branagh obviously follows the rules of classical realistic cinema. Like some realist novels, a classical realistic film displays knowledge of how things really are through a subjective viewpoint that is not revealed as such, thus conveying a specific ideology in a much stronger way than in drama. In a play, the different cues can be attributed easily

---

[62] Laurence Olivier, 'An Essay in *Hamlet*', in *The Film 'Hamlet': A Record of its Production*, ed. Brenda Cross (London: The Saturn Press, 1948), pp. 11–12.

to each character. Their origins are distinctly stated. According to drama theorist Manfred Pfister, 'As a speech-act, the dramatic speech constitutes its own particular speech situation. This is in contrast to dialogue in narrative texts, in which the fictional speech situation can be constituted by the narrator's report.'[63]

The words that are heard in a play are, therefore, presented as the responsibility of the one that utters them, and of that one only. There is no generalization made by a narrative, superior and/or omniscient prose saying what speech, action or decision is 'good' or 'bad', 'true' or 'wrong', 'valid' or 'invalid'. A clear, unambiguous ideology is thus less likely to be produced. In classical cinema, the role of narrative prose is taken over by the unfolding of events in front of the camera's eye. Camera angles, movements and editing create a narrative which offers a specific point of view, revealing what goes on and telling a certain kind of 'truth' against which the dialogues can be assessed. However, wherever the camera is placed, its viewpoint can never be objective. It can never record how things 'truly' are. But, as the conditions of filming are never disclosed in classical cinema – in order to construct realistic diegesis – the camera's subjectivity is not questioned. The film plays at presenting events as if they were really happening here and now, as if they had been recorded in an objective manner.

At the level of the screenplay, however, the conditions of creation are not yet hidden. In fact, they are extensively displayed. In contrast to the novel, screenplays are not works of art in themselves. They are only intermediary steps coming before the completed works that are the films. Screenplays generally include many metafilmic directions describing the way in which the shots are filmed and assembled. Just like Shakespeare stories by Francis Brett Young or Marchette Chute, Shakespearean screenplays are written in the present tense and regularly disclose enunciation through the adoption of an exterior viewpoint that reveals the film's articulations. In each screenplay, the writer can choose to focus on certain kinds of articulations such as camera angles and movements, the composition of shots and/or editing.

In his screenplay for *Hamlet*, Almereyda discloses very few details of the film's construction. He often indicates when editing occurs with expressions such as 'cut to:', but he does not include any reference to the way action is filmed. The only references to camera can be found in passages like:

ANGLE ON WALL-MOUNTED HOTEL SURVEILLANCE CAMERA.
The camera stares after him [Hamlet].[64]

---

[63] Manfred Pfister, *The Theory and Analysis of Drama* (Cambridge University Press, 1991), p. 6.
[64] Almereyda, *William Shakespeare's 'Hamlet'*, p. 87.

But, in this excerpt, the camera referred to does not represent the master camera with which the action of the film is shot: this camera belongs to the story of the film, to diegesis itself. Almereyda's film, focusing as it does on high technology and on the paranoia it induces, features many surveillance cameras that often spy on the characters. Though the positions and motions of the technical apparatus are never commented upon in the screenplay, the description of many cameras inside the story certainly introduces an effect of *mise-en-abyme*, allowing the spectators to indirectly reflect on the construction of the movie.

Zeffirelli's screenplay includes many indications of editing ('cut to' and 'dissolve to') but it also provides the reader with details on how the action is shot. Firstly, it specifies the point of view adopted by the camera, as in this extract:

27 – EXT. COURTYARD DAY
Hamlet's P.O.V. – Claudius and Gertrude appear on a terrace below.
HAMLET (V.O.)
. . . married with my uncle . . .[65]

Claudius and Gertrude are here seen by Hamlet. Their image occupies the field of the camera while Hamlet's voice can be heard. The screenplay also indicates the scale of shots used by the camera, especially when dealing with close-ups:

167 – C.U. Claudius's eyes widen and he rises, reaching out a helpless hand.[66]

Finally, the movements of the camera are commented on, as in the following examples:

We follow the clear waters that ripple over a bed of pebbles till we pull up to a willow tree.[67]

WE PULL BACK to see the throne room turned charnel-house.[68]

Zeffirelli's screenplay is, therefore, relatively complete in its apprehension of the filmic process – point of view, scale of shot, movement and editing. Laurence Olivier goes even further in the details his screenplay provides regarding filming. The movements of the camera are described with extreme precision, as in these extracts at the start and end of the 'Mousetrap' sequence:

---

[65] Devore and Zeffirelli, 'The Screenplay of *Hamlet*', p. 12. Abbreviations in this and following extracts are: 'Ext.', exterior; 'P.O.V.', point of view; 'V.O.', voice over; 'C.U.', close-up.
[66] *Ibid.*, p. 113.   [67] *Ibid.*, p. 97.   [68] *Ibid.*, p. 120.

173 – STAGE AND FORUM (PLAY) NIGHT
Camera is on a track.
It is centred on the King's party descending a flight of stairs in the background of the set on their way to take their seats for the play. As the King and Queen and their followers reach the middle foreground Hamlet enters from left and takes the Queen from the King.
Camera tracks back before the procession and pauses in front of the thrones placed before the stage.[69]

Camera on crane.
The camera starts from the position on the stairs that had been taken by the King. A panic-stricken torch-bearing crowd rush up the stairs towards the camera and over the camera. As this happens, the camera rises over the rushing people.[70]

The camera movements (here, tracking and rising) are carefully composed in advance. It is as if Laurence Olivier was considering each shot as a moving painting. The angle or viewpoint is emphasized, determining at every moment which scale of shot is used and from where this 'moving painting' is observed:

Close shot on Hamlet and Ophelia, but from farther away and more to the side than Scene 177. They react to Prologue Player.[71]

The Player Poisoner . . . comes in again, seeming to lament with him; the dead body is carried away. At this point in the play the camera should be immediately behind the King.[72]

For an actor originally coming from the theatre, one who has often been accused of being too 'stagey', Olivier displays a striking awareness of shot composition. While a more traditional form of subtext – such as the exclusive description of actions and feelings – might have been expected, it is surprising to note that Olivier's screenplay focuses much more on metafilmic comments. Even in the more conventional subtext describing what happens in front of the camera, Olivier makes the reader of the screenplay aware that what is depicted is a filmic experience. A case in point is the following excerpt:

A noise off causes Polonius to look over his left shoulder. An open fire burns. Out of this fire a log has fallen, and this has been the cause of the noise we have heard.[73]

---

[69] Laurence Olivier, *Hamlet: The Film and the Play*, ed. Alan Dent (London: World Film Publications, 1948), no pagination (p. 14, my pagination).
[70] *Ibid.*, pp. 20–1.   [71] *Ibid.*, p. 17.   [72] *Ibid.*, p. 18.   [73] *Ibid.*, p. 68.

Instead of saying merely that 'Polonius hears a noise caused by a log in the fire', Olivier uses the pronoun 'we' to report the action. We – the audience of the film – have heard the noise as much as Polonius. Instead of composing a very realistic subtext, Olivier prefers to make us conscious of film reception, and therefore of construction and discourse. Olivier's screenplay does not represent as much an attempt to create a realistic novel out of a play as a guide to the camera operator to reproduce as faithfully as possible the director's precise pictorial vision of the play.

Branagh's screenplay is distinctive in its close interweaving of Stanislavskian subtext and metafilmic commentary. When Horatio, Marcellus and Barnardo come across the Ghost of Old Hamlet, the screenplay has the following passage:

Exterior / MAIN COURTYARD **Night.**
The statue comes to life! They run for their lives! We are way above them in the night air. The GHOST's P.O.V. as the Camera rushes from a great height, swooping down on the retreating figures racing across the snow. We almost reach them, but no! Just in time they fling themselves behind a pillar.[74]

Sentences such as 'The statue comes to life' describe the action and draw attention to a character or an object, while notes such as 'The GHOST's P.O.V. as the Camera rushes from a great height' give indications on the way action is filmed. However, in addition to Olivier's, Branagh's screenplay offers information on the way the camera is moved. It provides not only details on the directions taken by the camera, but also on how such movements are handled. The comment on the movement thus includes either an adverb or a comparison to help apprehend the shot as precisely as possible:

Camera moves slowly back to reveal the sleeping peaceful monarch resting under a tree.[75]

The Camera creeping like an animal, pans left to reveal, a hundred yards away, ELSINORE, a gorgeous Winter Palace.[76]

Adverbs such as 'slowly' or comparisons such as 'creeping like an animal' create a new kind of subtext, very specific to Branagh, which is not applied to the action itself but to the filming of that action. It is as if the camera had a life of its own or was another character in the story. The screenplay also contains frequent comments on the effects the filmic choices have upon meaning:

[74] Branagh, *'Hamlet'*, p. 5. [75] *Ibid.*, p. 37. [76] *Ibid.*, p. 1.

Cut to a Close shot of Hamlet as he stands up – holding his sword in front of him. A still, mystic moment.[77]

The explicit notice of editing ('Cut to') and of scale ('Close shot') is immediately followed by the screenwriter/director's personal reading of the shot ('a still, mystic moment'). The result of the filmic decisions is interpreted here by the film-maker himself. Branagh, therefore, provides not only a guide for the camera operator but also for the spectator. The screenplay encodes the filming, but it also decodes it. In a way, Branagh provides his own response to his film in an attempt to channel the spectators' response to it.

In this survey of several scripts from *Hamlet*, a double discourse has been identified, one governing the different stages of cinematic creation. The first discourse comes directly from stage *mise-en-scène* and states decisions regarding the actors' moves, delivery and emotions, settings and props. With this form of subtext, directors offer a personal reading of the plays. To some scenes in which the situation remains ambiguous in Shakespeare's text they add a narrative that suppresses the original polysemy. By alternating dialogues and focused realistic narrative, the screenplays tend towards the sketching of a realistic, psychological novel meant to remain virtual, a mere step between the play and the film. However, the screenplays generally channel meaning rather than focus on the play's ambivalence. The composed subtexts bring consistency and psychological depth to the characters. They offer an interpretation of the play, but they also inevitably remove some of the play's ambiguities.

The second discourse deals with technical apparatus: it involves choices in terms of framing, shooting angles, camera and microphone movements, length of shots, and editing. Generally, each screenwriter favours one discourse over another.

With the example of *Hamlet*, Zeffirelli and Almereyda both put the emphasis on the first kind of discourse, but if Zeffirelli stresses the actors' moves and gestures as well as the geographical situations, Almereyda prefers rather to concentrate on a typical Stanislavskian subtext with many references to the characters' emotions. Olivier focuses much more on the second kind of discourse, offering many insights into the process of framing the shots and moving the camera. Branagh provides a combination of the two kinds of discourse, composing an abundant Stanislavskian subtext that applies not only to the characters in the film, but also to the camera itself.

---

[77] *Ibid.*, p. 39.

The screenplay's discourse regarding camerawork and editing can generally be considered the basis for a *mise-en-scène* of the first *mise-en-scène*. If, in the theatre, movement only concerns the actors on stage, in the cinema it also concerns the public's point of view. In fact, cinema appears as an organization of theatre both in space and time. Therefore, to adapt Shakespeare on screen would be to move to another medium which, in contrast to theatre, creates a permanent tension between the movement *in* the visual field and the movement *of* the field, i.e. between the movement *in front of* the camera and that *of* the camera.[78] Screenplays provide details on those two kinds of movement, the movement inside the field being diegetic and the movement of the field being extradiegetic. Screenplays regularly alternate between descriptions of the action in progress, the narrative through a certain viewpoint (or focalization), Shakespeare dialogues and interventions of the film director/narrator regarding filmic directions. The repeated use of the personal pronoun 'we' to introduce the different ways of filming and assembling the images ('we cut to . . .', 'we move to . . .', 'we track into . . .') reveals the director/screenwriter as an articulator, i.e. an enunciator. But this pronoun can also designate the spectators, who witness the movements of the image. These metafilmic descriptions thus display a constant consciousness of enunciation as well as reception. So, the screenplays often emphasize the fact that they are constructed, mainly through the use of articulating pronouns that reveal the camera's viewpoint as a subjective choice of the director's team. But this articulation most often disappears in the completed films, as there are no shots showing the technical apparatus, which could have disclosed the decisions governing the camera's viewpoints. In fact, a Shakespeare film shot in the mode of classical realistic cinema lacks the ability to subvert its own dominant discourse, unable as it is to deal with several contradictory narrative discourses and viewpoints within itself. The classical realistic film seems to resolve every contradiction; it puts the audience in a position of omniscience and dominance, compatible with the acceptance of the film's constructed ideology. The only way for a film to become more subversive would be to reveal that it is a constructed product and so to disclose the articulations of production. But even that is problematic as a film's illusion is always difficult to destroy completely: even if a director films a camera, this very act of filming will not be disclosed. Screenplays represent only a mere step in the cinematic creation, but they allow the reader – who saw or will see the completed film – to perceive the work as a constructed piece. With the different layers of discourse it usually

---

[78] See Pierre Maillot, *L'écriture cinématographique* (Paris: Méridiens Klincksieck, 1994), pp. 122–33.

includes, a Shakespeare screenplay makes the play into a narrative, but it also deconstructs the forthcoming film. The Stanislavskian subtext turns the original play into a realistic novel, while the metafilmic discourse reveals the film as a series of subjective choices. A screenplay, therefore, appears as hybrid: it creates ideology through a prose situating the dialogues in relation to a so-called objective truth, but at the same time it can deconstruct ideology by revealing each shot in the film as a subjective one.

CHAPTER 6

Case studies

It is now appropriate in this final chapter to offer detailed aesthetic comparisons between key scenes from different adaptations of the same play. By
identifying distinct visual strategies chosen by film directors to appropriate
the same scene, this concluding chapter illustrates how film aesthetics can
condition meaning, suggesting some guidelines for the study of sequences
in Shakespeare adaptations. Scenes will be closely examined in terms of
time, space, camera moves, editing, sound and music, dialogue, focusing
and identification, and cultural as well as cinematic codes.

The first case study, 'Fear on screen', analyses the scene of the Ghost's
appearance in *Hamlet*, in the productions of Laurence Olivier (1948), Tony
Richardson (1969), Franco Zeffirelli (1990) and Kenneth Branagh (1996),
putting the stress on the appropriation of codes and techniques from *films
noirs*, thrillers and horror films.

The second case study, 'Dream on screen', examines the night preceding
the battle of Bosworth in *Richard III*, as it is represented in the films of
Laurence Olivier (1955), Richard Loncraine (1996) and Al Pacino (1996),
highlighting the directors' decisions in terms of cinematic alienation and
realism.

The third case study, 'Trance on screen', considers the 'ocular proof' and
'fainting' scenes in *Othello* in the adaptations by Orson Welles (1952) and by
Oliver Parker (1995), discussing the choices between metaphorical and literal film-making, as well as between editing and uninterrupted shots.

The fourth case study, 'Power on screen', explores the scene of Antony's
speech in *Julius Caesar*, in the films directed by Joseph Mankiewicz (1953)
and Stuart Burge (1970), noting how changes in camera angles can reflect
shifts in authority.

The last case study, 'Wooing on screen', investigates the conquest of
Princess Katherine in *Henry V*, showing how the adaptations of Laurence
Olivier (1944) and Kenneth Branagh (1989) are positioned in regard to the
gender issues raised by the text of the play.

FEAR ON SCREEN: THE GHOST'S APPARITION IN 'HAMLET'

An in-between time: midnight. An in-between place: the ramparts, neither outside nor inside Elsinore Castle. Hamlet, Marcellus and Horatio are keeping the watch. Hamlet waits for the Ghost of his father to appear before him. The scene (1.v) that follows offers an instructive example of how fear can be communicated on screen through dramatic elements but also through specific cinematic aesthetics.

By definition, the apparition of a ghost is linked to both death and the supernatural. Old Hamlet's spectre is neither dead nor alive, coming back to haunt his son and confide a painful secret to him. The ultimate stage of death, a symbol of anguish and complete separation, has been overcome, as the Ghost comes back from the 'undiscovered country', possibly from Purgatory or maybe even Hell. Hamlet, therefore, sees his father in an in-between state, at the same time reborn and on the verge of disappearing once more into limbo.

This sequence in the film productions of Laurence Olivier (1948), Tony Richardson (1969), Franco Zeffirelli (1990) and Kenneth Branagh (1996) can be divided into five parts, each one working on a different kind of fear: the quest (or the fear of the maze), the waiting (or the fear of irruption), the apparition (or the end of homogeneity), the tale (or the contamination by the monster) and the final departure (or the fear of separation).

In the four films, the sequence begins with a search, a quest. The spectre appears briefly and orders Hamlet to follow him. The son is, therefore, following his father. The traditional code of terror is here reversed: the Ghost does not pursue, but is the one pursued. Anguish lies in what Hamlet could endure if he was to join the Ghost. His friends have already tried to talk him out of this quest by warning him that the Ghost could drive him to the cliffs or make him mad. Hamlet not only risks losing his way but also his mind. Directors have emphasized this fear of getting lost spatially and mentally. In his 1948 film, Laurence Olivier chooses to have the character of Hamlet lost in a frightening mist and uses the camera movements to evoke endless meandering. Stairs seem to stretch indefinitely in an atmosphere reminiscent of German expressionism. The fortress of Elsinore becomes a terrifying maze in which every geographical landmark is erased. This Hamlet, in fact, loses his own markers from the start of the sequence, as he faints and falls to the ground. Olivier adds quasi-mystical and religious aspects to the quest: the camera draws attention to the sword that Hamlet carries like a cross, on the slow walk upwards that recalls a pilgrimage, and on the kneeling at the sight of the father.

In Tony Richardson's version, the same idea of the maze can be found, but this time in the damp underground and sewers of Elsinore. Hamlet does not know any longer which way to take in order to find his father. The quest that was turned towards the sky and the divine in Olivier's film is here linked to the earth below and to Hell in Richardson's version. In Zeffirelli's film, the search takes place on the castle battlements, in open air. The impact of a maze effect is not only created by the location (a complex system of paths between the stone walls), but also through editing, which rapidly alternates between shots, each revealing a different piece of space. Hamlet's disorientation and confusion is expressed through this jerky and fragmented succession of shots. Hamlet keeps turning round to check behind him in the hope (or fear) of finding the Ghost. Editing reflects this frenzy by brusquely alternating shots/counter-shots of Hamlet and his point of view. Fear is born from this spatial fragmentation, as the viewer does not know when or from where danger may spring.

Kenneth Branagh uses thriller codes as far as the first part of this sequence is concerned. The Ghost is a military statue that comes to life, evoking the Commander in Mozart's *Don Giovanni*. As the spectre orders Hamlet to follow him, a breathless pursuit begins in the forest, a symbolic location for losing one's way. The branches appear as inextricable obstacles to sight and progression, creating hidden, mysterious and worrisome zones. The earth quakes and cracks open, liberating some bubbling white smoke. As in Zeffirelli's version, the rapid rhythm of editing mirrors the emotional fever of the character. Moreover, the camera follows Hamlet in steadicam, alternating between shots of his running and shots of his subjective viewpoint. Inserts emphasize the supernatural nature of the Ghost and his strange return to life: a shot in flashback shows Old Hamlet dead in his mausoleum; another shows the earth exploding to evoke the leaving of the tomb; another reveals the threatening moving statue. Branagh places this sequence, intentionally or not, in line with the genre of B-movie horror films. The scene recalls, for example, Jacques Tourneur's *Night of the Demon* (1957), when Dana Andrews is pursued in the forest by a ball of fire in the midst of smoky curls.

In the four adaptations, directors have, therefore, exploited the fear of getting lost, of losing spatial markers through location (mist, maze, forest) and/or speedy, frenetic editing.

If Richardson's and Olivier's films go directly from the quest to the Ghost's irruption, Zeffirelli's and Branagh's adaptations both use the codes of horror films, introducing what could be called 'buffer scenes'. After the agitation of the pursuit, a much calmer scene takes place, but it is paradoxically meant to convey even more fear to the viewers. Zeffirelli anaesthetizes a certain zone of space with a shot of the rampart wall where nothing can be spotted. Then, he activates it by filming the Ghost's apparition at this very same place, using a contrapuntal technique of editing and enhancing the feeling of surprise and shock. Branagh, instead, prefers to activate a zone of space through a succession of subjective pan shots in which Hamlet scans the forest environment, before anaesthetizing this zone: the Ghost will not burst out in front of Hamlet but behind him. In addition, Branagh makes the spectators hear the Ghost before he is shown on screen. His voice is cold, metallic, linked to Hell, recalling Darth Vader's speech in Lucas's *Star Wars*. By hearing the spectre before seeing him, the audience is encouraged to anticipate the irruption on screen and to fear the sight of a creature whose voice is so chilling.

Neither Zeffirelli nor Branagh use dramatic irony in this sequence. The audience's knowledge is never greater than the character's. The viewers never see what Hamlet does not see himself. On the contrary, they find themselves in the same position as him, sharing what little information he has. Both Zeffirelli and Branagh, therefore, favour the unexpected aspect of the Ghost's irruption as well as a complete identification with the Danish prince. The audience will only discover where the Ghost really is at the same time as Hamlet. The fact that no director has chosen to use dramatic irony can be explained by the nature of the sequence. This is not a usual pursuit: Hamlet is not hunted; on the contrary, he is the one who hunts. Fear lies, therefore, in the mixture of apprehension and desire that governs this quest for the Father. It plays on the effect of surprise and not on an irony that would make the audience connive with the Ghost.

In Laurence Olivier's and Tony Richardson's adaptations, the Ghost's apparition happens in the mode of amazement and stupefaction. Hamlet stops moving while the filmic flow is not interrupted by editing. In Olivier's film, a semi-subjective shot shows Hamlet from behind and his viewpoint at the same time. The audience watches Hamlet in the state of watching. Olivier again uses mist to make the apparition mysterious and quasi-mystical. The audience hardly makes out the Ghost's face under his armour and the cloud of smoke that surrounds him. In Richardson's version, the sequence also concentrates on stupefaction: the camera lingers on Hamlet's amazed face, lit by a white halo. By contrast, in Zeffirelli and Branagh's films, irruption is treated in the mode of shock and opposition, through both action and film aesthetic. In order to exploit the 180° angle of cinematic fear (in horror films, sudden appearances usually happen either from behind or in front of the character), the two directors have chosen to use the technique of shot/counter-shot to film the irruption. In Zeffirelli's version, the Ghost appears behind Hamlet. The character turns round, and immediately the film cuts to show his viewpoint: the spectre is there at the very spot that Hamlet had scanned earlier without noticing anything. The director plays on a shot/counter-shot editing that intensifies the contrast between absence and sudden presence. In Branagh's film, the apparition happens in the mode of violence and brutality. It actually takes place at the end of a shot, thus creating a formal break. The surprise of the bursting in is accompanied by another kind of fear – that of being choked, crushed, scratched. The first shot on the Ghost is, in fact, a hand that grabs Hamlet by the neck and throws him against a tree with frightening strength. This quasi-autonomous hand and the fragmentation of the body in general are recurrent features in horror films. The Ghost goes through a cinematic anatomization that immediately renders him monstrous. This hand arriving from nowhere notably recalls another film by Branagh, *Mary Shelley's Frankenstein* (1994) in which the audience discovers the Creature through the bloody hand it suddenly lays on the immaculate snow of a glacier.

The father's story is the part of the sequence that presents the greatest aesthetic differences when the four adaptations are compared. However, the four films concur in their use of one theme – that of the echo, whether it be through sounds or images. The confrontation between the father and the son can only be emphasized by the very nature of cinema, which generally works on an action/reaction pattern and implies a dialogue both verbal and visual between the characters on screen. The directors have thus favoured the shot/counter-shot technique to film the unfolding of the story. Consequently, if in the theatre the spectators can distance themselves from the action taking place on stage, if they can watch the meeting from outside, they can hardly do the same in the cinema. They are obliged to adopt the camera's viewpoint of the son watching his father, and that of the father watching his son. This cinematic alternation of viewpoint recalls the ambivalent nature of fear itself: the viewers are afraid *of* the spectre and frightened *for* Hamlet at the same time, through the processes of identification. In this part of the sequence, Zeffirelli plays on a contrast between the frightening darkness of the night and the light projected onto the faces. The confrontation between Hamlet and his father is treated in the mode of equality. Zeffirelli shoots all the sequence in shot/counter-shot, without any specific angle, positioning the two characters at the same level and insisting on the human aspect of the Ghost, who inspires pity more than fear. In Richardson's film, it is not darkness but light that is a source of fear. The audience never sees the Ghost. His presence is merely suggested by the illuminated face of Hamlet. The lighting here provokes panic and implies a supernatural apparition. However, sound is the most important element of the sequence in creating fear. The spectre's voice is, actually, none other than that of Hamlet and could be the hallucination of a disrupted mind. The voice also features an echo and a strong resonance, notably on the most striking words of the Ghost's speech, such as 'murder' or 'incest'.

In Olivier's version, in contrast to those of Zeffirelli and Richardson, the story is constructed around a flashback in which Old Hamlet is murdered. These past images are presented as Hamlet's mental pictures as he hears his father's speech. A shot shows Hamlet close his eyes, followed by a camera move towards the prince's head before dissolving into the flashback. The past images are surrounded by a dream-like blur that gives them the shape of a brain. In Olivier's version, the Ghost's whole speech, therefore, goes through the prism of Hamlet's thoughts. The murder is exhibited on screen rather than simply heard, satisfying the audience's scopic urges through the protagonist's imagination. Moreover, as in Richardson's film, the voice of the Ghost is the same as that of Hamlet. Laurence Olivier chose to dub the spectral character with a slight transformation of his voice. In this version, Hamlet's voice and that of his father are one and the same. Again, the notion of echo is exploited, with a voice that is both unique and double, though Olivier does not use the same reverberation effects as Richardson.

Branagh's film favours a relation of strength. The audience discovers the Ghost through a forward travelling shot in low angle, which is mirrored immediately by a high-angle shot of Hamlet. The Ghost's power and charisma are intensified through these two shots, which at once reflect the superiority of the father over his son. In contrast to what happens in Zeffirelli's film, Branagh's sequence does not present a relationship based on equality, but one based on intimidation. The Ghost appears before his son as a huge warrior in armour, evoking a fairy-tale ogre living in the woods. Branagh's sequence, like Olivier's, also offers flashback inserts that borrow from the codes of horror films. Branagh emphasizes the revolting side of the regicide: the poisoned ear explodes in a quasi-subliminal shot when the Ghost refers to his murder for the first time. This shot is shown again during the tale in a longer flashback where slow-motion adds a dream-like aspect to the past event. Editing also expresses a contamination from father to son. The Ghost confides his secret to Hamlet, but by doing so he contaminates his son and makes him monstrous too. The film cuts immediately from an extreme close-up of the Ghost's mouth, which orders 'Revenge his foul and most unnatural murther' (i.v.25), to an extreme close-up on Hamlet's mouth as he reacts by shouting 'Murther?' (i.v.26), thus creating a strong effect of visual echo. The mouth seen in extreme close-up directly recalls the childhood fear of being swallowed by a fairy-tale ogre. The camera lingers on the Ghost's mouth and teeth, which occupy the whole screen for a while as though they were ready to devour and engulf the spectators themselves. However, this anatomization of the face is not limited to the mouth. The sequence is also constructed around gazes. The eyes of the two characters almost speak to one another as three extreme close-ups of Hamlet's blue eyes directly respond to three extreme close-ups of the Ghost's own eyes, whose steel blue colour is strikingly strange. The Ghost has the eyes of a creature that knows the secrets of Purgatory. He contaminates Hamlet through his speech, just as his representation on screen contaminates that of Hamlet. The Danish prince is filmed in a monstrous, fragmented way, in symmetric relation to the shots of the Ghost's mouth and eyes. When the Ghost describes how his son would look if he knew the secret of after-death, he uses words that transform Hamlet into a monstrous figure:

> But that I am forbid
> To tell the secrets of my prison-house,
> I could a tale unfold whose lightest word
> Would harrow up thy soul, freeze thy young blood,
> Make thy two eyes like stars start from their spheres,
> Thy knotted and combined locks to part,
> And each particular hair to stand on end,
> Like quills upon the fearful porpentine.   (i.v.13–20)

The bulging eyes and the hair standing on end recall the mythic Medusa from whose head snakes burst. The way of filming the spectre and Hamlet in echoing extreme close-ups, therefore, reflects the theme of monstrous contagion that governs the scene in Shakespeare. In Branagh's film, Hamlet is contaminated by his father and becomes, in his turn, an unnatural character. If Olivier and Richardson point up a vocal contamination (as Hamlet and the Ghost share the same voice), Branagh works on contamination that is, above all, visual.

Fear of separation is one of the great fears of childhood. It means separation from the mother, a new vulnerability, the first unprotected exposure to pain and physical danger. This kind of fear is very much present at the end of the sequence – Hamlet has just found his father only to learn that he must be separated from him again. Three adaptations out of four put the stress on this separation through the characters' hands. In Olivier's film, Hamlet extends his arms towards his father, who is disappearing into the mist. Olivier emphasizes the son's submission, the filial love Hamlet feels for his father. The pain of separation is reflected in Hamlet's sudden fainting and through a fast, backwards travelling shot that shrinks the character, showing him as if crushed by a superior force. In the Zeffirelli version, by contrast, the Ghost is the one who extends his arms towards the audience, who has adopted Hamlet's subjective viewpoint. Zeffirelli here emphasizes fatherly love and the pressure that this love exerts on the son. In Branagh's film, Hamlet and the Ghost both extend a hand towards each other. Filial and fatherly loves are on the same level. The anxiety of separation is felt by both characters simultaneously. The two hands try to meet and touch, but that of the Ghost soon vanishes and Hamlet's hand can only close on thin air as an ultimate symbol of childlike frustration.

This scene of the Ghost's apparition in *Hamlet* combines different kinds of fear – the fear of strangeness, of losing one's way, of sudden irruption, of being devoured, of separation. Directors have used various cinematic processes to reflect these fears: frenetic editing or labyrinthine locations to communicate the fear of getting lost; shots/counter-shots, anaesthesia or activation of spatial zones to render the surprise of irruption; extreme close-ups of mouths to evoke engulfing; emphasis on the hands to awaken our psychological fear of separation. However, if directors have chosen different means to shoot the sequence and create fear, the film aesthetics all meet on two related themes – echo and contagion. As the Ghost delivers his secret to his son, he somehow reproduces the murder he was victim of, poisoning Hamlet's ear. Cinematic aesthetic acknowledges this poisoning through echoing, visual or sound effects. Eventually, Hamlet is made the bearer of confidential information but also of a certain form of monstrosity.

DREAM ON SCREEN: THE EVE OF BATTLE IN 'RICHARD III'

In Act v, scene iii of *Richard III*, Richard and Richmond are both sleeping on the eve of the battle of Bosworth. Ghosts of people killed on Richard's orders suddenly appear, bringing curses to Richard and encouragement to Richmond. The ambiguity of the scene lies in the ghosts' problematic nature. Do they spring up from Richard's tormented dreams or are they really present near the two men? Richmond, indeed, when he wakes up, states that he heard them too. In the theatre, the ghosts of Henry VI, Clarence, Rivers, Grey, Vaughan, the two young princes, Hastings, Lady Anne and Buckingham generally come on stage in the flesh. In Michael Grandage's 2002 theatre production at the Crucible Theatre in Sheffield, Richard lay in a wheeled traction machine stretching his limbs. The ghosts emerged from behind pillars and pushed the wheeled bed back and forth, spinning it around, taking advantage of Richard's captive state. The two princes even climbed onto the bed, springing from it as though on monkey bars. Richard was transformed into a kind of toy. After playing with the other characters, he was being played with. In Michael Pennington's 1986 English Shakespeare Company production, filmed for television and video, the *mise-en-scène* emphasizes the power of words and their capacity to hurt physically. Richard cannot fall asleep serenely as each ghost's speech makes him experience terrible pain. Birmingham even makes this forceful power of words literal by shooting bullets with his gun. If the ghosts' words to Richard follow the original text, those addressing Richmond are completely removed, thus suppressing the dramatic symmetry of the scene and the ambiguity of the ghosts, as they are seen by Richard only. This suppression can be found again in three cinematic adaptations of the play, a choice guided either by a desire for realism or a desire to add dramatic power.

In Richard Loncraine's 1995 adaptation, the dream sequence is brief and only includes some sentences already heard earlier in the film. Richard is lying on his bed, his face lit by a blue, almost mystical light. The text of the original scene is totally suppressed in favour of a sound flashback made up of words uttered by Lady Anne, the two young princes and Richard's mother. No ghost appears near Richard to circumvent cinematic realism. The dream is constructed like an ordinary fantasy, with sounds and voices already heard by Richard and the spectators, who are put in a situation of sound identification with the royal character. The sequence insists on memory, obsession and trauma. The analeptic aspect of the dream predominates.

In Laurence's Olivier's 1955 version, the dream sequence lies between Loncraine's realistic presentation and the original play's physical apparitions. Olivier chooses to let the ghosts appear, but to film them according to the usual cinematic codes of spectral apparition, i.e. by using superimposed images that emphasize the ectoplasmic and evanescent nature of the ghost-like characters. The sweetness of Lady Anne's white face, on which tears of light slowly roll, is opposed to the violence with which Hastings rushes onto Richard's face. Richard is filmed with a high-angle shot, lying on his bed, until his head and that of Hastings visually collide in one single shot for a brief, violent moment. The spectres, the editing and the final fall of Hastings onto Richard's body make the sequence nightmarish and extremely stylized and artificial at the same time. In Olivier's film, the dream seems to have a two-fold nature. It is analeptic through this succession of characters coming out of their tombs to haunt Richard; but it is also proleptic as the ghosts are superimposed on the battlefield itself, transforming it into a doomed place for Richard on the following day. The sequence also anticipates Richard's death by the repetition of the sentence 'Despair and die!' As far as the nature of the spectres is concerned, Olivier retains a certain ambiguity to the scene as the spectators do not know if the ghosts are 'real' entities or if they only belong to Richard's imagination.

In Al Pacino's 1996 adaptation, the sequence of Richard's dream is eminently complex as it involves several levels of enunciation and different time dimensions. The audience is alienated from the fiction through metafilmic comments from the actors themselves and through images showing Pacino the actor, holding the play text in his hand, in the process of playing the part of Richard. The dream sequence includes three different kinds of text: the metafilmic comments from the actors, sentences belonging to previous scenes of the film, and words belonging to the original scene in the play (including the familiar 'Despair and die!'). The sequence, aggressive through its fast editing and, at the same time, dream-like through its disorganization/deconstruction, is scattered with quasi-subliminal flashes taking the viewers to the past or to the future. In contrast to Richard Loncraine's version, these flashbacks and flashforwards are not only composed of sounds, but also of images. The audience, in the same dream-like position as Richard, sees distorted shots of events already shown in the film, as well as shots that will be seen later during the battle. In the latter shots, Richard catches a glimpse of himself already dead. The sight of an executioner rapidly bringing his axe down is evocative of people executed on Richard's orders in the past as well as Richard's own death in an imminent future. Pacino's version emphasizes the dream's two-fold status – both analeptic and proleptic – even more than the Olivier film. Through these bits and pieces of films-within-the-film, Pacino constructs a cinematic *mise-en-abyme* that reflects the metadramatic aspect of the original scene, as each ghost represents a piece of history that springs up again within the narrative.

Three distinct strategies can, therefore, be identified for adapting and appropriating this sequence on screen. Loncraine turns the physical, troublesome apparitions of the ghosts into a real-life dream enlivened with flashback sounds. The film aims at erasing the alienating effect of spectres that could disrupt cinematic realism. Olivier adopts a more theatrical approach, showing the ghosts, but limiting their apparitions to transparent presence. The stylized and artificial-looking sequence gives rise to alienating effects that circumvent the ideology of a consistent, realistic world of fiction. Pacino's version includes many alienating devices in the form of extradiegetic, metafilmic commentaries, as well as numerous flashcuts

breaking the film's space and time continuity. However, no ghost is actually present in the sequence. Pacino's film paradoxically achieves, through
a multiple array of alienating devices, the impressions of a real dream, filled
with disorganized images and sounds.

TRANCE ON SCREEN: THE 'OCULAR PROOF' AND 'FAINTING'
SCENES IN 'OTHELLO'

The scene of the 'ocular proof' (Act III, scene iii) and that of the 'fainting'
(Act IV, scene i) in *Othello* are two examples of how anger, violence and
trance are represented on the screen. In the former scene, Othello asks
Iago to provide him with the 'ocular proof' of Desdemona's infidelity. In
the latter scene, Iago provides the supposed proof, leading to Othello's
fainting. The screen versions of Orson Welles (1952) and of Oliver Parker
(1995) resort to distinct cinematic means to present these scenes, reflecting
the two divergent ways of filming Shakespeare plays, either using metaphors
or literal illustrations.

Welles cuts a fair amount of the words in his 'ocular proof' scene to concentrate on the power of the images even more. Iago (played by Micheál
MacLiammóir) first comes into view on a deserted grey background. He
is presented as a figure in a vacuum, a nihilistic character arriving from
nowhere, with no specific reason nor motivation for his malevolence. His
manipulative power is expressed through a low-angle shot that proclaims his
strength as soon as he enters the camera field. The confrontation between
Iago and Othello becomes, through Welles's camera gaze, a duel of high
and low angles with chiaroscuro lighting. As Iago is asked to give proof for
his words, he finds himself trapped for the first time in the play. In Welles's
film, this dramatic situation is reflected by the background setting. Othello
progressively leads Iago to move backwards, towards the dangerous edge of a
cliff overhanging a raging sea. The confrontation never turns into a physical
fight, but remains psychological. The major threat for Iago in the sequence
does not lie in Othello's bodily strength but in the height of the cliff and the
sea below. Othello's fury is not rendered literal through strangling (as it was
in the 1986 RSC production directed by Trevor Nunn, for example), but
is reflected in metaphorical images of foamy waves crashing in the background. As the waves only break in the background of the shot, they never
actually reach Iago, but if the viewer sees the shot as a two-dimensional
picture, it is as though the waves splashed on Iago's face, metaphorically
displaying Othello's raging desire to drown his opponent. The building
tension between the two characters is expressed through acceleration in

editing. The rapid change in shot angles results in a loss of spatial markers and a growing sense of danger: the spectators do not know any longer where Iago stands in relation to the edge of the cliff and if he is about to fall or not. As Othello is filmed over Iago, we are encouraged to feel that, for a short while, Othello is in command. But this cinematic work on vertical lines soon gives way to more peaceful horizontal lines. It is as if Iago has let the storm pass and now can continue to exert his manipulative skills.

If Welles's adaptation is constructed around metaphorical drowning, Parker's film is much more literal. The sea is again present in the scene, but this time it shares the immediate space of the actors. It is no longer a metaphorical element in the background. Parker emphasizes the realistic, exterior setting. The sea somehow becomes a player in the scene, on the same level as the two protagonists. Violence is above all expressed through physical actions. Othello first threatens Iago with his body language, then grabs him, strangles him and finally forces him under water. The editing, in contrast to what happens in Welles's version, is much less frenetic. Tension and danger are not reflected through rapid changes in shots but through rarely interrupted shot-sequences. The sense of action happening 'live' aims at making the drowning shot spectacular. As Iago is kept under water for a certain period, the feeling of real time, without editing, enhances the sense of threat: how long will he be able to stay alive without breathing?

The sequences by Welles and Parker are not only representative of the contrast between metaphorical and realistic camerawork in terms of images, but also of the opposition between two cinematic philosophies as a whole, one advocated by Sergei Eisenstein and the other recommended by André Bazin. Welles's sequence is based on Eisenstein's view of cinema, with highly stylized angle shots and metaphorical editing. Parker, rather, maintains the suspense of the scene through a preservation of space. There is less editing in an attempt not to disrupt the flow of action. Parker tries to reproduce a sense of real events happening here and now, whereas Welles reconstructs reality through space and time dislocation and stylized reorganization.

In Welles's *Othello*, the 'fainting' scene (Act IV, scene i) is built around a major metaphor that also runs through the whole film. From Iago's words 'And out of her own goodness make the net / That shall enmesh them all' (II.iii.361–2), Welles uses camerawork, lighting and setting to create shots with many criss-cross lines, evoking the trap in which Iago wants to catch Othello. In Welles's sequence, after Iago has coldly and dryly announced to Othello that Desdemona's infidelity has been reported and proved, a distressed Othello starts running beneath a lattice-work of branches. The camera, placed above the branches, makes Othello appear as if he is caught in a labyrinthine cage. Again, Welles uses fast editing and complex camera angles to express a loss of spatial markers. Othello is losing his mind as much as he is losing the sense of where he is. Space is rendered chaotic, while rhythmic, atonal music comments on Othello's anguish without empathy. The camera suddenly stops following Othello. Instead of seeing the character himself, the viewers now witness what the character sees. A shot in subjective camera makes us share Othello's sight. The camera moves to reveal an extreme low-angle shot of the castle and the sky, suggesting that Othello has fallen to the ground, experiencing a quasi-epileptic fainting fit. If space was made chaotic earlier in the sequence, Welles now makes time uncertain. As Welles films the sky and the passing of birds in discontinuous editing, the audience does not know how long Othello has been unconscious. The notion of real time disappears in favour of psychological time. As in the 'ocular proof' sequence, Welles has deconstructed and reconstructed space and time to achieve tension and anxiety within the characters as well as in the audience.

In Oliver Parker's 'fainting' sequence, the spectators are also brought to share Othello's experience of an epileptic crisis, but with a different form of subjective camera shot. In this version, Iago (played by Kenneth Branagh) appears much more sympathetic when he delivers the so-called truth to Othello (played by Laurence Fishburne). He acts as if he did not want to tell the truth in order to spare Othello, but finally appears to give in after much insistence from his 'friend'. As Othello's crisis starts, Parker's subjective shots do not show what the character sees with his eyes as in Welles's version, but what he sees in his mind. Literal images springing from Othello's own imagination appear on the screen, showing Desdemona actually in bed with Cassio. These images are highly problematic as they are very similar to a flashback and could lead the viewers to ask themselves if this love affair has really happened. The very fact of seeing the entwined couple on screen questions Desdemona's faithfulness. The bodies of the two lovers are shown through faster and faster editing. The close shots only present bits of skin at the same time, dislocating the bodies into space and time, turning the lovers into fleshy, pornographic monsters. With this speedy editing, Othello's fantasy becomes feverish. The epileptic crisis almost becomes an orgasmic trance. As we go back to 'objective' shots of Othello himself, we see him with his back to the wall, his head shaking in pain and his hands attached to heavy metal chains. These shots prolong the sexual imagery of the fantasy with a sado-masochistic picture of a man in a handcuff-like apparatus. At the same time, according to Stephen Buhler, the shot portrays Othello as a slave tied up with chains: 'the chain suggests that Parker intends we see Othello enslaved not only by his jealousy but by the racist categories Iago has led him to internalize'.[1] Parker's sequence, therefore, presents sexual and racial issues intermingled in the character of Othello. Made and released during the much publicized and voyeuristic trial of O. J. Simpson (accused of murdering his wife and an acquaintance), and featuring Laurence Fishburne (who played another brutal husband in the 1993 film, *What's Love Got to Do With It*) as Othello, Parker's film constructs and develops an intertext of sex, violence, voyeurism and racial anxieties.

The fainting sequences in Welles's and in Parker's films both bring the spectators into another dimension, away from an objective space and time. However, if Welles works on metaphorical suggestions, Parker chooses a much more literal film-making. Welles's camera makes us share the eyes of Othello and makes time melt into unconsciousness. Instead of showing the fall and crisis, Welles modestly suggests them to the viewers, who experience the event from an inner point of view. By contrast, Parker's version makes us penetrate Othello's thoughts in a voyeuristic sequence of sexual fantasies and racial imagery. While Welles hides the body in pain from our view, Parker puts the bodies on display, that of a suffering Othello as well as those of Cassio and Desdemona, made monstrous through dislocating, frenetic *découpage*. Suggestion has here given way to exhibition.

POWER ON SCREEN: ANTONY'S SPEECH IN 'JULIUS CAESAR'

In Act III, scene ii of *Julius Caesar*, Mark Antony's speech that follows Brutus's attempt to justify the plot against Caesar appears as a rhetorical bravura, acknowledging the capacity of words for shifting political power. The screen adaptations by Stuart Burge (1970) and Joseph Mankiewicz (1953) both present this scene with realistic human resources – a whole crowd of Roman citizens is shown near the Senate, waiting to be pacified by the orators or to let their rage out in mutiny. The sequence in the two films is constructed around a 'taming of the throng', but this is achieved through different strategies in terms of *mise-en-scène* and cinematic processes.

In Stuart Burge's 1970 film, with Charlton Heston in the part of Antony, the sequence is based more around Heston's performance than on complex cinematic work. Editing alternately shows the crowd and Heston, generally in close-shots. There are no establishing shots revealing how huge the

[1] Stephen Buhler, *Shakespeare in the Cinema: Ocular Proof* (Albany: State University of New York Press, 2002), p. 26.

crowd is. Instead, the camera separates relatively small groups of people in different shots. This formal division, perhaps due to the need for production economies, lessens the threatening potential of the throng, as it is transformed into an accumulation of identifiable individuals rather than an anonymous, uncontrollable mob. The camera often lingers on Heston and his facial emotions in close-ups. Antony is performed as a sincere man who does not manipulate the crowd to gain power for himself but who genuinely believes in the justice of his cause. Heston plays no Machiavel, instead carrying with him the echoes of Moses and Ben Hur – virtuous, righteous and courageous men. Even the rhetorical pause in his speech ('My heart is in the coffin there with Caesar, / And I must pause till it come back to me' III.ii.106–7) is not designed to assess the effect of his talk on the Romans, but is caused by an outbreak of real emotion. This Mark Antony is not a manipulative performer, but an earnest man who is certain to follow the path of truth. His attempts at convincing the crowd manifest themselves as much in his words as in his gestures. He starts speaking by addressing a few people near him, grabbing their hands and arms. Before displaying the corpse of Caesar, he takes a woman's face between his hands to prepare her for the shock to come. Antony remains very close to the people, staying physically among them. There is no marked cinematic work opposing him to the citizens and locating him in the margins. All shots are relatively similar to one another and do not include extreme angles. No party seems more powerful than the other. Only when the Romans' mutiny starts does Antony finds himself all alone, unhurriedly walking up the stairs to the Capitol. However, he does not look proud of what he has just triggered. It is as though he is working for a stronger force, continuing dutifully to serve a godlike Caesar. In this version, the mutiny is filmed in different shots, showing the Romans destroying everything and bringing chaos around them. Again, the crowd is divided into small groups of people. No establishing shot provides the audience with information on the scale of the event. The sequence of Antony's speech in Stuart's production does not present a Machiavellian man working for his own future, but a Moses-like salvager who wishes to guide (or almost convert) the Roman people towards the light of truth and justice.

Mankiewicz's 1953 film, in contradistinction, features a highly manipulative Antony, played by Marlon Brando. The sequence works on a strong opposition between an impressive throng and a lonely man. In the course of the scene, the shift of authority from the citizens to Antony is made perceptible through changes in camera angles. Low-angle and high-angle shots in turn reflect the power that one side gains over the other.

Near the end of the speech delivered by Brutus (played by James Mason), a shot draws attention to a woman in the crowd, blurting out a loud scream. The audience may think at first that she is reacting to Brutus's allusion to Caesar's death, but the following shot reveals the actual cause of her distress: Mark Antony has suddenly come out of the Capitol, carrying Caesar's dead body in his arms. Mankiewicz here reverses the usual pattern of the shot/counter-shot technique. Instead of presenting an action and then a reaction to this action, he shows the woman's response before disclosing the event that has induced it. This reversal produces an effect of both surprise and expectation before the audience discovers what the character's outburst is about. Here, this also emphasizes Antony's entrance, making it more spectacular and emotional. Antony is filmed with a low-angle shot stressing his charismatic, arresting persona. Editing alternates high-angle shots of Brutus down the stairs and low-angle shots of Antony at the top of the stairs. *Montage* thus constructs a duel of gaze and characters, each one assessing the other for a brief moment, with Antony immediately appearing as more imposing and commanding than Brutus. As Antony slowly and dramatically goes down the steps, heavy silence reigns over the crowd. It is only when the film comes back to a spectacular, establishing shot of the throng gathered in front of the Senate that noise invades space. As the crowd becomes loud and agitated, editing constructs another duel – between the throng and Antony. However, this time, Antony does not appear in a position of superiority. He is filmed with a high-angle shot, vulnerable and isolated in the frame, all alone against the threatening gathering of citizens. With the camera placed at the exterior edge of the crowd, Mankiewicz makes us share the view of Roman citizens far at the back. This subjective shot gives a sense of scale, demonstrating how difficult it is to make oneself heard and seen by everyone in such an impressive crowd. This is followed by a shot on the throng from the front. In this extremely deep-focus shot, the audience in the cinema sees the small figure of Mark Antony (viewed from the back) in the foreground, surrounded by a daunting number of people in the background. No horizon or sky can be seen any longer: the whole space is filled with populace. This semi-subjective shot makes us share Antony's frightening experience of having to face this animal-like crowd all by himself. It is as if a whole human wave was about to crash on him and drown him. This striking image also presents a metafilmic aspect, as the audience in the cinema sees itself reflected in this vertical display of another audience on screen, listening to Antony. The latter is obliged to shout his first line ('Friends, Romans, countrymen, lend me your ears!' III.ii.73) before eventually succeeding in imposing silence. A soundless confrontation follows, through shot/counter-shot editing, between Antony and some individual leaders among the crowd. Antony, now in command, starts delivering his speech without being interrupted either by Romans or by film editing. The camera follows his moves, as if it is totally under his control. Only a few shots of the crowd's leaders show how attentive they have become. As these leaders look at one another knowingly in medium shots, we are encouraged to understand that Antony has begun to convince them.

Antony's supposedly emotional pause comes, in fact, as a rhetorical device to ensure that his speech is working. For the first time in the sequence, Antony is filmed in close-up, as he turns his back to the crowd. His facial expression is displayed to the audience in the cinema with much dramatic irony. We are witnessing something that remains hidden to the crowd – Antony's cunning little smile as he glances behind him to check whether his scheme is working out as planned. From this moment forth, we are made certain of Antony's manipulative skills and Machiavellian attitude. While he has his back turned on purpose, the leaders in the crowd discuss in echoing close-ups, approving what Antony has said. The crowd is now aesthetically split into many smaller, less threatening groups. They are no longer filmed in low-angle shots, reflecting how the danger they represent has lessened. For the first time, they are filmed on the same level as Antony. When the latter resumes his oration, a subjective shot from the crowd's viewpoint focuses on Antony in a low-angle shot. Formally, Antony is gaining power. When he brandishes Caesar's will, the film cuts to a shot of the crowd, seen for the very first time in high-angle shot. This is followed by a series of shots in which the leaders, still filmed with a high angle, are shown in a position of supplication, as they beg Antony to read them the will. Antony, in a low-angle shot on the Capitol stairs, takes advantage of his commanding position. One man among the crowd addresses his line 'They were traitors; honourable men!' (iii.ii.153) not to Antony but to the populace behind him, turning around to face his comrades. Mankiewicz, all through this sequence, emphasizes the notion of relay between Antony, recognizable leaders and anonymous citizens. Taming a crowd, in this film, means convincing a few leaders of opinion, who will then rally all the people behind them, herding them as if they are mere sheep.

As Antony goes down the stairs to join the crowd ('Shall I descend? and will you give me leave?' iii.ii.160), an unusual shot breaks the cinematic rhythm unexpectedly. The camera suddenly focuses on the profile of the sightless old man who had delivered the prophecy of the Ides of March at the start of the film. This shot reminds us of the tragedy being announced and foretold from the beginning. The old man's face is directed away from the whole event as if, after being ignored, he did not feel concerned or involved any longer.

When Antony tears Caesar's toga to display his gruesome wounds to the crowd, Mankiewicz uses the same reversal of the usual action/reaction shot that he has already employed for Antony's entrance. The crowd's heartfelt reaction is filmed before the corpse itself, enhancing the horror through suggestion: we are asked to imagine the state of the body according to the people's responses before we even see it. In a slow and silent pan, the camera moves along the citizens' faces as they look upon the body in dismay and shame. It is as if the Romans were digesting Caesar's death before exploding into mutiny. As Antony attempts with difficulty to contain their rage by reminding them of the will, he is again seen in a vulnerable, slight high-angle shot for a short while. He strolls around the people, grabbing their arms and shoulders to gain their confidence. This finally succeeds, and the angles are again reversed – Antony is filmed in a low-angle shot while the crowd, at last tamed and won over, is shot in an extreme high-angle shot. As Antony's voice rises in an outstanding crescendo ('Here was a Caesar! when comes such another?' III.ii.252), confusion erupts among the throng in a final spectacular shot in deep focus. The ensuing destruction is not filmed in different shots as in the Burge version, but presented in all its extensive scale in one establishing shot. Chaos invades the whole screen as people move everywhere; scaffolds are brought down; columns and statues are smashed. Only Mark Antony remains poised and impassive. Filmed in the foreground of the chaotic activity, he walks slowly towards us, contemplating his work and smiling ironically. This last shot in the sequence emphasizes Antony's victory over a manipulated, giddy crowd. If Burge's adaptation presented the sincere speech of a righteous man serving a godlike Caesar and addressing himself to small groups of people as their guide, Mankiewicz concentrates on the size of the event with constant shifts in power made ostensible through changes in camera angle. While Burge's sequence puts the stress on Charlton Heston's acting and earnestly felt emotions, Mankiewicz's is based more on meaningful cinematic work that turns the speech into the epic oration of an eminently complex character.

WOOING ON SCREEN: THE CONQUEST OF
KATHERINE IN 'HENRY V'

In the play of *Henry V*, the French princess always appears subordinate to masculine ploys.[2] She seems to be only a pawn in men's schemes and a

---

[2] See Joan Lord Hall, *Henry V: A Guide to the Play* (London: Greenwood Press, 1997), p. 110.

subject of sexual innuendos.[3] Henry V first uses her as an excuse to start war against France. The French king proposes her to England in order to try and avoid the conflict, but Henry finds the offer too modest, rejects it and turns it into a reason to conquer France. The Chorus informs us at the beginning of the third act that:

> the King doth offer him
> Katherine his daughter, and with her, to dowry,
> Some petty and unprofitable dukedoms.
> The offer likes not.   *Henry V*, iii, Chorus, 29–32

However, at the end of the play, Henry considers Katherine as the main stake of the political negotiations:

> Yet leave our cousin Katherine here with us:
> She is our capital demand, compris'd
> Within the fore-rank of our articles.
>   *Henry V*, v.ii.95–7

This passage presents an ironic contrast with Henry's initial reaction. Henry believes his marriage with Katherine is a necessary condition for peace although he categorically rejected that possibility at the beginning of the military campaign. Thus, Katherine turns out to be the one who starts and ends the war, the one who is first offered by her father and who is then won by Henry. First given as a present, she is rejected, and eventually stands as the main plunder of England. Nevertheless, before being conquered by military force, the princess is subjugated through words that invade her voice and her intimate space during the English lesson in Act iii, scene iv. According to Carol Rutter, Katherine is, in this scene, 'blazoning her own body – so that body parts produce parts of speech: "de hand", "de fingers" – she learns to name the material that is going to be demanded in exchange for peace'.[4] The English lesson is framed by two military and political scenes, presenting Katherine as a diplomatic stake. The scene follows the threat to the governor of Harfleur, and precedes the meeting of the French Council that has to make a decision regarding the start of war. The violent transition between the frightening speech addressed to the governor of Harfleur and the intimate scene in which the princess learns how to speak English establishes a correlation between Henry's

---

[3] The dialogue between Henry and Burgundy, after the wooing scene, typically reifies woman, as Katherine is compared to a fortified town that has to be taken.

[4] Carol Chillington Rutter, 'Looking at Shakespeare's Women on Film', in *The Cambridge Companion to Shakespeare on Film*, ed. Russell Jackson (Cambridge University Press, 2000), p. 243.

description of raped women[5] and the sight of this cloistered princess who will soon become the property of the English king. The scene of the lesson actually extends itself in the scene of the wooing. Before even meeting the princess physically, Henry has already won her through words. Vocal conquest has preceded sexual conquest. When Katherine appears for the first time in the play, she thus can be seen as a prey or a possible victim, already invaded by the enemy voice, an asset, a toy and a stake in a war which is decided and led by men.

When Henry undertakes to seduce Katherine at the end of the play, he therefore proceeds onto a field which is almost conquered beforehand. However, Katherine achieves a small victory when she obliges Henry to speak French. The usual balance of power between man and woman is inverted, creating both an echo and a discrepancy with the English lesson. In the play, winning comes down to conquering the other's language. Henry's behaviour during the wooing scene has often been questioned by scholars. Is he sincere or is he revealing his manipulating skills another time? According to Bert O. States, the two readings keep clashing and producing a schism within each spectator: '[T]here is still a question as to how romantic and political goals can coincide so neatly in a single enterprise . . . [I]t would not necessarily indicate a "fundamental division in the writer's mind" but that the writer wanted to put a division in his character's and in our own minds.'[6]

In Laurence Olivier's 1944 film, Katherine's English lesson does not follow the speech in which Henry threatens the governor of Harfleur, as this speech has been entirely suppressed. Therefore, Katherine is not at first introduced as a potential victim of warlike rape. However, she is presented as a goal for Henry. After the victory at Harfleur, Henry looks towards the heavenly horizon of a painted, colourful countryside, inspired by the fifteenth-century illuminated manuscript *Les très riches heures du duc de Berry*. With harmonious, dream-like music, the sight dissolves into a model shot of the French palace, which dissolves again into the garden terrace of the palace in which the French princess is about to ask her gentlewoman Alice for an English lesson. This transition, which makes the audience discover Katherine through Henry's surveying gaze, shows that the English king is already thinking of conquering her. Henry is somehow presented as the Prince Charming of a fairy tale, who has to face many fights and obstacles before romantically

[5] 'What is't to me, when you yourselves are cause, / If your pure maidens fall into the hand / Of hot and forcing violation? . . . [L]ook to see / The blind and bloody soldier with foul hand / Defile the locks of your shrill-shrieking daughters' (III.iii.19–35).

[6] Bert O. States, 'Hamlet's Older Brother', *The Hudson Review* (Winter 1987), 548–9.

reaching the beautiful princess in her golden, secluded world. In the garden of the palace, Katherine learns English serenely and light-heartedly: she cuts flowers while repeating her new words. The place of the lesson, outside in a garden, yet on a terrace above, provides the princess with a protected feeling of limited freedom. Camerawork remains straightforward all through the scene, with a sequence-shot following the movements of Katherine and Alice. Cross-cutting between the two women only happens during the learning of the 'foot' and the 'coun', emphasizing complicity and laughter. Katherine appears only as a distant witness of all the war negotiations. The audience shares her gaze in two subjective shots starting and ending the English lesson. As a fanfare sounds, the princess leans over the balcony and looks at French nobles entering and leaving the palace. They acknowledge her presence by greeting her, but Katherine remains above at a distance, impenetrably thoughtful but forbidden to interact. Though Olivier chooses to have her join the French nobles for dinner in the following scene (iii.v), she is kept aloof from the discussions. Alice and Queen Isabel are actually appalled that the men should speak such profane language in front of the princess, and react with outraged shrieks at the nobles' insults to the English ('Normans, but bastard Normans, Norman bastards!' iii.v.10) and at their claim that French women 'will give / Their bodies to the lust of English youth / To new-store France with bastard warriors' (iii.v.29–31). This decision to involve Katherine in this scene may spring from Olivier's wish to present the princess as a potential victim of English concupiscence, thus compensating for the absence of the violent speech at the Harfleur siege. Consequently, in Olivier's version, Katherine is turned into an impending sufferer of rape only in the words of the French and not in those of Henry, who ideologically remains a model of courteous, spotless kingship.

In Act v, scene ii, Olivier has retained the role of the French queen, Isabel, which is often cut in production. When Isabel states that Katherine 'hath good leave' (v.ii.98) to stay with Henry while the nobles go and discuss the last articles of the peace settlement, extradiegetic fairy-tale music arises, creating a dream-like, romantic atmosphere for Henry's first encounter with the princess. In a symmetrically constructed shot, Henry and Katherine stand on each side of the frame's foreground while the court proceeds to leave in the centre background. Olivier's Henry watches them go as if to be sure his wooing will have no witness. As he walks towards Katherine, the camera follows his move to the left, as if controlled by Harry's bold determination – only to reveal the princess's gentlewoman, Alice, in the left corner of the screen. By hiding and then disclosing space, the camerawork becomes a source of ironic surprise. Henry will not be alone with Katherine as he wished. He will have to face two persons instead of one. This two-to-one confrontation is reflected in the following cross-cutting that alternates between shots of Henry alone and shots of Kate and Alice together. Olivier's Henry is first presented as a pursuer, always on the move, turning around Katherine, going in and out of the camera field. He often chuckles and laughs, taking the whole wooing as some joyful sport. He also touches the princess's hands many times, a part of her body that she has learned to name during her English lesson. Olivier's screenplay presents the following notes: 'He takes Katharine by the hand',[7] 'King Henry kisses her hand',[8] 'we see King Henry's hand clasping Katharine's'.[9] The princess appears very much reined in, physically and emotionally trapped. Henry often holds her by the wrist. The set metaphorically mirrors her situation as she is filmed near or through the prison-like bars of the windows. She cannot rebel against what is happening nor escape from Henry's sometimes brusque, irritated attitude. Even Alice sides with Henry, as she encourages her, through a nod, to reply favourably to Henry's proposal to 'clap hands and a bargain!' (v.ii.129–30). Comic relief only comes when Henry and the princess both laugh at the king's efforts to speak French. When the two characters finally kiss, the film displays at the same time a romantic and a political reading of the scene. The return of the dream-like music signals a fate-induced and amorous match, while the heraldry of England and France on the rings of their fingers is shot in close-up, insisting on the political imperatives of the marriage. Olivier's filmic interpretation, therefore, points in two directions, preserving the ambivalence present in the original text. Olivier also interpolates a crowning scene in another symmetrical shot: Henry and Kate, on each side of a priest, face the camera, dressed in white robes. As the camera moves backwards, it reveals the Globe theatre. The viewers have been subtly moved out of realistic diegesis to return to the original place of performance. While Henry is still played by Olivier, Katherine is now played by a boy actor, thus following the Elizabethan convention. By disclosing the conditions of performance, Olivier nostalgically calls attention to Shakespeare's original staging at the Globe, while constructing the wooing scene as play-acting in every sense. Henry would only be a performer in a play about performance.

In Kenneth Branagh's 1989 film version of the play, Branagh emphasizes the seclusion of the princess. The scene begins with a shot of a bird cage:

---

[7] Laurence Olivier and Alan Dent, *Henry V, Produced and Directed by Laurence Olivier* (London: Lorrimer Publishing, 1984), p. 84.
[8] *Ibid.*, p. 88.　　[9] *Ibid.*, p. 89.

'At the bars of her doves' lattice-work enclosure we see Princess Katherine of France, gently waking the caged birds in the bright morning light.'[10] Branagh's movie likens the princess to a dove trapped in a cage, thus stressing her vulnerability in the face of outside events. Branagh retains the threat to the governor of Harfleur and, therefore, the brutal transition to Kate's lesson. This violence, which rules the passage between the warlike and peaceful universe, makes us realize Katherine's complex and painful situation. Branagh's script commentary focuses on this aspect: 'As the Princess sits down at her dressing-table, and Alice begins to comb her hair, Katherine resigns herself to the fact that she must learn to speak English.'[11]

In Branagh's movie, the English lesson is less a play activity than an imposed exercise. The princess feels obliged to learn her enemy's language, as if she is anticipating the outcome of the war. The correlation between the vocal conquest and the sexual conquest is made explicit when the princess repeats her English words another time from the space of her bed. The scene becomes progressively more joyful, as the princess happily leaps around the room, forgetting the political agenda of her lesson. However, the end of the scene brings a change of mood. Katherine opens the door of her room, and finds herself face to face with her father followed by his court. Branagh's script provides this comment: 'Their mood is grim and Katherine is immediately quiet and serious. The men move on towards the Council Chamber and the Princess, slowly, sadly closes the door.'[12] The French king looks as if he understands that his daughter is learning English and that she has lost faith in the French victory. Although Katherine is locked in her golden cell, she has acquired an awareness of war. The joy she felt during the English lesson is reduced to nothing as soon as she is reminded of the political realities.

At the end of the film, in Act v, scene ii, Kate is dressed in black and wearing a veil, clearly in mourning. She seems apprehensive and frightened, not knowing where to look and grasping her father's hand for comfort. As the role of Queen Isabel has been cut for the film, the line, 'She hath good leave', is given to the French king, who delivers it with tangible sadness. The wooing starts awkwardly, with Henry and Kate sitting on each side of a long table, and Alice standing behind Kate. Branagh first cross-cuts between the king, who is seen in full face, and Katherine, who is shown in profile. This lack of angle symmetry denies, through editing, any direct gaze or communication between the two characters. The script commentary

---

[10] Kenneth Branagh, *Henry V: A Screen Adaptation* (London: Chatto & Windus, 1989), p. 63.
[11] *Ibid.*   [12] *Ibid.*, p. 66.

Branagh uses to introduce the wooing scene clearly states the doubts and nervousness experienced by the king: 'The King and all the nobles retire from the room to go over the terms of the treaty, leaving a surprisingly nervous Henry to get this bit of the deal over with as quickly as possible.'[13]

In an ideological reversal, the man becomes the one who experiences fear and embarrassment. When Henry finally moves towards Kate, she remains still, delivering very coldly '*Sauf votre honneur*, me understand well' (v.ii.131). Henry resumes his speech in a triangular shot – Henry and Katherine are on each side of the camera field, with Alice in the middle. As Kate and Henry now share the same shot, it is as if communication is finally established, but still needs to go through an intermediary person. Alternating shots of the two characters then become closer and closer, emphasizing faces and emotions. Branagh's film begins to focus on the romantic side of the wooing and on the strong personality of Katherine, notably through an intertext that helps to guide the audience's expectations throughout the sequence. The princess is played by Emma Thompson, Branagh's partner in real life at the time. The political stratagem that is part of the wooing moves into the shadow, starting to be replaced by a true marriage of the heart and soul. As Henry delivers 'If thou would have such a one, take me' (v.ii.165), emotional, extradiegetic music comes in. Cross-editing goes from Kate's face to Henry's, denying Alice's presence and presenting the two characters as lovers alone in the world, communicating directly with each other. Despite his position of strength, Branagh's Henry suggests that Katherine still has the possibility of making a choice. He notably insists on the conditional mark in 'thou hast me, *if* thou hast me, at the worst; and thou shalt wear me, *if* thou wear me, better and better' (v.ii.231–3). Henry's French-speaking comes to break the rhythm of the romantic wooing: the music ends and Alice comes back into view in another triangular shot, this time displaying comic relief. As the English king struggles with the French words, his abnegation and humility seem to wipe out the reluctances of the princess. According to Branagh's commentary, Katherine begins to laugh at the king's attempt to speak French: 'He begins his Herculean task . . . Katherine controls her laughter at the King's efforts.'[14]

From this laughter stems their complicity and understanding, denying any political manipulation and glorifying the sentimental romance. A close shot then shows Kate in full face with Henry in profile speaking gently near her, literally pouring in her ear the words that might definitely convince her. As two close-ups reveal Alice at the same time sentimentally moved

[13] *Ibid.*, p. 119.   [14] *Ibid.*, p. 121.

and amused at the sight of the two of them, the audience is led to see Henry and Kate as two genuine lovers. Our reception of the scene is, in fact, ideologically guided by Alice's reactions. Having started the scene as a middle woman between the two protagonists, Alice is now presented as an intermediary between the audience and the 'couple'. Henry and Kate's first kiss is filmed in close-up with both their faces in profile, suggesting the match of two equals. When the French nobles return, Henry's line, 'Here comes your father' (v.ii.279–80), is spoken with the comic guilt of a teenager caught red-handed, thus emphasizing their new loving complicity. However, Katherine looks grim again when she is kissed a second time in the presence of the nobles. It seems that, with the return of official conventions, Katherine is made aware again of the political stakes behind her marriage. After Henry's last speech, the shot freezes suddenly, turning the line of nobles behind the table into a 'tableau' from a nineteenth-century play. The Chorus then closes a wooden door on the picture, reminding us that Henry's glory will not endure. Branagh, like Olivier, ends the film with a return to meta-drama, to a reminder that the whole show was merely performed and constructed before our eyes. The frozen shot points to the artificiality of cinema, while the Chorus paradoxically negates this very stillness of time by referring to the future.

In their treatment of the two feminine scenes, the movies by Branagh and Olivier clash in terms of space. In Olivier's version, the lesson sequence is presented in an open place. The film then evolves towards a princess who is more and more captive and subjugated in the wooing scene. On the contrary, in Branagh's version, the film tends to liberate and emancipate Katherine. During the English lesson, she is first presented in a closed place and assimilated like prey. But the scene of the wooing shows her as a strong and determined woman, free to escape from Henry's physical ascendancy and able skilfully to resist his verbal assaults. Yet, Branagh also suppresses the part of Queen Isabel, therefore refusing to give the final, peaceful speech to a woman. The last word is still given to a man, who, in Samuel Crowl's words 'utter[s] his own dream of union and assimilation'.[15] Branagh's movie tends to free Katherine by suggesting that she is making a marriage of true love, but eventually does not seem to question the masculine warlike values.

[15] Samuel Crowl, *Shakespeare Observed: Studies in Performance on Stage and Screen* (Athens, OH: Ohio University Press, 1992), p. 173.

Bibliography

Albert, Stuart. 'Physical Distance and Persuasion'. *Journal of Personality and Social Psychology* 15, 3 (1970): 265–70.

Allen, Norman. 'McKellen on Richard III'. *American Theatre* (April 1996): 34–5.

Almereyda, Michael. *William Shakespeare's Hamlet: A Screenplay Adaptation.* London: Faber & Faber, 2000.

Alter, Iska. '"To See or Not To See": Interpolations, Extended Scenes, and Musical Accompaniment in Kenneth Branagh's *Hamlet*'. In *Stage Directions in Hamlet: New Essays and New Directions*, ed. Hardin L. Aasand, pp. 161–9. Cranbury, London and Mississauga: Associated University Presses, 2003.

Althusser, Louis. *For Marx.* Trans. Allen Lane. Harmondsworth: Penguin Books, 1969.

Aristotle. *Poetics.* Trans. James Hutton. Toronto: W. W. Norton, 1982.

Aumont, Jacques, Alain Bergala, Michel Marie and Marc Vernet. *Esthétique du film.* Paris: Nathan, 1999.

Balazs, Béla. *Theory of the Film.* Trans. Edith Bone. New York: Dover Publications, 1970.

Ball, Robert Hamilton. *Shakespeare on Silent Film.* London: George Allen and Unwin, 1968.

Bate, Jonathan and Russell Jackson, eds. *Shakespeare: An Illustrated Stage History.* Oxford University Press, 1996.

Baudry, Jean-Louis. *L'effet cinéma.* Paris: Editions Albatros, 1978.

Bazin, André. *What is Cinema?* Trans. Hugh Gray. Berkeley and Los Angeles: University of California Press, 1967.

Orson Welles: A Critical Review. Trans. Jonathan Rosenbaum. London: Elm Tree Books/Hamish Hamilton, 1978.

Bergala, Alain. *Initiation à la sémiologie du récit en images.* Les cahiers de l'audiovisuel. Ligue Française de l'Enseignement et de l'Education Permanente, [1977].

Berthomieu, Pierre. *Kenneth Branagh: traînes de feu, rosées de Sang.* Paris: Editions Jean-Michel Place, 1998.

Bevis, Richard W. *English Drama: Restoration and Eighteenth Century 1660–1789.* London and New York: Longman, 1988.

Bidaud, Anne-Marie. *Hollywood et le Rêve américain: cinéma et idéologie aux Etats-Unis*. Paris, Milan and Barcelona: Masson, 1994.

Bordwell, David, Janet Staiger and Kristin Thompson. *The Classical Hollywood Cinema*. London: Routledge, 1985.

Boose, Lynda E. and Richard Burt, eds. *Shakespeare, the Movie*. London: Routledge, 1997.

Booth, Michael R. *Theatre in the Victorian Age*. Cambridge University Press, 1991.

Branagh, Kenneth. *Beginning*. London: Chatto & Windus, 1989.

'Hamlet' by William Shakespeare: Screenplay, Introduction and Film Diary. London: Chatto & Windus, 1996.

Henry V: A Screen Adaptation. London: Chatto & Windus, 1989.

'Much Ado About Nothing' by William Shakespeare: Screenplay, Introduction and Notes on the Making of the Film. London: Chatto & Windus, 1993.

Brecht, Bertolt. *Brecht on Theatre*. Ed. and trans. John Willet. London: Eyre Methuen, 1964.

Buchman, Lorne M. *Still in Movement: Shakespeare on Screen*. Oxford University Press, 1991.

Buhler, Stephen M. *Shakespeare in the Cinema: Ocular Proof*. Albany: State University of New York Press, 2002.

Burch, Noel. 'How We Got into Pictures: Notes Accompanying Correction Please'. *Afterimage* 8–9 [1981]: 24–38.

Burnett, Mark Thornton and Ramona Wray, eds. *Shakespeare, Film, Fin de Siècle*. London: Macmillan, 2000.

Burt, Richard. *Unspeakable ShaXXXspeares: Queer Theory and American Kiddie Culture*. New York: St Martin's Press, 1998.

Carter, Thomas. *Stories from Shakespeare*. London: George G. Harrap, 1913.

Cartmell, Deborah and Michael Scott, eds. *Talking Shakespeare*. Houndmills: Palgrave, 2001.

Cartmell, Deborah. 'The *Henry V* Flashback: Kenneth Branagh's Shakespeare'. In *Pulping Fictions: Consuming Culture across the Literature/Media Divide*, ed. Deborah Cartmell, I. Q. Hunter, Heidi Kaye and Imelda Whelehan, pp. 73–83. London and Chicago: Pluto, 1996.

Chillington Rutter, Carol. 'Looking at Shakespeare's Women on Film'. In *The Cambridge Companion to Shakespeare on Film*, ed. Russell Jackson, pp. 241–60. Cambridge University Press, 2000.

Chion, Michel. *Audio-Vision: Sound on Screen*. Ed. and trans. Claudia Gorbman. New York: Columbia University Press, 1994.

La musique au cinéma. Paris: Fayard, 1995.

Chute, Marchette. *Stories from Shakespeare*. London: John Murray, 1972.

Cobley, Paul. *Narrative*. London: Routledge, 2001.

Coursen, H. R. *Reading Shakespeare on Stage*. London: Associated University Presses, 1995.

'Words, Words, Words: Searching for *Hamlet*'. *Shakespeare Yearbook* 8 (1997): 306–24.

Crowdus, Gary. 'Shakespeare in the Cinema: a Film Directors' Symposium, with Peter Brook, Sir Peter Hall, Richard Loncraine, Baz Luhrmann, Oliver Parker, Roman Polanski and Franco Zeffirelli'. *Cineaste* 24.1 (1998): 48–55.

'Shakespeare is up to Date: an Interview with Sir Ian McKellen'. *Cineaste* 24.1 (1998): 46–7.

Crowl, Samuel. 'Much Ado About Nothing'. *Shakespeare Bulletin* (Summer 1993): 40.

Shakespeare at the Cineplex: The Kenneth Branagh Era. Athens, OH: Ohio University Press, 2003.

Shakespeare Observed: Studies in Performance on Stage and Screen. Athens, OH: Ohio University Press, 1992.

Crunelle, Anny. 'All the World's a Screen: Transcoding in Branagh's *Hamlet*'. *Shakespeare Yearbook* 8 (1997): 349–69.

Davies, Anthony. *Filming Shakespeare's Plays*. Cambridge University Press, 1988.

De Banke, Cécile. *Shakespearean Stage Production Then and Now*. London: Hutchinson, 1954.

Dent, Alan, ed. *Hamlet: The Film and the Play*. London: World Film Publications, 1948.

Devore, Christopher and Franco Zeffirelli. 'The Screenplay of *Hamlet* Freely Adapted from William Shakespeare's Tragedy'. Date of draft: 3 April 1990. Unpublished screenplay. Consulted at the Shakespeare Institute Library, April 2003.

Dorval, Patricia and Jean-Marie Maguin, eds. *Shakespeare et le cinéma, Actes du Congrés 1998 de la Société Française Shakespeare*. Paris: ENS, 1998.

Dover Wilson, John. *What Happens in 'Hamlet'*. Cambridge University Press, 1964.

Doyle, Patrick. 'Music'. In *Hamlet* (introductory notes). Random Century Audiobooks, RTC in association with BBC Radio Drama, RC100, 1992.

Dudley Andrew, J. *The Major Film Theories: An Introduction*. Oxford University Press, 1976.

Edmonds, Robert. *The Sights and Sounds of Cinema and Television: How the Aesthetic Experience Influences Our Feeling*. New York and London: Teachers College Press, 1992.

Elam, Keir. *The Semiotics of Theatre and Drama*. New York and London: Methuen, 1980.

Fabiszak, Jacek. 'Branagh's Use of Elizabethan Stage Conventions in His Production of *Hamlet*'. Paper given at the 'Shakespeare on Screen' conference organized by the University of Malaga, Benalmadena (Spain), 21–4 September 1999.

Finkel, Alicia. *Romantic Stages: Set and Costume Designs in Victorian England*. Jefferson and London: McFarland, 1996.

Fitter, Chris. 'A Tale of Two Branaghs: *Henry V*, Ideology and the Mekong Agincourt'. In *Shakespeare Left and Right*, ed. Ivo Kamps, pp. 259–75. New York and London: Routledge, 1991.

Fortier, Mark. 'Speculations on *2 Henry IV*, Theatre Historiography, the Strait Gate of History, and Kenneth Branagh'. *Journal of Dramatic Theory and Criticism* 7 (Fall 1992): 45–69.

Foucault, Michel. *Madness and Civilisation*. Trans. Richard Howard. London: Random House, 1965.

The Archeology of Knowledge. Trans. Alan Sheridan. London: Tavistock Publications, 1973.

Freud, Sigmund. *The Essentials of Psychoanalysis*. Ed. Anna Freud. Trans. James Strachey. Harmondsworth: Penguin Books, 1986.

Five Lectures on Psycho-Analysis. Trans. James Strachey. Harmondsworth: Penguin Books, 1995.

Fuchs, Cynthia. 'Looking Around Corners. Interview with Michael Almereyda'. <http://www.popmatters.com/film/interviews/almereyda-michael.html> Consulted on 2 March 2003.

Garfield, Leon. *Shakespeare Stories*. London: Victor Gollancz, 1985.

'The Penny Whistle: the Problem of Writing Stories from Shakespeare'. *Essays by Divers Hands* 46 (1990): 92–108.

Gaudreault, André. *Du littéraire au filmique: système du récit*. Paris: Méridiens Klincksieck, 1988.

Gaudreault, André and François Jost. *Cinéma et récit II: Le récit cinématographique*. Paris: Nathan, 1990.

Geduld, Harry. *The Birth of the Talkies: From Edison to Jolson*. Bloomington: Indiana University Press, 1975.

Genette, Gérard. *Narrative Discourse: An Essay in Method*. Trans. Jane E. Lewin. Ithaca, NY: Cornell University Press, 1980.

Palimpsests: Literature in the Second Degree. Trans. Channa Newman and Claude Doubinsky. Lincoln and London: University of Nebraska Press, 1997.

Paratexts: Thresholds of Interpretation. Trans. Jane E. Lewin. Cambridge University Press, 1997.

Gorbman, Claudia. *Unheard Melodies: Narrative Film Music*. Bloomington: Indiana University Press, 1987.

Green, André. *'Hamlet' et Hamlet*. Paris: Balland, 1982.

Gritten, David. 'The Film's the Thing'. *The Daily Telegraph*, 11 January 1997, A1.

Gunning, Tom. 'The Cinema of Attractions: Early Film, its Spectator and the Avant-Garde'. In *Early Cinema: Space, Frame, Narrative*, ed. T. Elsaesser and A. Barker, pp. 56–62. London: British Film Institute, 1990.

Guntner, Lawrence and Peter Drexler. 'Recycled Film Codes and the Study of Shakespeare on Film'. *Deutsche Shakespeare* (1993): 31–40.

Gurr, Andrew. *The Shakespearean Stage*. Cambridge University Press, 2nd edn. 1992.

Guthrie, Tyrone. *A Life in the Theatre*. London: Readers Union, 1961.

Hall, Edward T. *The Silent Language*. New York: Doubleday, 1959.

Hapgood, Robert. 'Shakespeare on Film and Television'. In *The Cambridge Companion to Shakespeare Studies*, ed. Stanley Wells, pp. 273–86. Cambridge University Press, 1986.

Hatchuel, Sarah. 'Making Melodies for Branagh's Films: an Interview with Patrick Doyle'. *Shakespeare* 2.1 (Winter 1998): 12–13.

Hatchuel, Sarah and Pierre Berthomieu. '"I Could a Tale Unfold", I Could a Tale Enlighten: Kenneth Branagh ou l'art de la clarté'. In *Shakespeare et le cinéma, Actes du Congrès 1998 de la Société Française Shakespeare*, ed. Patricia Dorval and Jean-Marie Maguin, pp. 131–40. Paris: ENS, 1998.

Howlett, Kathy M. *Framing Shakespeare on Screen*. Athens, OH: Ohio University Press, 2000.

Irace, Kathleen O., ed. *The First Quarto of 'Hamlet'*. Cambridge University Press, 1998.

Iselin, Pierre. *'Hamlet* and the Rhetoric of Secrecy'. In *Hamlet*, ed. Pierre Iselin, pp. 141–59. Paris: Didier Eruditions – CNED, 1997.

Jackson, Russell. 'Diary'. In *'Hamlet' by William Shakespeare: Screenplay, Introduction and Film Diary*, Kenneth Branagh, pp. 179–213. London: Chatto & Windus, 1996.

'Kenneth Branagh's Film of *Hamlet*: the Textual Choices'. *Shakespeare Bulletin* 15.2 (Spring 1997): 37–8.

'Shakespeare's Comedies on Film'. In *Shakespeare and the Moving Image*, ed. Anthony Davies and Stanley Wells, pp. 99–120. Cambridge University Press, 1994.

'Shakespeare on the Stage from 1660 to 1900'. In *The Cambridge Companion to Shakespeare Studies*, ed. Stanley Wells, pp. 187–212. Cambridge University Press, 1986.

Jackson, Russell, ed. *The Cambridge Companion to Shakespeare on Film*. Cambridge University Press, 2000.

Jenkins, Harold. *'Hamlet* Then Till Now'. In *Aspects of Hamlet*, ed. Kenneth Muir and Stanley Wells, pp. 16–27. Cambridge University Press, 1979.

Jorgens, Jack J. *Shakespeare On Film*. Bloomington and London: Indiana University Press, 1977.

Jost, François. *L'œil-caméra. Entre film et roman*. Presses Universitaires de Lyon, 1987.

Kellog, Robert and Robert Scholes. *The Nature of Narrative*. New York and Oxford: Oxford University Press, 1966.

Kennedy, Dennis. *Looking at Shakespeare: A Visual History of Twentieth-Century Performance*. Cambridge University Press, 1993.

Kennedy Sauer, David. 'Suiting the Word to the Action: Kenneth Branagh's Interpolations in *Hamlet*'. *Shakespeare Yearbook* 8 (1997): 325–48.

Keyishian, Harry. 'Shakespeare and Movie Genre: the Case of *Hamlet*'. In *The Cambridge Companion to Shakespeare on Film*, ed. Russell Jackson, pp. 72–81. Cambridge University Press, 2000.

King, Norman. 'The Sound of Silents'. In *Silent Film*, ed. Richard Abel, pp. 31–44. London: The Athlone Press, 1996.

Kliman, Bernice W. 'Branagh's Henry: Allusion and Illusion'. *Shakespeare on Film Newsletter* 14.1 (December 1989): 1, 9–10.

'The Unkindest Cuts: Flashcut Excess in Kenneth Branagh's *Hamlet*'. In *Talking Shakespeare*, ed. Deborah Cartmell and Michael Scott, pp. 151–67. Houndmills: Palgrave, 2001.

Kozintsev, Grigori. *Shakespeare: Time and Conscience.* London: Dobson, 1967.

Lacan, Jacques. *Ecrits: A Selection.* Trans. by Alan Sheridan. London: Tavistock Publications, 1977.

Laffay, Albert. *Logique du cinéma.* Paris: Masson, 1964.

Lamb, Charles and Mary. *Tales from Shakespeare.* London and Glasgow: Collins, 1953.

Langer, Susanne. *Feeling and Form.* New York: Scribner's, 1953.

Lebel, Jean-Patrick. *Cinéma et idéologie.* Paris: Editions Sociales, 1971.

Lehmann, Courtney. *Shakespeare Remains: Theater to Film, Early Modern to Post-modern.* Ithaca, NY, and London: Cornell University Press, 2002.

Linden, George. *Reflections on the Screen.* Belmont: Wadsworth, 1970.

Loehlin, James N. '"Top of the World, Ma": *Richard III* and Cinematic Convention'. In *Shakespeare, the Movie,* ed. Lynda E. Boose and Richard Burt, pp. 67–79. London: Routledge, 1997.

Lord Hall, Joan. *Henry V: A Guide to the Play.* London: Greenwood Press, 1997.

Luhrmann, Baz and Craig Pearce. *Romeo and Juliet.* London: Hodder Children's Books, 1997.

MacCabe, Colin. 'From Realism and the Cinema: Notes on Some Brechtian Theses'. In *Contemporary Film Theory,* ed. Antony Easthope, pp. 53–67. Harlow: Longman, 1993.

Mackintosh, Iain. *Architecture, Actor and Audience.* London and New York: Routledge, 1993.

Macleod, Mary. *The Shakespeare Story Book,* with Introduction by Sidney Lee. London, 1902.

Maher, Mary Z. *Modern Hamlets and their Soliloquies.* Iowa University Press, 1992.

Maillot, Pierre. *L'écriture cinématographique.* Paris: Méridiens Klincksieck, 1994.

Manheim, Michael. 'The English History Play on Screen'. In *Shakespeare and the Moving Image,* ed. Anthony Davies and Stanley Wells, pp. 121–45. Cambridge University Press, 1994.

Manvell, Roger. *Shakespeare and the Film.* London: J. M. Dent, 1971.

Theater and Film: A Comparative Study of the Two Forms of Dramatic Art, and the Problems of Adaptation of Stage Plays into Films. Cranbury: Associated University Presses, 1979.

Mariette, Amelia. 'Urban Dystopia: Reapproaching Christine Edzard's *As You Like It*'. In *Shakespeare, Film, Fin de Siècle,* ed. Mark Thornton Burnett and Ramona Wray, pp. 73–88. London: Macmillan, 2000.

Metz, Christian. *L'énonciation impersonnelle ou le site du film.* Paris: Klincksieck, 1991.

Essais sur la signification au cinéma. Vol. 1. Paris: Klincksieck, 1978.

Essais sur la signification au cinéma. Vol. 2. Paris: Klincksieck, 1981.

'The Imaginary Signifier'. In *Film and Theory: An Anthology,* ed. Robert Stam and Toby Miller, pp. 408–36. Oxford: Blackwell, 2000.

Milling, Jane and Graham Ley. *Modern Theories of Performance.* Palgrave: New York, 2001.

Morris, Pam. *Realism.* London: Routledge, 2003.

Murfin, Ross and Supryia M. Ray. *The Bedford Glossary of Critical and Literary Terms*. Boston, MA: Bedford Books, 1997.

Naughton, John. 'The Return of The Magnificent Eight?' *Premiere*, September 1993, 60–4.

Olivier, Laurence. 'An Essay in *Hamlet*.' In *The Film 'Hamlet': A Record of its Production*, ed. Brenda Cross, pp. 11–15. London: The Saturn Press, 1948.

Olivier, Laurence and Alan Dent. *Henry V, Produced and Directed by Laurence Olivier*. London: Lorrimer Publishing, 1984.

Pavis, Patrice. *Dictionnaire du théâtre*. Paris: Editions Sociales, 1980.

Voix et images de la scène: pour une sémiologie de la réception. Villeneuve d'Ascq: Presses Universitaires de Lille, 1985.

Perrin, J. B. *Contes Moraux Amusants et Instructifs, à l'usage de la Jeunesse, tirés des Tragédies de Shakespeare*. London, 1783.

Pfister, Manfred. *The Theory and Analysis of Drama*. Cambridge University Press, 1991.

Plato. 'The Republic III'. In *The Portable Plato*, ed. Scott Buchanan, trans. Benjamin Jowett, pp. 364–412. Harmondsworth: Penguin Books, 1976.

Price, Cecil. *Theatre in the Age of Garrick*. Oxford: Basil Blackwell, 1973.

Price, Curtis A. *Music in the Restoration Theatre*. Ann Arbor, MI: UMI Research Press, 1979.

Pursell, Michael. 'Playing the Game: Branagh's *Henry V*'. *Literature/Film Quarterly* 20 (1992): 268–75.

'Zeffirelli's Shakespeare: the Visual Realization of Tone and Theme'. *Literature/Film Quarterly* 8.4 (1980): 210–18.

Rasmus, Agnieszka. 'Michael Almereyda's *Hamlet*: the Film is the Thing . . .? Metatheatre vs. Metacinema'. <http://www.geocities.com/britgrad/2001/rasmus.html> Consulted on 8 July 2003.

Rathburn, Paul. 'Branagh's Iconoclasm: Warriors for the Working Day'. *Shakespeare on Film Newsletter* 15.2 (April 1991): 14, 16.

Reader, Keith A. 'Literature/Cinema/Television: Intertextuality in Jean Renoir's *Le Testament du Docteur Cordelier*'. In *Intertextuality: Theories and Practices*, ed. Michael Worton and Judith Still, pp. 176–89. Manchester and New York: Manchester University Press, 1990.

Rothwell, Kenneth S. *A History of Shakespeare on Screen: A Century of Film and Television*. Cambridge University Press, 1999.

'Kenneth Branagh's *Henry V*: the Gilt [Guilt] in the Crown Re-Examined'. *Comparative Drama* 24 (1990): 173–8.

'Representing *King Lear* on Screen: from Metatheatre to "Meta-cinema"'. In *Shakespeare and the Moving Image*, ed. Anthony Davies and Stanley Wells, pp. 211–33. Cambridge University Press, 1994.

'Shakespeare for the Art Houses'. *Cineaste* 24.1 (1998): 28–33.

Rowell, George. *The Victorian Theatre 1792–1914*. Cambridge University Press, 1978.

Royal, Derek. 'Shakespeare's Kingly Mirror: Figuring the Chorus in Olivier's and Branagh's *Henry V*'. *Literature/Film Quarterly* 25.2 (1997): 104–10.

Saada, Nicolas. 'Le théâtre apprivoisé'. *Les Cahiers du Cinéma* (January 1991): 65–6.

Schoch, Richard W. *Shakespeare's Victorian Stage: Performing History in the Theatre of Charles Kean.* Cambridge University Press, 1998.

Shurgot, Michael W. *Stages of Play: Shakespeare's Theatrical Energies in Elizabethan Performance.* London: Associated University Presses, 1998.

Sinyard, Neil. *Filming Literature: The Art of Screen Adaptation.* London and Sydney: Croom Helm, 1986.

Smith, Emma. '"Either for Tragedy, Comedy": Attitudes to *Hamlet* in Kenneth Branagh's *In The Bleak Midwinter* and *Hamlet*'. In *Shakespeare, Film, Fin de Siècle*, ed. Mark Thornton Burnett and Ramona Wray, pp. 137–46. London: Macmillan, 2000.

Sotinel, Thomas. 'Prendre les spectateurs au collet: entretien avec Kenneth Branagh'. *Le Monde (Dossiers et Documents Littéraires)*, issue 19, April 1998, 4.

Souriau, Etienne, ed. *Vocabulaire d'esthétique.* Paris: Presses Universitaires de France, 1990.

Southern, Richard. 'The Picture-Frame Proscenium of 1880'. *Theatre Notebook* 5.3 (1951): 59–61.

Speaight, Robert. *William Poel and the Elizabethan Revival.* London: William Heinemann, 1954.

Spencer, Hazelton. *Shakespeare Improved.* New York: Frederick Ungar, 1963.

Spencer, T. J. B. 'The Decline of *Hamlet*'. In *'Hamlet': Stratford-upon-Avon Studies* 5, ed. John Russell Brown and Bernard Harris, pp. 185–99. London: Edward Arnold, 1963.

Stanislavski, Constantin. *An Actor Prepares.* London: Methuen, 1980.

Building a Character. London: Methuen, 1968.

Creating a Role. London: Methuen, 1981.

Starks, Lisa S. 'Cinema of Cruelty'. In *The Reel Shakespeare*, ed. Lisa S. Starks and Courtney Lehmann, pp. 121–42. London: Associated University Presses, 2002.

States, Bert O. 'Hamlet's Older Brother'. *The Hudson Review* (Winter 1987): 537–52.

Styan, J. L. *The English Stage: A History of Drama and Performance.* Cambridge University Press, 1996.

Talouarn, Bruno. 'Interview avec Patrick Doyle'. *Main Title* (June 1993): 11–18.

Taymor, Julie. *Titus: The Illustrated Screenplay.* New York: Newmarket Press, 2000.

Todorov, Tzvetan. *The Poetics of Prose.* Ithaca, NY: Cornell University Press, 1977.

Vanoye, Francis. *Cinéma et récit I: récit écrit, récit filmique.* Paris: Nathan, 1989.

Vanoye, Francis and Anne Goliot-Lété. *Précis d'analyse filmique.* Paris: Nathan, 1992.

Vardac, Nicholas. *Stage to Screen.* Cambridge, MA: Harvard University Press, 1949.

Wells, Stanley. 'Shakespeare Productions in England in 1989'. *Shakespeare Survey* 43 (1991): 183–203.

'Tales from Shakespeare'. *Proceedings of the British Academy* 73 (1987): 125–52.

Willems, Michèle. 'Verbal–visual, verbal–pictorial or textual–televisual? Reflections on the BBC Shakespeare Series'. In *Shakespeare and the Moving Image*, ed. Anthony Davies and Stanley Wells, pp. 69–85. Cambridge University Press, 1994.

Willson, Robert F. "*Henry V*: Branagh's and Olivier's Choruses." *Shakespeare on Film Newsletter* 14.2 (April 1990): 1–2.

'Lubitsch's *To Be or Not To Be* or Shakespeare Mangled'. *Shakespeare on Film Newsletter* 1.1 (December 1976): 2–3; 6.

Index

186